# CUTTING EDGE

## STARTER

### TEACHER'S RESOURCE BOOK

chris redston

with sarah cunningham    peter moor

PEARSON
Longman

# Contents

# Introduction

*Cutting Edge Starter* is a course aimed at adults and young adults studying general English at complete beginner or false beginner level. It provides material for up to 120 hours' teaching, depending on how much photocopiable material is used from the *Teacher's Resource Book*. It is suitable for students studying in either a monolingual or multilingual classroom situation.

| | |
|---|---|
| **STUDENTS' BOOK**<br><br>**CLASS CASSETTES/<br>AUDIO CD** | The *Cutting Edge Starter Students' Book* is divided into twelve modules, each consisting of approximately 6–8 hours of classroom material. In each module you will find:<br><br>• Three double-page **Focus** sections containing a balance of:<br>  – **grammar**<br>  – **vocabulary**<br>  – **reading** and/or **listening** activities<br>  – **practice activities** and extended **speaking tasks**<br>• **Real life** (everyday survival language)<br>• **Do you remember?** – quick spot-check revision<br><br>In addition there are **Consolidation sections** after Modules 4, 8 and 12.<br><br>At the back of the book you will find:<br><br>• **Communication activities**<br>• a detailed **Language summary**<br>• **Tapescripts** of the material on the Class Cassettes/Audio CD<br><br>**Vocabulary Book**: in the back cover pocket of the *Students' Book* is the *Cutting Edge Starter Vocabulary Book*, which contains pictures, examples and phonemic transcriptions for approximately 500 words and phrases from the *Students' Book*.<br>The **Class Cassettes/Audio CD** contain(s) all the listening and pronunciation exercises in the *Students' Book*, as well as many of the answers to the practice exercises. |
| **WORKBOOK**<br><br>**STUDENTS' CASSETTE/<br>AUDIO CD** | The *Cutting Edge Starter Workbook* is divided into twelve parallel modules, consisting of:<br><br>• additional **grammar** practice<br>• additional **vocabulary** practice<br>• skills work: **Listen and read** and **Improve your writing** sections<br>• **pronunciation** exercises<br>• **spelling** exercises<br><br>The optional **Students' Cassette/Audio CD** contains all the *Listen and read* texts and pronunciation exercises in the *Workbook*, as well as answers to many of the grammar exercises. |
| **TEACHER'S RESOURCE BOOK** | The *Cutting Edge Starter Teachers' Resource Book* contains:<br><br>• **Introduction** and **Teachers' tips**<br>• step-by-step **teachers' notes** for each module, including detailed language notes, alternative suggestions for different teaching situations, extra practice ideas and integrated answer keys.<br>• The **Photocopiable Resource bank**, which contains:<br>  – **communicative practice activities** which revise the key grammar and vocabulary in each Module of the *Students' Book*.<br>  – one **Vocabulary Booster** worksheet per Module of the *Students' Book*.<br>  – six pairs of **tests**, to be used after Modules 2, 4, 6, 8, 10 and 12. |

# The thinking behind *Cutting Edge Starter*

The *Cutting Edge Starter Students' Book* has a multi-layered syllabus, which includes a comprehensive grammar and vocabulary syllabus and incorporates systematic work on listening, speaking, reading and writing. It takes an integrated approach to pronunciation, and includes regular recycling and revision. We are particularly interested in helping learners to take an active approach to learning, and in encouraging them to use the language they know, even at this low level. We realise that learners need guidance and preparation to do this, and so we aim to take them step by step through new language and tasks, providing them with all the support they need in order to communicate successfully.

## Grammar

To enable learners to use the language confidently, *Cutting Edge Starter* provides a sound basis of grammar that includes all the key tenses and structures that students at this level need. This grammar is introduced a little at a time, so that students are not overloaded. Each module of the *Students' Book* has three double-page *Focus* sections, which introduce the new language in clear and meaningful contexts, then take the students through the important rules via clear and concise *Grammar* boxes. The illustrated *Language summary* at the back of the book provides extra information and examples of each grammar point.
All new language is practised actively through personalisation and other communicative pairwork activities. There are also many information gap-type exercises, which have additional material in the *Communication activities* section at the back of the book, and written exercises designed to improve accuracy. Further practice is provided via a range of photocopiable activities in the *Resource bank*, and there is also systematic written practice in the *Workbook*.

## Vocabulary

*Cutting Edge Starter* also places a strong emphasis on lexis, as we feel that students at beginner level need a solid foundation of key vocabulary in order to communicate successfully. Each module of the *Students' Book* introduces one or more lexical sets, such as food and drink, countries and places in a town, as well as other key vocabulary. However, we realize that even at Starter level students need to become familiar with simple collocations, common phrases and 'chunks' of language, and the *Students' Book* also focuses on this kind of lexis where appropriate. Students will find useful everyday language in the *Real life* sections, which focus on areas such as telling the time, ordering drinks and meals, and buying things in shops. It is important that learners are actively involved in improving their own vocabulary, so *Cutting Edge Starter* comes with its own *Vocabulary Book*. This contains all the most important words and phrases from the *Students' Book*, along with spaces for students to write their own translation. The *Vocabulary Book* also includes illustrations, phonemic transcriptions, simple collocations, quick revision lists, and spaces for students to add their own personal vocabulary. For more information on how to use the *Vocabulary Book* with your class, see page 11.
For classes that require extra vocabulary input, there are regular *Vocabulary booster* worksheets in the *Teacher's Resource Book* (one per module) which are designed to be used in class. These worksheets extend simple concrete areas of vocabulary (such as jobs and parts of the body) via illustrations and matching activities, as well as providing controlled and communicative practice. Note that the vocabulary introduced in the *Vocabulary booster* worksheets is **not** included in subsequent modules of the *Student's Book* or the *Workbook*. This means that you can use as many or as few of these *Vocabulary Booster* worksheets as you wish, depending on the needs of your class and the length of your course. For a list of all photocopiable activities, turn to pages 87 and 88.

## Speaking tasks

Complete beginners are often reluctant to express themselves in English, and we aim to develop their confidence in communicating orally by providing regular Speaking tasks. The focus in these tasks is on practising the language in a meaningful way, and they usually have a realistic end product or outcome. The tasks usually involve more extended communication than the other practice activities, and require students to do many of the things that they may have to do in real life, such as ask and give personal information, describe the place where they live, and talk about their family.
It is likely that learners will need most of the language they have encountered earlier in the module in order to accomplish the task. However, most beginners cannot 'just do' these kinds of tasks without additional support. Therefore speaking tasks are often preceded by a preparation stage, where students either write questions to ask their partner, prepare what they are going to say on their own, or listen to native speakers doing the same task. While working, students can also refer to the *Don't forget* boxes, which contain useful words and phrases for use during the task.
The teacher's notes on each Module provide step-by-step instructions on how to use these tasks, and suggestions for adapting them to particular teaching situations. For more ideas on how to make the most of the Speaking tasks, see *Using the Speaking tasks* section on page 8.

# Other important elements in *Cutting Edge Starter*

## Listening

*Cutting Edge Starter* places a strong emphasis on listening, and the *Students' Book* includes:
- short extracts and mini-dialogues to introduce and practise new language.
- longer texts (interviews, stories, songs and conversations) for more extensive listening.
- opportunities to check answers to exercises via listening.
- words and sentences to provide pronunciation models.

In addition, the *Workbook* has an optional *Student's Cassette*, which includes:
- extensive *Listen and read* texts.
- pronunciation exercises.
- some grammar exercises.

## Reading

There is a wide range of reading material in the *Students' Book*, both short extracts to contextualise new language (often stories or quizzes) and more extensive reading texts for general comprehension. The reading material is graded, ranging from very short, simple texts at the beginning of the book to longer and more complex texts as students progress. These texts are supported by a variety of comprehension exercises, vocabulary work and discussion. There are additional reading texts in every Module of the *Workbook*, which are usually followed by simple comprehension questions and exercises.

## Writing

The *Students' Book* includes a variety of writing exercises, ranging from very controlled exercises, which focus on areas such as word order and sentence completion, to more extensive pieces of personalised writing (for example, describing where you live). There are also writing activities based on real-life situations, such as filling in a form.
The writing syllabus is developed further in the *Workbook*:
- *Improve your writing* sections provide further practice of the topics and new language in the *Students' Book*, as well as focusing on specific areas such as punctuation and capital letters.
- Spelling exercises provide practice of difficult areas such as double letters, contractions, silent letters and problem words.
- There is also extra work on articles, prepositions and question formation.

## Pronunciation

The pronunciation work in the *Students' Book* is integrated into the sections which present new language (Grammar, Vocabulary and Real life) and focuses mainly on sentence stress, weak forms and word stress. Pronunciation exercises are presented in clearly labelled boxes, and place an equal emphasis on both recognising and reproducing the language.

The pronunciation syllabus is developed further in the *Workbook*, where there are additional exercises to practise sentence stress, word stress and problem sounds. These *Workbook* exercises can equally well be used in class. Note that the pronunciation activities in both the *Students' Book* and the *Workbook* are designed to be used in conjunction with the relevant cassette or audio CD, which provide models for students to copy.
For more information on teaching pronunciation at this level, see the section on *Helping students with pronunciation* on page 9.

## Revision

The *Students' Book* revises and recycles language in the following ways:
- *Do you remember?* sections at the end of every Module provide quick spot-check revision of the main areas covered.
- Consolidation units at the end of Modules 4, 8 and 12 combine grammar and vocabulary exercises with listening and speaking activities, and revise language from the previous four modules.
- There are also six pairs of photocopiable tests in the *Resource bank* (there are two alternative tests for teachers to choose from after every second module in the *Students' Book*).
- *Don't forget!* boxes in the Speaking tasks contain the relevant language from the module, and from previous modules, which students will need to do each task.

For more ideas on how to incorporate revision into your lessons, see the *Revision and Recycling* section on page 7.

# Teacher's tips

## WORKING WITH BEGINNERS

Beginner level students present teachers with particular challenges. Students can lack confidence and classes can be of very mixed levels – students may be weak or strong, or real or 'false' beginners. Here are some tips to deal with these different classroom situations:

### Building confidence

- Go slowly and thoroughly through the material. Make sure students have grasped each point fully before moving on.
- Spend time doing spoken repetition of new language together as a class, as well as giving individual repetition practice. Students will probably need a lot of this sort of practice of new items.
- If your class are all real beginners, consider introducing the new language yourself and doing the first activity in the book as practice. For example, at the beginning of Module 5 (page 40), if you think students won't know any of the family vocabulary, draw your own family tree on the board and use this to introduce the new words. You can then ask students to do Exercise 1 (a matching activity).
- Pre-teach important items of vocabulary before students do reading or listening activities.
- Integrate the use of the *Vocabulary Book* from the beginning of the course.
- Use exercises from the *Workbook* in class, to give students greater confidence with new language.
- Take the time to correct students who have problems, but be realistic about what students can achieve at this level.
- Build in extra revision and recycling stages into your classes, particularly at the beginning of each lesson.
- Use the activities from the *Resource bank* to give students more communicative practice of new language.
- If you have a monolingual class, you may want to give some instructions in the students' own language. If you do this, it is a good idea to say the instructions in English immediately afterwards, so that students can begin to understand the English versions.

### Working with mixed levels

- Move at the pace of the average student, not the strongest or weakest. Don't feel you have to wait until everyone has finished pair/group work. It's best to finish when most students have completed a task.
- Involve all the students. Make a conscious effort to encourage weaker/quieter students, for example by giving praise and asking them to answer easier questions.
- Allow students to check answers to exercises together. In class feedback ask a variety of students for answers, including weaker ones, especially if you know they have the correct answer.

- Give students time and space to think. Classes can get used to a strong student calling out the answer first. Encourage each member of the class to note down the answer or put their hands up when they know, so that all students in the class have time to think.
- When drilling new language individually, start with stronger students and finish with weaker ones. Be stricter when correcting stronger students, and make them feel that you're pushing them harder.
- Provide opportunities for students to work in pairs and groups. Weaker students are more likely to participate in small groups and are more likely to ask you for help. When you circulate during an activity, go first to weaker students and give them extra support.
- Experiment with pairing. If you put two strong students together, you may need to think of extra activities for them if they finish early. Consider pairing a strong and weak student together in an open-ended exercise, where students can answer according to their level, for example in many of the speaking tasks or in personalised practice activities.
- In dialogues, weaker students can use the tapescript or prompts in the *Students' Book* to practise the conversation, while stronger students can be encouraged to work without it.
- Focus on the effort made by each individual and help him or her to measure themselves against their personal standard. Perhaps they got four answers right today and only two yesterday.

### Using the board

Boardwork is especially important in beginners' classes. Here are some tips to help your students make the most of your board work:
- **board** This icon in the teacher's notes for each Module indicates stages in the lesson when it may be useful to use the board.
- Sometimes it may be useful to plan what you are going to write on the board before the lesson.
- Involve the students when you are writing on the board by asking them questions (e.g. What comes next? Where's the stress? etc).
- Write at least two or three examples of grammar structures, so students can see the underlying pattern.
- Mark the word stress on new vocabulary.
- Allow students enough time to write down your board work, and check everyone has finished before moving on. Remember beginners may take longer than other students to copy down from the board.
- You may find it useful to leave examples of new language on the board during practice activities, so that you can refer back to them when correcting students.

# REVISION AND RECYCLING

Beginners particularly need regular revision and recycling of new language. Here are some tips and ideas on how to incorporate revision and recycling into your lessons:

## Using Cutting Edge Starter

*Cutting Edge Starter* constantly recycles new language in the readings, listenings and practice exercises of each Module, which means that students will automatically revise much of what they have already covered. There are also other sections of *Cutting Edge Starter* that are specifically designed for revision:

- The exercises in the *Do you remember?* sections can be done all together, or used one at a time where necessary (e.g. in the last five minutes of a lesson). They can also be set for homework, and checked in class the next day.
- The three *Consolidation* sections include grammar exercises, listenings and vocabulary exercises, which recycle much of the language from the previous four Modules. Each *Consolidation* section also contains a well-known song.
- The *Workbook* is designed mainly for homework/self-study, but many of the exercises are also suitable for use in class as revision.
- The *Resource bank* contains between two and four communicative practice activities per module that can be used to revise key language areas.
- The *Resource bank* also contains *Tests* to be used after Modules 2, 4, 6, 8, 10 and 12. Note that there are two alternative tests that cover the same language areas, which means that you can give different tests to students sitting next to each other! If you don't use all the tests in class, consider giving the others for homework.
- The *Vocabulary Book* is also a good source of revision material. For ideas on how to use this, look at the section on *Making the most of the Vocabulary Book* on page 11.

## Warmers and fillers

These activities need no (or very little) preparation, and are particularly useful for the first or last five minutes of a class, after breaks, or whenever you feel students need a change of focus.

- Ask students to write down six or eight words they learnt last lesson, then compare their lists with their partner.
- Put students in pairs and ask them to ask each other questions to find four things they both have in their bags/can do well/usually do at the weekend/did last year, etc.
- Write five wrong sentences on the board based on a particular grammar point. Students work in pairs and decide how to correct them.

- Practise key verbs like *have*, *like* or *want* by asking students to write down five things they have/like/want, then comparing their answers with a partner.
- Write ten words on the board. Spell five of these correctly and five incorrectly. Students work in pairs and decide which words are correct.
- Ask students to write down three things they can do well/did last week/like doing in their free time, etc. Students then move around the room (or work in groups) and ask questions to find people with the same answers as them.
- Students write the names of two or three people they know well on a piece of paper. They must then tell their partner as much as possible about each person in five minutes. (This idea can also be used for question and answer practice.)
- Write half a dialogue on the board (e.g. from a *Real life* section in the *Students' Book*) and ask students to write the other half. Students can then practise the dialogue in pairs.

## Other revision ideas

- Put students into groups and ask them to make posters based on a particular topic (e.g. their home town, a famous person, their school, etc.). These can then be put up around the classroom for other students to read.
- Write twenty or thirty words on a piece of paper and photocopy it for the class. Students work alone or in pairs and organise the words into groups or lexical sets. They can then add two more words to each group.
- Make your own 'Find Someone Who …' worksheets. Write six to ten prompts on a piece of paper based around a topic or language area, like those in the Speaking tasks on pages 54 and 103 of the *Students' Book*. Photocopy the worksheet for the class, then ask students to find one person for each prompt.
- Write six questions on a worksheet, but with the words in the wrong order (e.g. *live/Where/you/do?*). Photocopy the worksheet for the class, and ask students to put the questions in the right order. They can then work in pairs and ask each other the questions.
- Prepare a short text with ten mistakes in it and photocopy it for the class. Students work in groups and correct the mistakes.

There are more ideas for revising vocabulary in the section on *Vocabulary* on page 10. Note that there are also ideas for extra practice on specific language areas in the *Additional suggestions* boxes in the teacher's notes.

# USING THE SPEAKING TASKS

The speaking tasks in *Cutting Edge Starter* mirror situations that students might encounter in real life, and give them a chance to use the language they have learned in a meaningful way. Here are some other tips for making the speaking tasks work well:

## Personalise the speaking tasks

Students using this course will vary in age, background, interests and ability. All these students need to find the Speaking tasks motivating and 'do-able', yet challenging at the same time. Do not be afraid to adapt the tasks to suit your class, for example by changing the prompts, making the questions more relevant to your students' backgrounds, doing the activity in groups rather than pairs, adding an extra preparation stage, etc. Often your students would find it more motivating if you provided your own model rather than always using the model in the book. The teacher's notes contain suggestions on how to adapt certain tasks where appropriate.

## Make the most of the Don't forget boxes

The *Don't forget* boxes are intended to remind students of language they need to perform the tasks, often words and expressions that have appeared in previous Modules. It is important to draw students' attention to the contents of the *Don't forget* boxes before they begin the task, and check that students understand (and can pronounce) this language. If necessary, do some repetition practice.

## Use the preparation stages

Most speaking tasks include a preparation stage, where students either write questions, draw a time line, make notes, or plan what they are going to say. This preparation stage is very important if beginner-level students are to produce the best language that they are capable of, and is particularly useful for building up the confidence of students who are normally reluctant to speak in class. Make sure you allow students enough time to complete the preparation stage, and if necessary check that students have done this stage successfully before moving on.

## Pay attention to seating arrangements

Whether you have fixed desks or more portable furniture, when working in groups or pairs always make sure that students are sitting so that they can hear and speak to each other comfortably. Groups should be in a small circle or square rather than a line, for example. Empty desks between students may mean that they have to raise their voices to a level at which they feel self-conscious when speaking English, and this can have an adverse effect on any pairwork or group-work activity.

## Let the students do the talking

If students are hesitant, it is easy (with the best of intentions!) to intervene and speak for them. Some students will be only too happy to let you do this, and before long they won't even attempt to formulate full sentences, knowing that you will usually do it for them. Remember that at beginner level any kind of speaking is a considerable challenge, so try to let the students do the talking. Don't worry if they have to think for a little while before they speak; they will get better at this eventually, but only if they get the opportunity to practise!

## Provide positive feedback

Allow enough time for you to give your feedback at the end ... and make it positive! Students of this level are bound to make a lot of errors in any kind of communication, and you may feel that you need to deal with these during the activity. However, it is usually best not to interrupt, but to make a note of any important points to deal with at the end. It is also important to provide feedback on the outcome of the task itself as well as on the language used. Generally, keep the emphasis on praise and positive feedback, and hopefully your students will be eager to do this kind of speaking task again!

# HELPING STUDENTS WITH PRONUNCIATION

When people say 'you speak good English', very often they are reacting to a student's pronunciation, and this illustrates the importance of pronunciation in creating a positive first impression. Setting high standards for pronunciation is probably the best practical way to help your students become clear speakers of English, and the best time to lay the right foundations for this is at beginner level.

## Give priority to pronunciation ... but be realistic!

There are Pronunciation boxes in the *Students' Book* which are designed to help students improve their pronunciation. However, don't wait for a Pronunciation box to come along – integrate pronunciation work whenever students have a problem. 'Little and often' is a particularly good principle with pronunciation. Also consider what you want your students to achieve: clarity and confidence are what most students need, rather than perfection in every detail. Individuals vary widely in what they can achieve, so don't push too much when a particular student is getting frustrated or embarrassed. A humorous, light-hearted approach also helps to relieve stress!

## Provide pronunciation models

Make sure students hear the correct pronunciation before you ask them to reproduce it. Even if students cannot yet produce the target pronunciation, it will improve their listening skills if they can at least hear it. All examples for pronunciation work are on the *Class Cassettes/Audio CD*, but you may prefer to model the new language yourself. At low levels it is often helpful to repeat the word or phrase two or three times before you ask students to say it. Sometimes you need to isolate and repeat individual words, syllables or sounds, and exaggerating the stress is often helpful.

## Drill

Choral and/or individual repetition is the simplest pronunciation activity to set up and possibly the most effective. It can help to build confidence, and is often popular with low-level students as long as you don't overdo it. When you are drilling students individually, correct any obvious errors in pronunciation on the spot, then ask the student to try again. Do your best to keep your feedback positive, and don't forget to let students know when they are pronouncing things correctly too!

## Pay attention to spelling

One of the biggest problems for learners of English is the relationship between sounds and spelling. Highlight and drill problem words on a consistent basis, and consider dealing with pronunciation before writing on the board. Also think about teaching students the phonemic symbols. This gives them a valuable tool for finding out problematic pronunciation themselves, and for writing it down. You can use the list of

sounds on page 64 of the *Vocabulary Book* to teach it – but only teach a few symbols at a time, and make constant use of them, otherwise students will soon forget them.

## Focus consistently on word stress ...

This is an easy area in which to correct students effectively. Get into the habit of focusing on word stress whenever you teach a new word. If students have problems, try one of the following ideas when you drill:
– exaggerate the stress;
– clap or click your fingers on the stressed syllable;
– isolate the stressed syllable first then add the other syllables.
Don't forget to mark stressed syllables when you write new words on the board, by underlining or drawing a blob over them, and encourage students to do the same when they copy the words. Also make sure that students know how word stress is marked in the *Vocabulary Book*.

## ... and sentence stress

Sentence stress is one of the most important elements in helping students to be easy to understand when they speak, just as punctuation makes their written work more comprehensible. Try to focus on it little and often, for example when you teach a new structure or phrase. You can use the same methods for word stress to help students to hear and reproduce the sentence stress.

## Pay attention to the schwa \ə\

This is by far the most common vowel sound in English, occurring in a very high percentage of multi-syllable words as well as in many weak forms of verbs and prepositions (e.g. *I was* /wəz/ *tired.*). Using the schwa correctly will help students to speak faster, and will greatly increase their comprehensibility. Focus on it whenever it occurs in new words or example sentences, but be careful not to stress it accidentally – syllables with a schwa in them are not normally stressed. To avoid this, drill new words starting with the stressed syllable, then add the schwa sounds either before or afterwards, for example:

**doc ... doctor**
\ə\

Consistently marking schwa sounds when you write words on the board will also help raise students' awareness.

## Dealing with correction

It is important to correct pronunciation errors in class, and don't forget that most students do want to be corrected. However, don't discourage students by overcorrecting, or feel you have to correct every pronunciation error you hear. When you do correct students, try to help them understand what the problem is – word stress, sentence stress, the wrong sound, etc. – before asking them to try again. Remember also that being corrected in front of the class can be stressful for less confident students, so consider waiting till the class are working in pairs or groups before helping these students with individual problems.

# TEACHING VOCABULARY

Having a good range of vocabulary is one of the most important factors in successful communication, and for beginner level students vocabulary is probably more important than grammar in fulfilling their basic communicative needs. Students at this level usually recognise this, and enjoy 'collecting' all the new words they learn. Here are some tips for teaching vocabulary to your students.

## See what students know

Very often in *Cutting Edge Starter* students are asked to match words to pictures. Of course, they may not know any, in which case you will have to teach the words yourself. However, always see if they can do any first. Even true beginners often know a few words and there may be others they can guess. This is an important skill to encourage, even from the beginning. If students really don't know anything, however, step in quickly. You do not want to undermine their confidence with long awkward silences.

## Use the Vocabulary Book

*Cutting Edge Starter* comes complete with its own *Vocabulary Book*, which contains all the key words and phrases from the *Student's Book*. For more information on this, see the next page.

## Make students aware of collocation

Even at beginner level, it is very important to make students aware of common collocations and 'chunks' of language, as well as traditional one-word items. These could be verb–noun combinations like *go for a walk* and *start work*, adjective–noun combinations such as *young people* and *new buildings*, and fixed phrases or sentences such as *Here you are.* and *I don't know.* When you teach these to your class, treat each 'chunk' as a single item of vocabulary, and use every opportunity to point out collocations and fixed phrases as they appear.

## Vocabulary boosters

If you feel your students can cope with some extra vocabulary, use the Vocabulary booster worksheets in the *Resource bank*. There is one Vocabulary booster worksheet for each Module, and each is based around a common lexical set (e.g. the weather, sports, nationalities). Note that this vocabulary is *not* required for students to do the relevant module in the *Students' Book*.

## Spelling

Many students have problems with spelling, and the fact that English is not a phonetic language has caused students problems for generations! It is therefore important to draw students' attention to non-phonetic spellings, double letters, silent letters, irregular forms, etc. when writing new vocabulary on the board. Use the spelling exercises in the *Workbook* as consolidation, and consider having quick spelling tests at the beginning or end of every week.

## Parts of speech

It is useful to teach students the basic parts of speech (verb, noun, adjective, etc.) if they don't already know them. This helps them organise the language in their own minds, and gives them underlying rules on how to use them. When writing new vocabulary on the board, check that students know what parts of speech they are when appropriate. You may also choose to write (*v*), (*n*), (*adj*), etc. after each word.

## Keep a written record

The simplest way to help your students remember new words is to get them into the habit of writing them down. The Personal vocabulary sections in the *Vocabulary Book* are specifically designed for students to note down any extra vocabulary that they wish to remember. It is sometimes useful to keep an area of the board reserved for noting down any new vocabulary that comes up during the lesson.

## Revise and recycle regularly

With all new language it is important to revise and recycle what has been taught, and this is particularly true for vocabulary. Here are some simple ideas for recycling vocabulary in class:

- Use the vocabulary exercises in the *Do you remember?* sections of the *Students' Book* and the *Workbook*, as well as the activities in the *Resource bank*. Remember that these can be used any time after the language has been taught, even six months later!
- Give students the 'headword' of a lexical set you have taught (e.g. family members, jobs, etc.), and ask them to write down as many words as possible in two minutes.
- Practise collocations by writing verbs down one side of the board and the corresponding nouns down the other side. Students match up the nouns and the verbs.
- If you take a break in the middle of a lesson and there is some new vocabulary on the board, rub out everything but the first letter of each word. When the students return to class, see if they can remember all the words from just their first letters.
- Cut pictures from magazines of vocabulary you have taught and put these on pieces of card. Stick these on the board and ask students to write down all the words. You can also hand the cards out to the class and ask them to test one another.
- Ask students to make posters based on lexical sets or topics to display around the room.
- Make your own wordsearches (like Exercise 4 in the *Do you remember?* on page 21) based on vocabulary that students are having problems with.

For more ideas, see *Making the most of the Vocabulary Book* section on the next page, and the *Revising and Recycling* section on page 7.

# MAKING THE MOST OF THE VOCABULARY BOOK

The *Cutting Edge Starter Vocabulary Book* has been especially designed to be useful to, and usable by, beginner students. It contains the following special features:

- places where students can write in translations of each new word and phrase;
- pictures of new words where appropriate, and if not, examples that are as self-explanatory as possible;
- the phonemic transcription of all new vocabulary, and a table of the phonemic symbols;
- clear organisation of collocations;
- check-lists of all the important vocabulary in each Module;
- places for students to keep a record of personal vocabulary;
- regular and irregular verb tables.

Here are some ideas on how to use the *Cutting Edge Starter Vocabulary Book* effectively with your students.

## The beginning of the course

Show students the *Vocabulary Book* at the beginning of the course. Explain what it is, and take a few minutes to point out all the features, including the spaces for translations, the personal vocabulary sections, the verb tables, the phonemic symbols page, etc.

## The Students' Book

The *Vocabulary Book* is designed to be used in class alongside the *Students' Book*, and at relevant points in the Students' Book you will see the following references:

 Vocabulary Book page 12.

Here are some ways to use these *Vocabulary Book* references in class:

- If the vocabulary reference relates to new vocabulary input, you may want your students to do as much of the exercise in the *Students' Book* as they can, then refer to the *Vocabulary Book* to check any words they don't know.
- If you have a class of real beginners, you may wish to use the *Vocabulary Book* to teach the words first, then use the exercise in the *Students' Book* as practice.
- If the vocabulary reference relates to a reading text, then you may wish to deal with this vocabulary before they read the text. Alternatively, students can refer to the *Vocabulary Book* while they are reading.

It is a good idea to experiment with how you use the *Vocabulary Book* in class, to see what works best for you and your students.

## Writing in the translations

After each lesson students should ideally go back over the new words in their *Students' Book*, look them up in their *Vocabulary Book* and fill in the translations in the appropriate places. This will provide invaluable revision and consolidation of what they have learnt. At the beginning of the course it would be useful to allow some time for this in class.

## Personal vocabulary

At the end of each Module in the *Vocabulary Book* there is space for students to write in their own vocabulary. This may be other words or phrases that have come up in class, or items that are particularly important for them to remember (e.g. their job title in English). Encourage students to use this section during and after class, and help students with any spelling problems where necessary.

## Collocations

The *Vocabulary Book* reinforces the collocations taught in the *Students' Book*, usually by using 'spider-maps' (e.g. page 13). Beginner students probably won't be aware that collocations in English are often different from in their first language, so whenever you focus on a word which has a problematic collocation, show how the *Vocabulary Book* examples can help with this.

## Revision in class

The *Vocabulary Book* can also be used for quick revision activities in class. Here are a few ideas:

- Students work individually and choose ten words they have already done. Students then work together and say the words to each other. Student A says a word, and Student B must convey the meaning of the word, either by mime, pointing, drawing, giving a clear example or definition, etc.
- Student A says words from the *Vocabulary Book*, and Student B must write them down with correct spelling.
- Students look at the list of important vocabulary at the end of each module and try to group the words into lexical sets.
- Students work in pairs with one *Vocabulary Book* between them. Student A chooses a page with a lot of pictures (e.g. page 17) and covers up all the pictures with a piece of paper, except those at the top of the page. Student B must say what the top two pictures are. The students can then move the paper down the page and test each other on the rest of the pictures.
- Students test each other on common collocations (e.g. page 42). One student says a noun, and his/her partner says an adjective.
- The teacher prepares a list of vocabulary already covered and distributes it to the class. Students tick each vocabulary item if they are sure they know it, put a '?' if they are not sure, and a ✗ if they don't know it. They can then find the words with ?s and ✗s in their *Vocabulary Book* and check the meaning.
- In a monolingual class, students can say the translations they have written in their *Vocabulary Book* and their partners must say the English word.

## Cutting Edge Companion Website

*Cutting Edge* has its own dedicated website, with a wide variety of resources for you and your students, designed specifically to complement each level of the course.

The site is updated regularly, taking into account your comments and suggestions (you can send them into us using the 'Contact Us' button on the web page below). Help make **www.longman.com/cuttingedge** your site by exchanging ideas and opinions with other Cutting Edge users, and with the authors and publishers of the course. The website includes separate pages for teachers and students. On the *Students'* page opposite you will see some of the resources available for students. Below you will see the resources available to teachers on the *Teachers'* page, with an explanation of each one.

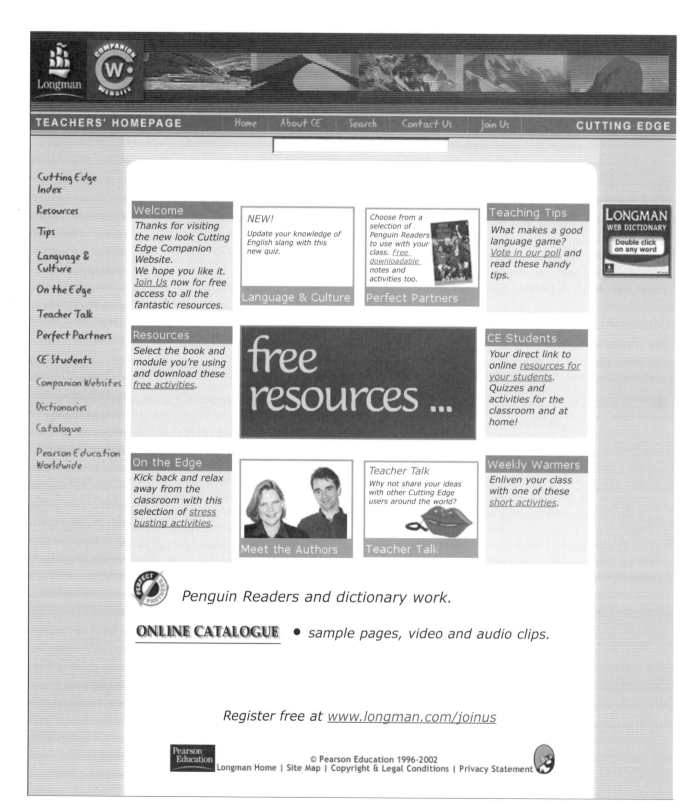

In addition to general *Cutting Edge* resources, there are specific web materials suggested for each module of the course. These are indicated by the *Cutting Edge* website logo at appropriate points in the teacher's notes for each Module.

**Module 1:** Activities to practise spelling and the use of the alphabet.

**Module 2:** Further consolidation with the downloadable worksheet on countries and nationalities.

**Module 3:** Your students can send ecards and write about their holidays online.

**Module 4:** Use the links to popular radio stations for up-to-date interviews.

**Module 5:** Which room am I in? Download the extra activities to use with your students.

**Module 6:** Find out the time around the world or ask your students to take the online quiz.

**Module 7:** Learn more about life in Britain with activities relating to British TV.

**Module 8:** Help your students with English spelling with the activities related to this module.

**Module 9:** The Internet has lots of sites related to the past – try one of our specially selected links and related activities.

**Module 10:** Use the Perfect Partners section of the website and see a selection of Penguin Readers.

**Module 11:** Practise writing emails and use the links to buy train tickets online.

**Module 12:** Shop online – see the latest fashions and use the activities as consolidation.

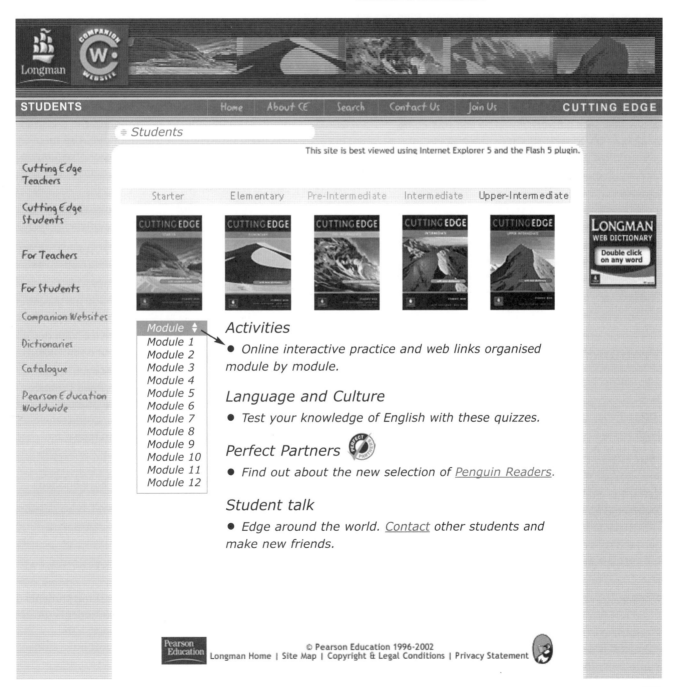

## Focus 1 (PAGES 6–7)

### Names and introductions

1 📠 [1.1] Focus students on the pictures on page 6. Play the recording and tell the students to follow the conversations in their books. Play the recording again if necessary.

## Grammar

**board** Write *…'m Rosa.*; *… name's Ebru.*; *Are … David?* and *What's … name?* on the board. Ask students to complete the gaps in these sentences, referring back to the dialogues if necessary. Alternatively, point at yourself and write *I'm +* (*your name*) and *My name's … .* on the board. Then choose different students in the class and ask *What's your name?* and *Are you (Marcos)?* Write these sentences on the board and underline *I*, *my*, *you* and *your*.

Highlight:

● the difference between *I* and *you*.

● the difference between *my name* and *your name*.

● the use of full stops, question marks and capital letters.

You may decide to look at *Language summary* 1A on page 113 of the *Students' Book* after teaching *he*, *she*, *his*, *her* in Focus 2.

LANGUAGE NOTE:
Students might ask you about the meaning of *'m*, *'s* and *are* in these sentences. Tell the class that they are part of the verb *be*, but encourage students to treat the new language as set phrases at this stage. The verb *be* is dealt with systematically in Modules 2, 3 and 4.

## Pronunciation

See *Teacher's Tips: Helping students with pronunciation* on page 9.

📠 [1.2] Play the recording and help students hear the main stress in each sentence by clapping at the same time, or by using hand gestures. Also check that students understand how stress is shown in the *Students' Book*. Play the recording again, stopping after each sentence and asking the students to repeat. Ensure that students say the contracted form of *be* when repeating the sentences.

**Exercise 1: additional suggestion**

Drill (i.e. say the language yourself, then ask students to repeat) the other useful words and sentences from the pictures, for example: *Hello, Hi, Nice to meet you.* and *I'm a student*. Ask students to repeat the dialogues across the class, then put all the students into pairs to practise the dialogues again.

2 Check example a) with the class, then allow them time to do the exercise individually or in pairs. Students can check their answers in different pairs or small groups. Check also that students know what *Mr* /ˈmɪstə/ and *Mrs* /ˈmɪsɪz/ mean, and how to pronounce these abbreviations.

**ANSWERS**
**a** your  **b** I; your; My  **c** you  **d** my; I  **e** you; I

LANGUAGE NOTE:
In many languages there are both formal and informal words for *you*. If this is the case in your students' language(s), point out that there is no difference in English between an informal *you* (e.g. *Are you David?* in Exercise 1) and a more formal *you* (e.g. *Are you Mrs Adams?* in Exercise 2).

**Exercise 2: alternative suggestions**

See *Teacher's Tips: Working with beginners* on page 6.

a *If your students aren't complete beginners*: consider doing Exercise 2 at the beginning of the lesson to test their knowledge of the language. Use their answers to highlight the meaning of *I, you, my* and *your,* and refer them to the *Grammar* box on page 6 if necessary.

b *If you have a mixed-ability class*: consider pairing false beginners with complete beginners for this activity.

3 a) 📠 [1.3] Play the recording and allow students to check their answers to Exercise 2. Check the answers with the whole class. Also check that students have included capital letters where appropriate (i.e. with the personal pronoun *I* and at the beginning of a sentence).

b) Play the recording again, stopping after each sentence and asking the students to repeat. Choose two students and ask them to do dialogue a) together in front of the class (students don't need to leave their seats). Correct their pronunciation if required, and ask them to repeat the dialogue if necessary. Repeat this procedure with different pairs. Students then work in new pairs and practise all the dialogues, changing roles when they have finished dialogue e).

## Speaking task

See *Teacher's Tips: Using the Speaking tasks* on pages 8.

1 **board** Write *My name's … .* and *I'm … .* on one side of the board. Go round the class asking students to say their names in turn. Write the students' names on the other side of the board. Practise the pronunciation of these names if you have students from different countries.

**2** Revise other expressions which are useful when meeting new people, for example: *Hello, Hi, Are you …? Yes, that's right. No, I'm … . Nice to meet you.* Write these on the board if necessary. Students then move around the room and meet as many students as possible, using the language from the lesson.

**Speaking task: alternative suggestions**

a *If your students already know each other*: ask them to imagine they are famous people.

b *If your class are false beginners*: you may decide to combine this activity with Exercise 5 on page 8 of the *Students' Book*, which introduces the vocabulary of jobs and *What's your job?*

c *If you have a large class*: students can turn around in their desks and work in groups of six or eight if there is not enough room for them to move around the class.

## ADDITIONAL PRACTICE

**Workbook:** Names and introductions, page 4

## Focus 2  (PAGES 8–9)

Vocabulary: jobs; *a/an*

See *Teacher's Tips*: *Teaching vocabulary* on page 10.

**1** Focus students on the pictures on page 8 of the *Students' Book*. Teach the word *job*, then put students into pairs or small groups and ask them to match the pictures with the job vocabulary in the box. Students will probably know one or two words already (e.g. *teacher* and *student*), and be able to match other words because they are similar in their own language. When they have done as much as they can, they can check their answers with you, or on page 3 of the *Vocabulary book*. (See *Teacher's Tips: Making the most of the Vocabulary book* on page 11.)

LANGUAGE NOTE:
With a strong class you may wish to teach *policeman* /pəˈliːsmən/, *policewoman* /pəˈliːsˈwʊmən/ and the female forms *actress* /ˈæktrɪs/ and *waitress* /ˈweɪtrɪs/ at this point.

**ANSWERS**
**a** businessman/businesswoman   **b** actor
**c** police officer   **d** student   **e** engineer   **f** waiter
**g** doctor   **h** teacher

**Exercise 1: alternative suggestions**

a *If your class are all complete beginners*: you may choose to present the vocabulary yourself, rather than asking them to try and match the pictures and the words. Point to each picture in the book and tell students the corresponding word. Alternatively, prepare flashcards of the jobs and hold these up in front of the class.

b *If this is easy for your class*: you may want to introduce some more jobs vocabulary (for example, words that refer to students' own jobs).

c *If your students are false beginners*: use the *Vocabulary booster*: *Jobs* on page 103 of the Resource bank (instructions on page 89). Note that this worksheet also practises *he, she, his* and *her*.

## Pronunciation

**1** board 💬 [1.4] Play the recording and allow students to listen to the words. Focus students on the main stress of each word by beating the stress with your hand, and/or marking the stress on the board:

tea·cher  stu·dent  ac·tor  wai·ter  doc·tor
en·gi·neer  busi·ness·man  busi·ness·woman
po·lice officer

**2** Play the recording again (or model the pronunciation yourself), pausing after each word and asking the class to repeat chorally and individually. Check the pronunciation of *businessman* /ˈbɪznɪsmən/ and *businesswoman* /ˈbɪznɪsˌwʊmən/. Also focus students on the /ə/ sound at the end of many of the words, for example, *actor* /ˈæktə/ and *doctor* /ˈdɒktə/.

**2** 💬 [1.5] Play the recording and ask students to write down each person's job, as shown in the example. Students check their answers in pairs or small groups. Play the recording again, stopping after each person to check the answers with the whole class. Note that these answers do not relate to the pictures on page 8.

**ANSWERS**
**1** doctor   **2** actor   **3** police officer   **4** engineer
**5** businesswoman   **6** waiter

**3** 💬 [1.6] Play the recording, pausing after each sentence to allow students time to write. Check the answers with the whole class on the board.

**ANSWERS**
**a** I'm a waiter.   **b** I'm an actor.
**c** I'm an engineer.   **d** I'm a businesswoman.

# Grammar

**board** Divide your board into two columns headed *a* and *an*. Teach the words *vowel* and *consonant*, and write the examples in the correct columns. Go through the rule with the whole class, emphasising that in English we always use *a* or *an* when talking about jobs. This is particularly important if this is not the case in your students' language,. or if their language does not use articles at all. (Note that the alphabet is taught later in the module on page 10.)

Refer students to *Language summary* 1B on page 113 of the *Students' Book*.

TEACHER'S NOTE:
It will be helpful for students if you always put *a* or *an* in front of countable nouns when you are writing new vocabulary on the board.

4 Students work in pairs and put the jobs from the box in Exercise 1 in the correct place. Check the answers with the whole class.

5 Drill the question *What's your job?* chorally (i.e. with the whole class) and individually. Students move around the room asking one another what their jobs are. Note any problems with *a/an* in their conversations.

LANGUAGE NOTE:
*What do you do?* is also a common question when asking about jobs, but at this stage we feel that it is important to keep the language simple here. If you have a class of false beginners you might choose to introduce this as an alternative to *What's your job?* before students do Exercise 5.

### Exercise 5: alternative suggestions

a *If none of your students have jobs*: use activity 1A *What's your job?* in the Resource bank on page 102 (instructions on page 89).

b *If you have a monolingual class*: consider teaching students the English words for their own jobs before they do Exercise 5.

c *If you have a large class*: students can turn around in their desks and work in groups of six or eight if there is not enough room for them to move around the class.

## ADDITIONAL PRACTICE

**Workbook:** Vocabulary: jobs; *a/an*, page 4
**RB** **Resource bank:** 1A *What's your job?*, page 102 (instructions on page 89)

---

## he/she/his/her

6  [1.7] Focus students on the pictures on page 9. Students do the exercise in pairs or individually. Play the recording to allow students to check their answers. Also check that students understand the following new vocabulary: *politician* /ˌpɒlɪˈtɪʃən/; *tennis player*; *footballer*; *singer*; *actress*, and refer them to page 3 of the *Vocabulary book* if necessary. Check the pronunciation of the new words with the whole class.

### Exercise 6: alternative suggestion

If you don't think your students will know the famous people mentioned, find pictures of people who are famous in their country and stick them on the board. This is also a good way to check the meaning of the new vocabulary in Exercise 6.

# Grammar

**board** Draw two columns on the board, headed with stick-figures of a man and a woman. Write *... name's Luis Figo. ...'s a footballer.* in one column, and *... name's Jennifer Lopez. ...'s a singer.* in the other column. Ask students to complete the sentences. Add sentences about Serena Williams and Tony Blair if necessary.

Highlight:

● the difference between *he* and *she*.

● the difference between *his name* and *her name*.

● the *'s* (= *is*) after *he*, *she* and *name*.

Refer students to *Language summary* 1A on page 113 of the *Students' Book*.

7 a)  [1.8] Play the recording and allow students to listen to the questions and answers. Play the recording again, pausing after each sentence for the students to repeat.

b) Demonstrate the activity by pointing to one of the pictures in the book and asking: *What's his/her name?*. Put students into pairs to continue the activity.

### Exercise 7b: additional suggestions

a Cut out pictures of about ten or twelve other famous people and stick them onto a piece of paper to be photocopied. Give a photocopy of the pictures to each pair of students to practise the language in Exercise 7a. (You will need to teach any additional jobs vocabulary and the expression: *I don't know.* before they begin.)

b Alternatively, give each student in the class a picture of a famous person. Students move around the room asking one another: *What's his/her name?* and *What's his/her job?*. If your students can't move around the room, they could do the activity by turning around in their desks and asking each other in groups.

c As a follow-up task to the above activities, students can write sentences about the people, similar to those in Exercise 6.

d *Vocabulary booster: Jobs* on page 103 of the Resource bank (instructions on page 89) can be used at any time after Exercise 7b.

## Reading

**8** Do the exercise with the whole class. Check the pronunciation of *full name* /fʊl neɪm/, *first name* /fɜːst neɪm/ and *surname* /ˈsɜːˌneɪm/.

**9** Check that students know the famous people and their jobs. Teach *He's a golfer.* for Tiger Woods if necessary. Go through the example a) with the whole class. Students do the rest of the exercise individually.

**10** Students work individually, then check their answers in pairs. Students don't need to practise the pronunciation of the names.

> **ANSWERS**
> **1** b  **2** c  **3** a  **4** d

## ADDITIONAL MATERIAL

**Workbook:** *he/she/his/her*, page 5; *I/my/you/your/his/her*, page 5

**RB Resource bank:** *Vocabulary booster: Jobs*, page 103 (instructions on page 89). This worksheet also contains further practice of *he*, *she*, *his* and *her*.

## Focus 3 (PAGE 10)

The alphabet; *How do you spell ...?*

**1** 🔲 [1.9] Play the recording and ask students to repeat each letter. Drill the letters chorally and individually, using the tape or yourself as a model. Pay particular attention to the pronunciation of *a, e, i, g, h, j, q, r, w* and *y*. Check if students remember the meaning of *vowel* and *consonant*, and ask them to name the vowels.

> **Exercise 1: alternative suggestions**
>
> a *If you have a class of false beginners*: ask students to write down the alphabet without looking at the book. Write their version of the alphabet on the board and use the recording to check if they are correct.

b *If you have a monolingual class*: it is useful to highlight any differences between the alphabet for their language and the English alphabet. These differences could be extra letters, the lack of accents, or how particular letters are pronounced.

### The alphabet: a phonemic approach

If you have a strong class you may choose to teach the alphabet via phonemic symbols. Draw up a table on the board with seven columns and write the phonemic symbols below at the top of each column. Teach the class the sound of each phoneme, then play recording [1.9] (or model the letters yourself) and ask the class which column the letters go in. The letters can then be drilled in same-sound groups. Alternatively, this approach can be used for revision later in the course.

| /eɪ/ | /iː/ | /e/ | /aɪ/ | /əʊ/ | /uː/ | /ɑː/ |
|------|------|-----|------|------|------|------|
| a | b | f | i | o | q | r |
| h | c | l | y |  | u |  |
| j | d | m |  |  | w |  |
| k | e | n |  |  |  |  |
|  | g | s |  |  |  |  |
|  | p | x |  |  |  |  |
|  | t | z |  |  |  |  |
|  | v |  |  |  |  |  |

Note: If you use this approach, also ensure that students learn the correct order of the alphabet (*a, b, c*, etc.) and are able to say the letters in order.

**2** 🔲 [1.10] Play the recording and ask the whole class to say the letters that have been replaced by a 'beep'. Alternatively, go round the class so that only one student answers for each 'beep'. Students can then do the same activity in pairs.

> **Exercise 2: additional suggestions**
>
> a Students work in pairs. Student A says a letter and Student B has to point to the letter on page 10 of the *Students' Book*.
>
> b Students work in pairs and say alternate letters of the alphabet. They can then repeat the activity by saying the alphabet backwards!

**3** Students work in pairs or small groups and practise saying the company names.

> **Exercise 3: additional information**
>
> *EMI* is an international record company.
>
> *IBM* is an American computer company.

*BBC* is a British television channel.

*KLM uk* is an airline based in Holland.

*DKNY* is an American clothing company.

*BMW* is a German car manufacturer.

**4** **a)**  [1.11] Choose one student and play the first question on the recording. As he/she spells the word, write it up on the board and ask the rest of the class if they think it is correct. Repeat this procedure with the rest of the questions on the recording.

**b)** Drill the question *How do you spell ...?* chorally and individually. Tell the students to choose five English words they know. Students then work in pairs and ask each other to spell the words they have chosen. Move around the room and help any students with pronunciation or spelling difficulties.

### Exercise 4b: additional suggestions

a   *Bingo*: draw a grid with sixteen spaces on the board and ask students to copy it. Students then fill in letters at random on their own bingo card. Call out letters in random order. (It is useful to make a list of the letters yourself and tick them off as you call them out.) The student who completes a line – or the whole card – first is the winner.

b   *Guess the word*: think of a word students know and write it on the board as a series of dashes, with one dash for each letter. (e.g. *actor* would be _ _ _ _ _ ). Students say a letter they think will be in the word. If they are correct, write it in the appropriate space. If the letter doesn't appear in the word, write it in a box on one side of the board. If the class guesses the word before there are eight letters in the box, they win the game. After demonstrating this a few times with the class, students can continue to play in pairs or small groups.

c   Consider using Exercise 6 on page 6 of the *Workbook* in class as further practice.

 Find activities to practise spelling and the use of the alphabet in the Resources section of the website.

## Speaking task

**1**  [1.12] Focus students on the picture on page 10. Play the recording and allow students to fill in the missing words in the questions. Drill the questions chorally and individually, either by playing the recording again and pausing after each question for students to repeat, or by modelling the questions yourself.

### ANSWERS
**a** surname   **b** what's   **c** full name   **d** how; spell

**2** Students walk around the room, asking the questions from Exercise 1 and filling in the gaps in their *Students' Books*. If it is not possible for students to move around the room, they should talk to four students sitting near them. Encourage students to aim for accuracy in spelling during the activity, and to use *Thanks* or *Thank you* to close each conversation.

### Exercise 2: additional suggestions

a   Students work in pairs and tell each other the names they have found out. Remind students to use *his* and *her* in their conversations. This idea can also be used for students who finish the speaking task early.

b   *If you have a monolingual class*: consider doing the speaking task before teaching the alphabet, as students probably won't need to spell names to each other during the activity.

c   Activity 1B *What's his surname?* on pages 104 and 105 of the Resource bank (instructions on page 89) provides extra practice of *he/she* questions and spelling.

## ADDITIONAL MATERIAL

**Workbook:** The alphabet; *How do you spell...?*, pages 6 and 7

**RB Resource bank:** 1B *What's his surname?* on pages 104 and 105 (instructions on page 89)

## Real life   (PAGE 11)

*hello* and *goodbye*

**1**  [1.13] Focus students on the pictures, and allow students a few moments to look through the dialogues. Play the recording, then ask students to compare their answers in pairs or small groups. Play the recording again so that students can check their answers. The following new language appears in the conversations: *This is ... ; How are you? Fine, thank you. And you? I'm very well, thanks. Goodbye/Bye. See you (later).*

### ANSWERS
See tapescript Module 1, recording 13 on page 119 of the *Students' Book*.

### Exercise 1: alternative suggestion

*If you have a class of false beginners*: ask them to put the dialogues in order before listening to the recording. Then play the recording for them to check their answers.

**2** [cassette] Play the recording again, this time stopping the tape after each sentence for students to repeat. Encourage students to sound interested when responding.

**3** Put students into pairs and ask them to practise the conversations a few times, referring to the *Students' Book* when necessary. When they feel confident with the language, students move around the room and practise the conversations with other students. Students can also act out the conversations in front of the class before or after they mingle.

## Focus 4 (PAGE 12)

Numbers 0–20

**1** [cassette] [1.14] Play the recording to allow students to hear the numbers. Play the recording again, pausing after each number for the students to repeat.

**2** Put the students into pairs. Students take it in turns to write a number on a piece of paper, and his/her partner says the number in English. As they are working, move around the room and check pronunciation.

**3** **a)** Students do the activity individually or in pairs. Although complete beginners will not have seen these words before, they should be able to match most of them by referring back to the numbers in Exercise 1.
**b)** [board] [cassette] [1.15] Play the recording and write the numbers and words on the board. Play the recording again, pausing to allow students to repeat each word.

TEACHER'S NOTE:
When drilling the words for 13–19, highlight the fact that the -teen syllable is usually stressed. While we recognise this is not always the case (when counting, for example, native speakers often stress the first syllable), we feel that at this level it's more helpful to give students a clear rule that will avoid confusion and be correct in most instances.

**4** Divide the students into three groups, A, B and C. Ask Group A to turn to page 108, Group B to turn to page 110 and Group C to turn to page 112 of the *Students' Book*. Call out the numbers 0–20 yourself in random order, and tell the class to cross out the numbers they hear on their cards. The first person to cross out all the numbers on his/her card is the winner. (It is useful to make a list of the numbers yourself and tick them off as you call them out, and don't forget to include *zero*.) You may wish to demonstrate this activity on the board before you begin.

**Exercise 4: additional suggestions**

a *Bingo*: play bingo again by drawing a grid on the board and asking the students to copy it. Students then fill in numbers 0–20 at random on their own bingo card. Call out the numbers in random order. The student who completes a line – or the whole card – first is the winner.

b *Counting activities*: put students into pairs and ask them to count alternately from 0 to 20. Students can also count backwards from 20 to 0, or count using only odd (1, 3, 5 …) or even (2, 4, 6 …) numbers. These counting activities can also be played around the class.

c *Mutual dictation*: students write down ten of the numbers in any order. Students then work in pairs and take it in turns to dictate the numbers to their partner.

## ADDITIONAL MATERIAL

**Workbook:** Numbers 0–20, page 7

## Real life (PAGE 13)

Classroom language

**5** Check the meaning of the vocabulary in the box by asking students to point to the items in the classroom. Drill the words with the whole class and highlight the pronunciation of *picture* /ˈpɪktʃə/. Put students into pairs. Student A points to a person or thing in the classroom, and Student B says what it is.

**6** Put students into pairs and ask them to match the phrases and pictures. While little of this language has been formally taught so far, students will probably have picked up some of these words and expressions from previous lessons. Check the answers with the whole group, or ask them to check for themselves in the *Vocabulary book* on page 5. Drill the new vocabulary with the whole class, paying particular attention to the pronunciation of *listen* /ˈlɪsən/; *close* /kləʊz/ and *work* /wɜːk/.

**ANSWERS**
**a** open your book   **b** write your name   **c** look
**d** say your name   **e** work in pairs   **f** listen
**g** read your book   **h** close your book

**Exercise 6: additional suggestion**

*If you have a class of false beginners*: teach them a few more classroom instructions that they might find useful. For example: *Look at me/the board/the picture*; *Listen to the tape*; *Work in groups of three/four*; *Stand up*; *Walk around the room*; *Look at the picture on page 5*. Highlight the prepositions in these expressions where appropriate.
The Classroom language worksheet on page 101 of the Resource bank (instructions on page 89) introduces useful questions in the classroom, and is designed to be used at any time in the course. If your

students are false beginners, you may wish to use this worksheet at the end of Module 1. For a class of real beginners, it is probably more appropriate to use this worksheet later in the course.

**7** 📼 [1.16] Play the recording. All the students should respond to the instructions on the tape at the same time. If there are any instructions that do not elicit the appropriate response, deal with any difficulties by playing the recording again.

**8** Students work in pairs and give each other five instructions to act out. Encourage students to think of one or two different instructions to the ones in Exercise 2, for example: *Write your first name; Say your surname; Open/Close your Vocabulary book/Workbook.*

## ADDITIONAL MATERIAL

RB **Resource bank:** *Classroom language,* page 101 (instructions on page 89)

# Do you remember? (PAGE 13)

See *Teacher's Tips*: *Revision and recycling* on page 7.

**ANSWERS**

**1** a  What's your full name?
   b  How are you?
   c  What's his job?
   d  How do you spell 'Antonia'?
   e  What's her surname?

**2** 1  tennis player        6  engineer
   2  doctor                7  actor
   3  police officer        8  singer
   4  businessman           9  waiter
   5  teacher              10  student
   The extra job is 'politician'.

**3** a  five          d  seven
   b  thirteen      e  four
   c  twelve        f  twelve

**4** a  Hello         f  well
   b  Hi            g  this
   c  How           h  Nice
   d  fine          i  meet
   e  thanks

# module 2

## Focus 1 (PAGES 14–15)

### Vocabulary: countries

**1 a)** Focus students on the map on pages 14 and 15 and teach the word *country*. Put students into pairs and ask them to match the countries with the numbers. Although the students probably won't know all of them, they should be able to match those that are similar in their own language.

**b)** [2.1] Play the recording and allow the students to check their answers. Alternatively, students can refer to the *Vocabulary book* on page 7.

> **ANSWERS**
> **1** the USA  **2** Brazil  **3** Great Britain  **4** France
> **5** Spain  **6** Italy  **7** Poland  **8** Turkey  **9** Russia
> **10** Japan

### Pronunciation

**board** [2.2] Play the recording (or model the words yourself), and draw students' attention to the stress on each word. Write all the words for countries on the board, with a 'stress blob' over the correct syllable, and highlight the use of capital letters with countries in English.

Brazil  Turkey  Italy  France  Russia
Poland  Great Britain  Spain  the USA  Japan

Drill the words with the class. You may also like to point out that you haven't marked the word stress on *France* and *Spain* because they are one-syllable words.

**2** Students work in pairs. Student A says a number, and his/her partner says the country. Students should swap over after a minute or two.

### *be* with *I* and *you*

**3** **board** Ask the students if they know how to say their country/countries in English, and write the word(s) on the board. Mark the stress on the words, and drill these words chorally (i.e. with the whole class repeating together) and individually. Students can also write any new countries on the map on pages 14 and 15 of the *Students' Book*.

### Exercise 3: additional suggestion

a *If you have a monolingual class*: consider teaching the English words for the countries that border the students' own country, and any other countries that have particular significance for them. Students can write these in the personal vocabulary section on page 11 of their *Vocabulary books*.

b *If you have a class of false beginners*: consider teaching the English words for the continents/regions, for example *North America* /nɔːθ əˈmerɪkə/, *South America* /saʊθ əˈmerɪkə/, *Asia* /ˈeɪʒə/, *Europe* /ˈjʊərəp/, *Africa* /ˈæfrɪkə/, *The Middle East* /ðə ˈmɪdl iːst/, etc. Students can then practise these in pairs by asking each other where various countries are, for example: *'Where's Kenya?' 'It's in Africa.'*

c *If you have a monolingual class*: use activity 2A *Where are you from?* in the Resource bank on page 106 (instructions on page 90) after Exercise 3. Note that this activity also revises names and jobs from Module 1. You may also wish to deal with the language in the *Grammar* box first.

d *If you have a multilingual class*: students can move around the room and ask each other where they are from. Activity 2A in the Resource bank (see above) can then be used as revision in a future lesson.

e *If you have a large class*: either of these activities can be adapted by telling the students to talk to the people that are sitting near them.

## Grammar

**board** Write *Where ... you from? I ... from France.* and *... you from Italy? No, I ... from Spain.* on the board, and ask the students to complete the sentences with the verb *be*.

Highlight:

- *am* and *are* are parts of the verb *be*.
- we use *am* with the pronoun *I*, and *are* with the pronoun *you*.
- *I'm* is a contraction of *I am*.
- the word order changes in the questions: *you are* > *are you*.
- *are* is usually pronounced /ə/, for example in *Where are* /weərə/.

You may decide to look at *Language summary* 2 on page 113 of the *Students' Book* later in the lesson.

LANGUAGE NOTES:
a) The verb *be* is particularly problematic for students whose own languages don't have an equivalent verb. If you have a multilingual class, consider asking your students if they have the verb *be* in their language. This will help you understand why some students might be making mistakes.
b) It is important students realise that contractions (*I'm, you're, he's,* etc.) are extremely common in both spoken and written English, and is not 'lazy' language use as it is sometimes perceived. We suggest that you teach the contractions as the 'standard' form, and then explain what the contracted words are.

## Listening

**4** [2.3] Students do the exercise individually before checking in pairs.

**5** **a)** Students work in pairs or individually and put the conversation in order. Early finishers can check in pairs.

**b)** Play recording [2.3] again to allow students to check their answers. Play the recording again, pausing after each sentence for students to repeat. Students work in pairs and practise the conversation. When they have practised a few times, students can close their books and see if they can remember the conversation. You may wish to deal with the language in the *Grammar* box at this point.

> **ANSWERS**
> **1** a  **2** d  **3** c  **4** f  **5** e  **6** b  **7** g

**6** Students work in pairs and write a conversation similar to the one in Exercise 5a, using different countries, towns and jobs. Move around the room while they are working and help them with their conversations as required. Each pair should then practise their conversations until they have memorised them. Choose a few pairs to perform their conversations in front of the class (they do not have to leave their seats).

## Grammar

**board** Write *I …… from Moscow, I'm from St Petersburg.* and *You …… from Great Britain. You're from Poland.* on the board. Ask students to complete the sentences with the verb *be* in the negative.

Highlight:

● the use of *not* to indicate a negative sentence.

● the contracted forms *I'm* and *aren't*.

Refer students to *Language summary* 2 on page 113 of the *Students' Book*.

LANGUAGE NOTE:
*You're not* is a common alternative to *You aren't*, and is included in the *Language summary*. We feel that students only need to be taught one version at this stage, and often acquire *You're not* naturally. Teach students both versions if you feel it is appropriate.

**7** **a)** Pre-teach the words *big, small, city* and *capital city*. Students work individually and mark the sentences true or false for them.

**b)** Again working individually, students correct the wrong sentences in Exercise 7a. Go through the example before they begin. Students can then compare their answers in pairs or with the whole class.

LANGUAGE NOTE:
You may like to use sentences b) and d) to point out that adjectives in English come before the noun.

## ADDITIONAL PRACTICE

**Workbook:** Vocabulary: countries, page 9; *be* with *I* and *you*, page 10; Negatives, page 10

**RB** **Resource bank:** 2A *Where are you from?*, page 106 (instructions on page 90)

## Focus 2 (PAGES 16–17)

Nationalities: *be* with *he, she* and *it*

**1** Students do the exercise individually. Check the answers with the whole class. Drill the nationalities chorally and individually, highlighting the stress on the following words: *American, Japanese, British, Russian, Italian*. Also highlight the use of capital letters for nationalities, particularly if this is not the case in your students' language(s).

> **Exercise 1: additional activities**
>
> *Vocabulary booster*: nationalities are covered in more detail in the *Vocabulary booster: Nationalities* on page 107 of the Resource bank (instructions on page 90).
>
> *If you have a multilingual class*: teach the nationalities of all the students in the group. Students can record these in the personal vocabulary section of their *Vocabulary books*.

**2** Pre-teach the following words: *blue, a mosque* /mɒsk/, *a company* /ˈkʌmpəniː/, *a car*. Students work in pairs or small groups and do the quiz.

**3** [2.4] Play the recording and allow students to check their answers.

> **ANSWERS**
> **1** b  **2** c  **3** c  **4** a  **5** a  **6** c

## Grammar

**board** Write *Leonardo DiCaprio's American. Anna Kournikova's a tennis player.* and *The Blue Mosque is in Istanbul.* on the board. Ask students which names should be replaced by *he, she* and *it*, and write the contracted forms *He's, She's* and *It's* in the correct place. Then write *Italian, a singer* and *Cairo* on the board and ask students to form the corresponding negative sentences.

Highlight:

● we use *is* and *isn't* with the pronouns *he, she* and *it*.

● the contractions *He's, She's, It's* and *isn't*.

● we can also say *He's not* instead of *He isn't*, etc.

Refer students to *Language summary* 2 on page 113 of the *Students' Book*.

**LANGUAGE NOTE:**
Point out that we also use contractions after people's names, e.g. *Rivaldo's from Brazil*.

**4** Students do the exercise individually. Check the answers with the whole group.

**ANSWERS**
**a** isn't; is or 's  **b** is or 's; isn't  **c** isn't; is or 's

**5** Go through the example with the class. Students work individually and correct the rest of the sentences. Allow students to compare their answers in pairs or groups before checking them with the whole class.

**LANGUAGE NOTE:**
Point out that we also use *an* in front of an adjective + noun (e.g. *an Italian car*) if the adjective begins with a vowel.

**ANSWERS**
**b** Tony Blair isn't an actor. He's a politician.
**c** A Rolls Royce isn't an Italian car. It's a British car.
**d** Rio de Janeiro isn't in Spain. It's in Brazil.
**e** Martina Hingis isn't an actress. She's a tennis player.
**f** Buckingham Palace isn't in New York. It's in London.
**g** Vladimir Putin isn't the President of the USA. He's the President of Russia.
**h** Fiat isn't a Spanish company. It's an Italian company.
**i** Hillary Clinton isn't French. She's American.

## Pronunciation

[2.5] Play the recording and focus students on the correct pronunciation of *he's* /hiːz/, *she's* /ʃiːz/, *it's* /ɪts/ and *isn't* /ˈɪzənt/. Play the recording again, pausing after each phrase or sentence for students to repeat.

**6 a)** Students write their sentences individually. Encourage students to look back at Exercise 5 for examples of the types of sentences that are needed.

**b)** Pre-teach the words *true* and *false* by using the example in the speech balloon. Students then work in pairs and say the sentences they have written to their partner, who must decide if they are true or false.

**Exercise 6: alternative suggestion**

This exercise can also be done in teams. Divide the class into an even number of teams and tell each team to write five true sentences and five false sentences. Teams then work together and take it in turn to say their sentences. Each team gets one point for each sentence they correctly identify as true or false, and one point for correcting the false sentence. The team with the most points (out of fifteen) are the winners.

## Questions

**7 a)** Focus students on the pictures on page 17. Check that students can pronounce all the countries correctly (particularly *Egypt* /ˈiːdʒɪpt/ and *Thailand* /ˈtaɪlænd/), and drill these if necessary. Students work individually and match the people with the countries.

**b)** [2.6] Drill the question and answer in the speech balloon with the class. Students then work in pairs and ask each other where the other people are from. Play the recording and allow them to check their answers.

**8** Students work in new pairs and ask each other where the rest of their classmates are from. Remind students of the questions *What's his/her name?* before they begin.

## Grammar

**board** Write the answers *He's from Australia.* and *She's from Thailand.* on the board, and ask students what the corresponding questions are. Write these next to the answers.

Highlight the contraction *Where's* /weəz/ in the questions. You may also like to add the questions *What's his/her name?* and *What's his/her job?*.

Refer students to *Language summary* 2 on page 113 of the *Students' Book*.

**Exercise 8: additional suggestions**

**a** *If you have a monolingual class*: students can mingle and ask each other which town, city or district they are from. Students should try to remember the answers, but are not allowed to write anything down. Students then work in pairs and ask each other where their classmates are from. If it is not possible for your students to move around the room, they should ask as many people as possible from their seats before working in pairs.

**b** If you haven't used Resource bank activity 2A *Where are you from?* on page 106 yet, this can be used to give practice in questions with *he/she* (see instructions on page 90).

**c** Cut out pictures of some famous people and stick them on a piece of paper. Photocopy the paper and distribute copies to the class. Students work in pairs and ask each other where the famous people are from. This can be extended to revise *What's his/her name?* and *What's his/job?* if required.

 Use the downloadable worksheet on countries and nationalities from the Resources section of the website.

## ADDITIONAL PRACTICE

**Workbook:** Nationalities, page 10; *is/are/am*, page 10; Questions, page 11

RB **Resource bank:** *Vocabulary booster: Nationalities,* page 107 (instructions on page 90)

## Focus 3  (PAGES 18–19)

Note: Ask your students to bring in some photos of their friends in preparation for Exercise 2 of the Speaking task activity on page 19.

### Numbers 21–100

**1** [2.7] Play the recording, pausing after each number for students to repeat. Point out that the stress in these numbers is always on the first syllable. You may want to revise the numbers 0–20 before beginning this exercise.

**2 a)** Focus students on how the numbers 21, 22 and 29 are written and highlight the use of hyphens in these numbers. Students then write the missing numbers individually.

**b)** board [2.8] Play the recording, and allow students to check their answers. Drill the numbers chorally and individually. Write the answers on the board, and highlight that these numbers are also hyphenated.

**c)** Students work in pairs and say the numbers on the lottery balls. Check the numbers with the class, and drill them if necessary.

**3** board [2.9] Play the recording and allow the students to write down the numbers. Check the answers on the board with the whole class.

**4** Demonstrate this activity with the whole class before allowing students to work in pairs.

### Exercise 4: additional suggestions

a  Use activity 2B *Bingo!* on page 108 (instructions on page 90), and/or activity 2C *The numbers game* on page 109 (instructions on page 90) of the Resource bank.

b  Students can work in pairs and take it in turns to count from 20–100 in threes, e.g. 20, 23, 26, etc. They can also do the same backwards from 100.

c  Draw up two columns, A and B, on the board. Write *13, 14, 15*, etc. in column A and *30, 40, 50,* etc. in column B. Check students can recognise the difference between the stresses on these numbers (e.g. *thirteen* v *thirty*.). Drill the numbers chorally and individually, then say a few of the numbers and ask students which columns they are in. Finally, students work in pairs. One

student says a number on the board, and his/her partner says which column it is in.

### Ages

**5** Focus students' attention on the photographs on pages 18 and 19. Teach the questions *How old is he/she?* and highlight the change in word order *he's > is he?*. Teach the meaning of *I don't know*. and *I think (she's about twenty-two).*, and drill all the new language chorally and individually. Students then work in pairs or small groups and ask each other how old they think the people are, using the ages in the box in their answers.

**6** [2.10] Play the recording and allow students to check their answers.

> **ANSWERS**
> **a** She's fifteen.  **e** He's twenty-two.
> **b** She's thirty-three.  **f** She's fifty-nine.
> **c** He's ninety-two.  **g** He's forty-seven.
> **d** He's forty-eight.  **h** He's two.

**7** Drill the question *How old are you?*, and highlight the weak form of *are* /ə/ in this question. Students move around the room and ask each other how old they are.

### Exercise 7: alternative suggestion

If you feel that asking one another's ages is inappropriate for your students, consider giving students the identities of famous or imaginary people. These new identities can be written on cards with the person's age (and nationality/job if required), and distributed to the class. Students then walk around the room asking people their names, ages, etc. If it is not possible for students to leave their seats, they should ask as many people as possible around them.

## Speaking task

**1** [2.11] Focus students on the photographs and the information next to them. Play the recording and allow students to write down the answers. Play the recording again if necessary. Students can compare answers in pairs before checking the answers with the whole group.

> **ANSWERS**
> **a** a waiter  **b** twenty-six  **c** Judit  **d** Budapest

**2** Check that the whole class can make the appropriate questions for the prompts in the table, and write them on the board if necessary. Students choose one of the two options and do the activity in pairs. If you want your class to bring in photos of their friends, make sure you tell them during the previous lesson. At the end of the activity, each student can tell the class about one of their partner's friends.

## ADDITIONAL PRACTICE

**Workbook:** Numbers 21–100, page 11; Ages, page 12

**RB** **Resource bank**: 2B *Bingo!*, page 108 (instructions on page 90); 2C *The numbers game*, page 109 (instructions on page 90)

## Real life (PAGES 20–21)

Phone numbers

**1 a)** Teach the phrase *phone number*, and ask students if they are able to say the numbers in the *Students' Book*. Explain that we usually say *'oh'* for 0, and 'double two/double nine', etc. for 22, 99, etc. when saying phone numbers.

**b)** 📼 [2.12] Play the recording and draw students' attention to the way the phone numbers are broken up into smaller groups of numbers. Play the recording again, pausing after each number for students to repeat.

**2** Drill the question: *What's your phone number?*, focusing on natural rhythm and stress. Highlight that the reply often begins with *It's …* . Students move around the room (or talk to people sitting near them) and ask their classmates for their phone numbers. Students should write each number down and check that it is correct before moving on to another person. Depending on your class, you might need to teach *I don't have a phone.* before you begin.

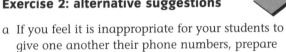

**Exercise 2: alternative suggestions**

a If you feel it is inappropriate for your students to give one another their phone numbers, prepare some cards with fictitious phone numbers on and distribute these to the students instead.

b If you have a strong group, or a class where most students work and/or have mobile phones, you might choose to teach them the questions: *What's your home number?*; *What's your work number?*; and *What's your mobile number?* before they begin the activity.

Listening

**3** 📼 [2.13] Focus students on the picture and the form on page 20. Go through the information on the form with the class and teach the following vocabulary: *single, married, age, home phone number* and *work phone number*, drilling the words as necessary. Play the recording and ask students to find and correct the four mistakes on the form. Play the recording again if necessary. Check the

answers with the whole group, referring back to the recording to clarify any disagreements.

**ANSWERS**
Her surname is Kirma**ni.**
She is **32.**
She lives in **Sang**ley Road.
Her work number is 020 **7322** 8424.

**Exercise 3: additional suggestion**

After you have done the listening with the class, ask the students to turn to the tapescript on page 120 of the *Students' Book* and play the recording again. Students listen and follow the conversation in their books at the same time. (This is often a useful follow-up activity to listening activities, and helps students connect sounds and words in English.)

**4** **board** Students work individually before checking their answers with the whole class. Write the sentences from Exercise 2 on the board in preparation for the pronunciation work.

**ANSWERS**
**a** 's **b** 's **c** Are **d** are **e** 's **f** 's **g** 's

## Pronunciation

1 **board** 📼 [2.14] Play the recording (or model the sentences yourself) and focus students on the sentence stress by clapping, tapping or 'beating' the stress with your hand. Mark the stressed words on the board. Also highlight the weak form of *are* /ə/.
*What's your surname? What's your address?*
*What's your first name? What's your phone number?*
*Are you married? What's your job?*
*How old are you?*

2 Play the recording again, pausing after each question to allow students to repeat chorally and individually.

## Speaking task

Filling in a form

Go through the form with the class and draw students' attention to the language in the *Don't forget!* box. Students work in pairs and interview each other, filling in the form as they go. Move around the room, helping students with any problems and noting down any common errors for discussion at the end of the activity.

## Speaking task: additional suggestions

a *If your class already know each other well*: use activity 2D *What's your address?* on page 110 of the Resource bank (instructions on page 91 – procedure 1), which provides role cards for the Speaking task.

b *Further practice of third person forms (he, she, his, her)*: when students have finished the Speaking task they can work in new pairs and tell their new partner about the person they have just interviewed. Alternatively, activity 2D *What's your address?* on page 110 of the Resource bank (instructions on page 91 – procedure 2) can also be used to provide practice of third person forms.

## ADDITIONAL PRACTICE

**Workbook:** Improve your writing, page 11

**RB** **Resource bank**: 2D *What's your address?*, page 110 (instructions on page 91)

# Do you remember? (PAGE 21)

**ANSWERS**

1 a are
   b 's
   c are
   d Is
   e 's

2 1 c
   2 e
   3 a
   4 d
   5 b

3 a forty, twenty
   b fifty-six, fifty
   c forty-eight, sixty
   d forty-four, fifty-three

**4**

| W | G | R | E | A | T | B | R | I | T | A | I | N | S |
|---|---|---|---|---|---|---|---|---|---|---|---|---|---|
| J | S | R | A | M | N | O | D | E | V | I | L | E | E |
| V | R | E | P | O | Y | N | N | A | F | T | A | R | S |
| P | B | G | E | R | M | A | N | Y | B | A | K | U | R |
| O | M | Y | S | S | O | T | F | Q | O | L | C | S | A |
| L | S | P | K | C | U | F | R | A | N | Y | I | S | T |
| A | I | T | H | A | I | L | A | N | D | M | R | I | Y |
| N | J | M | R | E | P | S | N | A | W | S | P | A | M |
| D | B | J | A | P | A | N | C | R | S | P | A | I | N |
| O | F | A | W | I | R | P | E | G | T | A | W | T | C |
| Q | B | O | N | L | L | A | M | S | S | K | R | A | M |

5 a city
   b car
   c capital city
   d company
   e address
   f phone number

# module 3

## Focus 1  (PAGES 22–23)

### Vocabulary: places; plural nouns

**1** Focus students on the pictures on pages 22 and 23. Students work in pairs and try to guess which countries the places are from. Compare answers with the whole class, and encourage students to give reasons for their answers where possible.

> **ANSWERS**
> **a** the USA (San Francisco)  **b** the USA (New York)
> **c** The United Arab Emirates  **d** England (London)
> **e** Australia

**2** Students work in pairs or small groups and try to find the vocabulary items in the pictures. Students can check their answers in the *Vocabulary book* on page 12, or with the whole class. Drill the new vocabulary chorally and individually.

LANGUAGE NOTE:

If your students speak a language that does not use articles, remind them to use *a/an* in front of a singular noun.

**3** Teach the meaning of *How many ...?* by going through question a) with the class. Check their understanding of *How many ...?* by asking how many people there are in the room. Check that students understand the plural nouns *children* and *people*, then allow them do the rest of the exercise on their own. Check the answers with the whole class. You may decide to focus on the language in the *Grammar* box before doing this exercise.

> **ANSWERS**
> **1** two  **2** twelve  **3** three  **4** five  **5** thirteen

## Grammar

**board** Draw three columns on the board, and write *a taxi* and *a car* in the first column, *a bus* and *a city* in the second column, and *a man, a woman, a child* and *a person* in the third column. Ask students how to form the plurals of these nouns, and write them on the board (in a different colour pen if possible).

Highlight:

- most nouns form the plural by adding -*s*.
- nouns ending in -*s* (e.g. *bus*) form the plural by adding -*es*.
- with nouns ending in -*y* (e.g. *city*), the -*y* changes to -*ies*.
- the existence of irregular plurals in English.

Refer students to *Language summary* 3B on page 114 of the *Students' Book*.

## Pronunciation

[3.1] Play the recording and allow students to hear the pronunciation of the plural forms. Highlight the fact that with nouns ending in -*s* (e.g. *bus*), the plural forms have an extra syllable that is pronounced /ɪz/. Play the recording again (or model the words yourself), and ask students to repeat the words chorally and individually. Pay particular attention to the pronunciation of *woman* /ˈwʊmən/; *women* /ˈwɪmɪn/ and *people* /ˈpiːpəl/.

**4** Students work individually and write the plural forms. Check the answers on the board with the whole class by writing them in the appropriate column (see *Grammar* box). Drill the plural forms with the whole class, highlighting the extra syllables in *actresses* /ˈæktrɪsɪz/ and *addresses* /əˈdrɛsɪz/, and the pronunciation of *businesswomen* /ˈbɪznɪsˌwɪmɪn/.

> **ANSWERS**
> **a** shops  **b** countries  **c** actresses
> **d** businesswomen  **e** teachers  **f** businessmen
> **g** houses  **h** companies  **i** addresses

### Exercise 4: additional suggestion

*If you have a class of false beginners*: ask students to work individually and write down ten more nouns that they know. Students work in pairs and swap papers with their partners. Students then write down the plural forms before checking back with their partners.

### *be*: plural

**5** Pre-teach the words *yellow, red, expensive, cheap* and *The Pyramids* /ðə ˈpɪrəmɪdz/. Students work in pairs and decide which three sentences are false. Check the answers with the whole group.

> **ANSWERS**
> **a** (The Pyramids are in Egypt.)  **c** (The Eiffel Tower is in Paris.)  **f** (Washington is the capital of the USA, not New York.)

## Grammar

**board** Write *The Pyramids ... in Egypt. New York taxis ... yellow.* and *London buses ... red.* on the board, and ask students to complete the sentences. Drill the sentences chorally (i.e. with the whole class) and individually.

Highlight:

- *are* is the plural form of *be* (as well as the *you* singular form).
- *are* is usually pronounced /ə/, as in the examples.
- we don't contract *are* to *'re* with plural nouns.

You may decide to look at *Language summary* 3A on page 114 of the *Students' Book* after you have dealt with *we* and *they* in Focus 2.

**6** **a)** Pre-teach the words *hot* and *cold*. Focus students on the three boxes a), b) and c), and go through the example with the class. Students work individually and write sentences using the language in the boxes. Encourage students to use the contraction *'s* where appropriate.

**b)** 📼 [3.2] Play the recording and allow students to check their answers.

**ANSWERS**
Paris and Madrid are capital cities.
Warsaw is in Poland.
Egypt and Oman are hot countries.
São Paulo and Rio de Janeiro are Brazilian cities.
Ferraris are expensive cars.
Scotland is a cold country.
Sydney and Melbourne are in Australia.

**7** Use the speech balloons to explain the activity, and check students remember the meaning of *true* and *false*. Students work individually and write four sentences. Students then work in pairs and say their sentences to their partner, who must say if they are true or false.

## ADDITIONAL PRACTICE

**Workbook:** Vocabulary: nouns, page 14; Plural nouns, page 14; *be*: plural, page 14

## Focus 2 (PAGES 24–25)
Reading and vocabulary

**1** Focus students on the pictures of the people on page 24, and the texts below these pictures. Students work individually and answer the questions. Check the answers with the whole class. Students should not read the postcard or the email at this stage.

**2** Use the happy/unhappy faces to teach the meaning of the words and phrases in the box, and check students understand which are strong adjectives. Drill the vocabulary with the whole class, paying particular attention to the pronunciation of *fantastic* /fæn'tæstɪk/, *nice* /naɪs/ and *awful* /'ɔːfʊl/. Students work individually and read the email and postcard. They should then complete the table by drawing the appropriate happy/unhappy face(s) in the table, as in the example.

|  | **Helen, Stewart and Amy** | **Renata and Claudia** |
|---|---|---|
| rooms | ☺ (nice) | ☹ (not very big) |
| food | ☺☺ (very good) | ☹☹ (awful) |
| weather | ☺☺ (fantastic) | ☺ (good) |
| other people | ☹☹ (awful) | ☺ (nice) |

**3** Discuss the question with the whole class. Encourage students to give reasons for their answers.

### *be* with *we* and *they*

**4** Focus students on the email on page 24, and give the students time to read the text again if necessary. Students then do the exercise individually. Check the answers with the whole class.

**ANSWERS**
**a** is **b** isn't **c** are **d** aren't **e** are **f** aren't

## Grammar

**board** Focus students on the email on page 24 and ask them to underline every *we* and *they*. Write some of these sentences on the board in two columns, with positive sentences in one column and negative sentences in the other. Alternatively, write the examples in the *Grammar* box on the board with gaps instead of *are/aren't* and ask students to complete the sentences.

Highlight:

- the meaning of *we* and *they*.
- the use of *are/aren't* with *we* and *they*.
- the contractions *we're*, *they're* and *aren't*.
- the use of *aren't* in negative sentences.

Refer students to *Language summary* 3A on page 114 of the *Students' Book*. Also draw students' attention to the plural question forms in the *Language summary*, or write them on the board.

LANGUAGE NOTE:
Point out that there is no polite plural form of *you*, as there are in many other languages, and that *you* in the plural is grammatically the same as *you* in the singular. You may also wish to use the examples in Exercise 4 to teach the possessive adjectives *our* and *their*.

## Pronunciation

**1** 📼 [3.3] Play the recording and ask students to tick the sentences they hear. Play the recording again if necessary. Check the answers with the whole group, referring back to the tape to deal with any problems.

2  Play the recording again, stopping after each sentence for students to repeat. Pay particular attention to the pronunciation of *we're* /wɪə/, *they're* /ðeə/ and *aren't* /ɑːnt/.

### ANSWERS
**1** b  **2** b  **3** b  **4** a

 Your students can send ecards and write about their holidays online.

**5** **a)** Focus students on the *People in London* box on page 25. Pre-teach the word *conference* if necessary. Allow students time to read the paragraphs, and check that students understand the basic information about each text (where the people are from, their jobs, etc.). Students work individually and complete the sentences with *is/isn't or are/aren't*. Encourage students to use contractions where appropriate. Students who finish early can check their answers in pairs.

**b)** [3.4] Play the recording and allow students to check their answers.

### ANSWERS
**A** are; are; are; are; is; isn't  **B** is; aren't; are; is; is
**C** are; are; are; is; aren't; is; are

**6** **a)** Students choose **one** group of people on pages 24 and 25, and write three sentences about them, using *They're* and/or *They aren't*. Go through the example with the whole class before they begin.

**b)** Students do the exercise in pairs. Alternatively, students can move around the room and say their sentences to different students.

..................................................................

### Exercise 6: alternative suggestion

Students work in pairs and write down ten sentences about the people on pages 24 and 25. Five of these sentences should be true, and five should be false. Put the pairs together so that students are working in groups of four. Each pair says their sentences and the other pair must decide if they are true or false. The pair that gets the most sentences correct are the winners. If necessary, demonstrate this activity with the whole class before they begin.

..................................................................

### Question forms with *they*

If you would like your students to practise question forms with *they*, use activity 2A *What are their names?* in the Resource bank, pages 111 and 112 (instructions on page 91).

## ADDITIONAL PRACTICE

**Workbook:** Opposites, page 15; *be* with *we* and *they*, page 15, *we're*, *they're*, *our*, *their*, page 15

**RB** **Resource bank:** 3A *What are their names?*, pages 111 and 112 (instructions on page 91)

## Focus 3  (PAGES 26–27)
Vocabulary: food and drink

**1** Focus students on the pictures in the *A Question of Food* quiz, and ask them to match these pictures with the vocabulary in the box. **Note that students should not actually do the quiz at this stage.** Allow students to compare their answers in pairs (or in their *Vocabulary book*, page 14) before checking the answers with the whole class.

### ANSWERS
**a** water  **b** rice  **c** eggs  **d** bread  **e** fruit
**f** cheese  **g** coffee  **h** meat  **i** vegetables  **j** pasta
**k** fish  **l** milk

LANGUAGE NOTE:
We have chosen not to introduce the concept of countable and uncountable nouns here, as we feel this would be unnecessarily complicated at this early stage. Students are therefore not asked to differentiate between countable and uncountable nouns in this module.

**2** Check the meaning of the words *food* and *drink*. Students do the exercise individually or in pairs. Check the answers with the whole class.

**3** [3.5] Play the recording, pausing after each word to allow students to repeat. Pay particular attention to the pronunciation of *vegetables* /ˈvedʒtəbəlz/ and *fruit* /fruːt/.

**4** **a)** Check the meaning of *I like …; I don't like …;* and *my favourite food/drink is …* by using things you like or don't like as examples. (We suggest that *I like …* and *I don't like …* are taught as set phrases, rather than using them to introduce the Present Simple.) Students then work on their own and complete the quiz. While they are working, circulate and help students with any new vocabulary they may need.

**b)** Draw students' attention to the language in the speech balloons, and drill these sentences with the whole class. Students work in small groups and compare their answers. Each student can then tell the class one thing they like or don't like.

..................................................................

### Exercise 4: additional suggestions

a Students move around the room and find another student who has the same favourite food or drink as them. Teach the expression *Me, too!* before they begin.

..................................................................

b Introduce the phrase *We both like ...* . Students work with a new partner and find four items of food and drink they both like. Each pair can then tell the class what they both like.

c The *Vocabulary booster: Food and drink* on page 113 of the Resource bank (instructions on page 91) can be used at any time after Exercise 4.

## ADDITIONAL PRACTICE

**Workbook:** Food and drink vocabulary, page 16

**Resource Bank:** *Vocabulary booster: Food and drink*, page 113 (instructions on page 91)

### *this, that, these, those*

5 [3.6] Pre-teach the words *bananas* and *shoes*, then focus students on the pictures in the left-hand column of page 27 in the *Students' Book*. Play the recording and ask students to circle the correct words in the conversations. Check the answers with the whole class. Play the recording again (or say the sentences yourself), pausing after each sentence and asking the students to repeat. Pay particular attention to the pronunciation of 'th' in *this* /ðɪs/, *that* /ðæt/, *these* /ðiːz/ and *those* /ðəʊz/. Students work in pairs and practise the conversations. You may choose to deal with the language in the *Grammar* box before doing this exercise.

> **ANSWERS**
> **a** this   **b** that   **c** these   **d** Those

**Exercise 5: alternative suggestion**

*If you have a class of false beginners*: ask the class to choose the correct words in conversations a)–d) before listening to the tape. Students can then listen and check their answers.

## Grammar

board Draw two columns on the board under the headings *singular* and *plural*. Write *this cheese* and *that car* in the first column, and *these bananas* and *those shoes* in the second column. Using hand gestures, ask students which words refer to 'here' and which words refer to 'there'. Guide students to form questions with *What ...?* for each word, and write these on the board.

Highlight:

• *this* and *these* refer to things that are close to the speaker, and *that* and *those* refer to things that are at a distance from the speaker.

• the difference in pronunciation of *this* /ðɪs/ and *these* /ðiːz/.

• the pronunciation of *What are ...?* /wɒtə/.

Refer students to *Language summary* 3C on page 114 of the *Students' Book*.

6 a) Students do the exercise individually. Early finishers can check their answers in pairs.

b) [3.7] Play the recording and allow students to check their answers.

> **ANSWERS**
> **a** that   **b** those   **c** These   **d** this; this

**Exercise 6: additional suggestions**

a Use activity 3B *What's this?* on page 114 of the Resource bank (instructions on page 91).

b Teach some more words of things in the classroom, e.g: *white/blackboard, board pens, windows, door, desk, table, chair, coat, pencil, bag, picture, poster, cassette player, noticeboard, video, wall, floor,* and anything that can be seen outside the windows. Teach the students the question *What's this/that/these/those in English?*. Students work in pairs or small groups and ask each other questions. As they are working, move around the room and help students with new words or pronunciation.

## ADDITIONAL PRACTICE

**Workbook:** *this, that, these, those*, page 16

RB **Resource bank:** 3B *What's this?*, page 114 (instructions on page 91)

## Real life   (PAGES 28–29)

In a café; prices

1 a) [3.8] Play the recording and allow students to put the prices in order. Play the recording again and check the answers with the whole group. Check the pronunciation of *euros* /ˈjʊərəʊz/, and explain that *p* is short for *pence* and is pronounced /piː/.

> **ANSWERS**
> **1** $12.50   **2** €4.00   **3** 6.25   **4** 45p   **5** 59.99
> **6** £3.70   **7** 7.90

b) Play the recording again, pausing after each price for students to repeat.

2 a) Focus students on the pictures at the top of pages 28 and 29 in the *Students' Book*. Students work in pairs and find the words in the box in the pictures. Check the answers with the whole group, or allow the students to check their answers in the *Vocabulary book* on page 15.

b) [3.9] Play the recording (or say the words yourself), and ask the students to repeat chorally and individually. Pay particular attention to the pronunciation of *sandwich* /ˈsænwɪdʒ/, *salad* /ˈsæləd/ and *burger* /ˈbɜːgə/.

**3** **a)** Students work individually and write the expressions in the box in the correct places in conversations a), b) and c). Early finishers can check their answers in pairs.

**b)** **board** 🔲 [3.10] Play the recording and allow students to check their answers. Write the dialogues on the board and check the meaning of the other new expressions in the dialogues: *Sure. Anything else?*; *Here you are*. Play the recording again, pausing after each sentence for students to repeat. Encourage students to say the sentences with correct stress, and to sound interested and friendly. You can mark the sentence stress on the board at this point. Students then work in pairs and practise the dialogues, changing roles when they have finished dialogue c).

**ANSWERS**
**a** A burger and chips, please.; No, thanks.
**b** Three coffees, please.; Thank you.
**c** How much is that?

**4** Students work in pairs and make new conversations using the items listed. When they have finished, ask some of the pairs to act out their new conversations in front of the class. You may wish to demonstrate this activity with the class before they begin working in pairs.

**5** 🔲 [3.11] Focus students on the waiter's order pad and teach the words *café* /ˈkæfeɪ/ and *customer* /ˈkʌstəmə/. Play the recording and allow students to tick the items that the customers order. Play the recording again, pausing at appropriate points to allow students to check their answers.

**ANSWERS**
See tapescript Module 3, recording 11 on page 121 of the *Students' Book*.

**Exercise 5: additional suggestion**

After you have done the listening with the class, ask the students to turn to the tapescript on page 121 of the *Students' Book* and play the recording again. Students listen and follow the conversation in their books at the same time.

## Speaking task

**1** Ask students to look at the menu on page 112 of the *Students' Book* and check they can say all the food items and prices. Put students into groups of three and tell them to write a conversation in a café.

**2** Students practise their conversations in their groups until they have memorised them. Ask each group to act out their conversations for the other students, either in front of the class or from where they are sitting.

**Speaking task: alternative suggestion**

If possible, reorganise the furniture in your classroom so that it resembles a café. Make some students waiters and bring them to the front of the class. Make the rest of the students customers and put them in groups of three or four. There should be the same number of groups as there are waiters. Tell the customers to turn to the menu on page 112 of the *Students' Book*. Each waiter then chooses a 'table' and takes the customers' orders. The waiters can then serve the 'food', and give the customers a bill at the end of the meal. (You might like to introduce the word *tip* here!). Repeat the roleplay with different waiters and new groups of customers.

## Do you remember? (PAGE 29)

**ANSWERS**

**1**
| a That | d This |
|--------|--------|
| b this | e those |
| c Those | f This |

**2**
| a bottles | e sandwiches |
|-----------|--------------|
| b vegetables | f countries |
| c addresses | g houses |
| d children | h women |

**3**
| a cold | e fantastic |
|--------|-------------|
| b hot | f nice |
| c awful | g good |
| d expensive | h big |

**4** **people:** a man, a woman, a child
**buildings:** a house, a hotel, a shop
**transport:** a bus, a taxi, a car

# module 4

## Focus 1 (PAGES 30–31)

### Vocabulary: places in a town

**1** Focus students on the pictures on page 30. Students work in pairs or small groups and try to match the vocabulary with the pictures. Check the answers with the whole group. Also check that students understand the meaning of *a cinema, a supermarket, a post office, a bus stop, a restaurant* and *a car park*, or ask students to refer to the *Vocabulary book* on page 17. (Pronunciation is dealt with in Exercise 3.)

> **ANSWERS**
> **a** a café  **b** a park  **c** a hotel  **d** a square
> **e** a bank  **f** a station

> **Exercise 1: additional suggestions**
>
> a *If you have a monolingual class*: you may also like to teach a few other words that are important in your students' city: e.g. *mosque, church, temple, underground station, bridge, river, cathedral.*
>
> b *If you have a class of false beginners*: consider using the *Vocabulary booster: Places in a town* on page 118 of the Resource bank (instructions on page 92) early in the module. Note, however, that the practice activities in this worksheet include *there is/there are*, so we suggest that most classes should use this worksheet after Focus 3.
>
> c *Memory game*: Allow students one minute to memorise the words in the box, then tell them to close their books. Students then write down as many words as they can remember in one minute.

**2** Focus students on the map on page 31 and allow them a few moments to study it. Teach the words *street* and *road*. Draw their attention to the language in the speech bubbles before students do the exercise in pairs.

> **ANSWERS**
> **1** a café  **2** a bus stop  **3** a restaurant  **4** a post office
> **5** a hotel  **6** a station  **7** a bank  **8** a park
> **9** a car park  **10** a cinema  **11** a supermarket

**3**  [4.1] Play the recording and allow students to check their answers. Play the recording again (or say the words yourself), pausing after each word for students to repeat chorally and individually. Pay particular attention to the word stress of *p·ost office, b·us stop, c·ar park, r·estaurant, c·afé* and *s·upermarket.*

### Prepositions

**4** **a)** Students work individually and match the prepositions with the diagrams, referring to the *Vocabulary book* on page 18 as necessary. Check the answers with the whole class, and refer students to *Language summary* 4C on page 114 of the *Students' Book*.

> **ANSWERS**
> **1** in  **2** on the left  **3** on the right  **4** near

**b)** Students look at the map and decide if the sentences are true or false. Check the answers with the whole class.

> **ANSWERS**
> **a** False  **b** True  **c** False  **d** True

LANGUAGE NOTE:
*The car park is* **on** *Station Road* is also correct, but we feel that students only need one option at this level.

> **Exercise 4: additional suggestion**
>
> *If you have a strong class*: use the map to teach the prepositions *next to* and *opposite* as well as those already introduced in the lesson. Students can then include these prepositions in their answers to Exercises 6 and 7.

**5** Go through the example with the class and allow students to do the rest of the exercise on their own. Students compare answers in pairs before checking with the whole class.

> **ANSWERS**
> **a** The bus stop's near the bank.
> **b** The car park's in Station Road.
> **c** The car park's on the right of the station.
> **d** The supermarket's on the right of the post office.
> **e** The bank's in New Market Street.
> **f** The bank's near the park.
> **g** The hotel's near the restaurant.
> **h** The bus stop isn't in the square.

**6** **board** Check the example on the board. Students work individually and write sentences based on the prompts. Allow students to compare answers in small groups before checking the sentences with the class. Write the correct sentences on the board for the students to copy.

**ANSWERS**

**a** The cinema is in Old Market Street.
**b** The café is in the square.
**c** The post office is on the left of the supermarket.
**d** The park is near/on the left of the bank.
**e** The cinema is near the café.
**f** The post office is in Station Road.
**g** The hotel is near/on the right of the park.

LANGUAGE NOTE:
Students may ask why we use *the* in these sentences, rather than *a* or *an*. Explain simply that we use *the* when there is 'only one' (e.g. on the map there is only one station). You can also compare 'a student' with 'the teacher' in your class.

7 Drill the language in the speech balloons with the class, and encourage students to say them with natural rhythm and stress. Also check students understand the meaning of *Excuse me* and *over there*. Students work in pairs and ask each other questions about the places on the map. You may like to demonstrate this activity before they begin.

**Exercise 7: additional suggestion**

Use activity 4A *Where's the cinema?* on pages 115 and 116 of the Resource bank (instructions on page 92).

## ADDITIONAL PRACTICE

**Workbook:** Vocabulary: places in a town, page 19; Prepositions, page 19

RB **Resource bank**: 4A *Where's the cinema?*, pages 115 and 116 (instructions on page 92)

## Focus 2 (PAGES 32–33)

### Listening

1 Focus students on the picture of a town square on page 32. Put the students into pairs and ask them to find the words in the box, referring to the *Vocabulary book* on page 18 if necessary. Drill the new words chorally and individually.

2 [4.2] Play the recording and ask students to decide which description is correct. (The answer is B). If there is disagreement, play the recording again to check. If possible, ask the students to give reasons for their choice.

**Exercise 2: additional suggestion**

You can use activity 4B *Vocabulary pelmanism* on page 117 of the Resource bank (instructions on page

92) at any time after you have taught the vocabulary in Exercise 1.

### there is, there are

3 Go through the examples with the whole class before allowing the students to do the rest of the exercise individually. Early finishers can compare their answers in pairs before you check your answers with the whole group.

**ANSWERS**

**a** False   **b** True   **c** False   **d** True   **e** False
**f** False   **g** True   **h** False   **i** False

## Grammar

board Draw two columns headed *singular* and *plural*. Write *There ... a hotel in the square.* in the first column and *There ... two dogs in the square.* in the second column, then ask the class to complete the sentences with the verb *be*. Elicit one or two more examples from the picture for each column, and drill the sentences on the board chorally and individually.

Highlight:

● the contraction in *There's* /ðeəz/.

● the weak form of *are* in *There are* /ðeərə/.

● that the main stress of the sentence comes on the words that follow *there is/there are* (e.g. *dog* and *five children* in the above examples).

You may decide to look at *Language summary* 4A on page 114 of the *Students' Book* after you have covered the negative and question forms of *there is/there are* in Focus 3.

4 board Refer students back to the incorrect sentences in Exercise 3 and ask students to correct them. After they have compared their answers in pairs you can write the correct sentences on the board in the appropriate column (*singular* or *plural*).

**ANSWERS**

**a** In the café, there's a man with his baby.
**c** There's one waiter in the café.
**e** On the right of the café there's a supermarket.
**f** There are three boys and one girl in the square.
**h** There's one tree in the square.
**i** There are two old men near the tree.

5 Students do the exercise individually. Ask them to check each other's sentences and help them when necessary. Each student can say one of their sentences to the class.

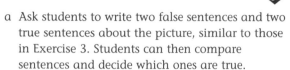

### Exercise 5: alternative suggestions

a  Ask students to write two false sentences and two true sentences about the picture, similar to those in Exercise 3. Students can then compare sentences and decide which ones are true.

b  Tell students to study the picture for a minute or two, then ask them to close their books. They must then write four or five true sentences about the square from memory.

### Exercise 5: additional suggestion

Write some words of things that the students can see in the classroom on the board, teaching the item if necessary. You may choose to include *table, chair, desk, man, woman, person, bag, white/blackboard, board pen, light, cassette player, window, coat, noticeboard, picture, poster*. Students work in pairs and write eight sentences using *There is/There are* about their classroom. Four of these should be be true and four should be false. The pairs then work together and say their sentences. The other pair must decide if the sentences are true or false. The pair who gets the most sentences right are the winners.

## Pronunciation

1  🔊 [4.3] Play the recording and ask students to listen to the 'th' sound /ð/ in the words shown. Play the recording again, pausing after each word for the students to repeat the words chorally and individually.

2  🔊 [4.4] Repeat the above procedure for the 'th' sound /θ/. For both sounds it may be useful to show students that they are made by putting the tongue between the teeth. Note that /ð/ is 'voiced' (i.e. you use your vocal cords) and /θ/ is 'unvoiced'.

## Speaking task

1  a)  Teach the following items of new vocabulary: *a chair, a bag*. Divide the class into two groups, A and B. Group A looks at the picture on page 33, and Group B should turn to the picture on page 111.

b)  Students from the same group work in pairs and make sentences about their picture using *There is* and *There are*. (Depending on your class, you may want students to write the sentences, or to just say them to each other.) Encourage them to think of as many sentences as possible and draw their attention to examples in the *Don't forget!* box above their pictures before they begin. Circulate and help students with any problems or vocabulary.

2  a)  Pair one student from Group A with a student from Group B. **Students are not allowed to look at each other's pictures.** Each pair takes it in turns to say sentences about their picture, and between them they must find eight differences between Picture A and Picture B. (Note that there are more than eight differences overall). You may also like to set a time limit of five or ten minutes to increase motivation.

b)  Ask each pair how many differences they have found, and invite the students to tell the class what they are. These differences can be written on the board if necessary. (Note that there are other small differences in the picture, but these are probably beyond the scope of the students' language.)

**ANSWERS**
1  In Picture A there are two dogs, in Picture B there are three.
2  In A there's one baby, in B there are two.
3  In A there are two tables, in B there's only one.
4  In A there are seven chairs, in B there are four.
5  In A there is one bag, in B there's two.
6  In A there's a bus, in B there are two buses.
7  In A there are two cars, in B there's one car.
8  In A there's a big tree on the right of the café, in B it's on the left.
9  In A the café is on the right of the lake, in B it's on the left.
10 In A there are three boys and one girl, in B there are three girls and one boy.

### ADDITIONAL PRACTICE

**Workbook:** *there is/there are*, Exercise 3, page 20

**RB** **Resource Bank:** 4B *Vocabulary pelmanism*, page 117 (instructions on page 92)

## Focus 3  (PAGES 34–35)

### Reading and vocabulary

1  Focus students on the pictures of the places and people on pages 34 and 35, and check students understand the heading *My home town*. Ask them to find out where all the people are from, but **not** to read everything on the page. (The people are from different places called Kingston.)

2  Ask students to answer questions a)–f) by looking at the pictures and captions for each place called Kingston. **Again students should not read the texts at this stage.** To increase motivation, set the students a time limit of one or two minutes. Check the answers with the whole class. You may need to pre-teach *a river, the sea* and *a lake* before beginning this exercise.

**ANSWERS**
**a** Jamaica  **b** England  **c** New Zealand
**d** England  **e** Jamaica  **f** New Zealand

**3** **a)** 🎧 [4.5] Ask students to read through sentences 1–9. Teach the class any words in bold that you think they don't know, and check the pronunciation of the new vocabulary with the whole class. Words that students usually have problems pronouncing are: *beaches* /ˈbiːtʃɪz/; *famous* /ˈfeɪməs/; *busy* /ˈbɪzɪ/; *interesting* /ˈɪntrɪstɪŋ/; and *mountains* /ˈmaʊntɪnz/. You may also wish to refer your students to the *Vocabulary book* on page 19 to consolidate these words. Play the recording and allow students to read the texts at the same time. (Alternatively, you may prefer your students to read the texts in their own time, and use the recording for consolidation later in the lesson.)

**b)** Students work in pairs or individually, and decide which three sentences in Exercise 3a are in the wrong place. Check the answers with the whole class.

**ANSWERS**
Sentence **3** should be in the **England** box.
Sentence **4** should be in the **New Zealand** box.
Sentence **8** should be in the **Jamaica** box.

*a, some* and *any*

**4** Students do the exercise in pairs. Check the answers with the whole group.

**SUGGESTED ANSWERS**
**a** New Zealand  **b** England  **c** Jamaica (or England)

# Grammar

**board** Draw two columns headed *singular* and *plural*. Write *There's ... famous train.* in the first column, and *There are ... parks.* in the second. Ask students to complete the gaps. Repeat this procedure for the negative sentences and questions. Alternatively, you can guide students to the sentences in the *Grammar* box (or examples from Exercises 3 and 4) by saying '*Kingston, New Zealand – famous train*', and '*Kingston, England – parks*', etc. Drill the sentences chorally and individually.

Highlight:

- we use *there isn't* and *there aren't* in negative sentences.
- the word order for questions: *There's > Is there ...?*; *There are > Are there ...?*
- in plural sentences we use *some* in positive sentences and *any* in negatives and questions.
- the weak pronunciation of *are* /ə/ and *some* /səm/, e.g. *There are some parks.* /ðeə ə səm pɑːks/.

Refer students to *Language summary* 4A and 4B on page 114 of the *Students' Book*.

LANGUAGE NOTES:
a) We realise that the 'use *any* in questions' rule is far from watertight, and there are many instances of *there is/there are* questions with *some*. However, at this level we feel it is important to give a general rule that always works for students, and leave the subtleties of *some* and *any* for later levels.

b) We also feel that *some* and *any* with countable nouns is enough for students to deal with at this early stage. Consequently, *some* and *any* with uncountable nouns and *there is* are not introduced in this book.

**5** Check that students know all the words in the box. Check also that they can pronounce the words correctly, particularly *mountains* /ˈmaʊntɪnz/. Each student thinks of a town they know (but **not** the town they live in) and writes sentences as in the examples. Students work in small groups and tell each other their sentences.

**Exercise 5: alternative suggestions**

a  *If you have a class of real beginners*: you may choose to do Exercise 7 in the *Workbook* on page 21, which gives controlled practice of *a, some* and *any*, before doing Exercise 5.

b  The *Vocabulary booster*: *Places in a town* on page 118 of the Resource bank (instructions on page 92) introduces more vocabulary on the same topic.

***there is/there are*: additional practice**

Students work in pairs and write questions using *Is there ...?/Are there ...?* based on the three Kingston readings on pages 34 and 35. Two pairs then work together and ask each other the questions. You may like to pre-teach *Yes, there is.* and *No, there isn't.* before doing this exercise.

## Speaking task

**1** **board** Go through the vocabulary with the class and teach any new words. Write the following examples on the board: *Is there a station near your house?*; *Are there any good restaurants near your house?* to show the class the kind of sentences required. Students work individually and write ten questions. Circulate and help students with any problems. Early finishers can work together and check their questions are correct.

**2** Draw students' attention to the sentences in the *Don't forget!* box, and drill these sentences if necessary. Students work in pairs and ask each other their questions. Circulate and help students as they are working. You may also like to note down errors, which can be written on the board after the activity for students to correct.

## Writing

**3** Focus students on the example, then allow them to write their paragraph individually. Alternatively, this exercise can be done for homework. Students can display their work around the classroom for other students to read. Encourage students to add some pictures to their descriptions if possible.

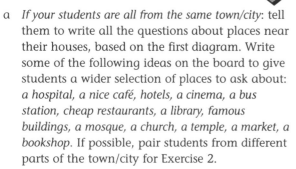

**Speaking task: alternative suggestions**

a *If your students are all from the same town/city*: tell them to write all the questions about places near their houses, based on the first diagram. Write some of the following ideas on the board to give students a wider selection of places to ask about: *a hospital, a nice café, hotels, a cinema, a bus station, cheap restaurants, a library, famous buildings, a mosque, a church, a temple, a market, a bookshop.* If possible, pair students from different parts of the town/city for Exercise 2.

b Activity 4C *Spot the difference* on pages 119 and 120 of the Resource bank (instructions on page 92) gives further practice in questions and statements with *there is/there are*.

### ADDITIONAL PRACTICE

**Workbook:** *there is/there are*, Exercises 4 and 5, page 20; Exercise 6, page 21; *a, some* and *any*, page 21; common adjectives, page 21

RB **Resource bank:** *Vocabulary booster: Places in a town*, page 118 (instructions on page 92); 4C *Spot the difference*, pages 119 and 120 (instructions on page 92)

## Real life (PAGES 36–37)

### In the street

**1** Focus students on the pictures on page 36 and allow them to do the exercise individually.

**2** [4.6] Play the recording and allow students to check their answers.

### Pronunciation

1 [4.7] Play the recording and ask students to listen to sentences in the *Students' Book*. Also draw their attention to the stress of each sentence, and the polite intonation used.

2 Play the recording again (or model the sentences yourself), pausing after each sentence for students to repeat chorally and individually. Encourage students to exaggerate the stress and intonation at first to help them achieve the correct voice pattern. If possible, explain to your students that if they sound too 'flat' they will be perceived as rude by native English speakers.

**3** Students practise the conversations in pairs, changing roles after conversation d). After they have repeated all the conversations a couple of times, ask them to say them again without looking at their books.

**4** board Ask the class for various different ways to end these sentences: *Is this …?*; *Excuse me, where's the …?*. Write their ideas on the board. Students then move around the room and have conversations with each other, similar to those on page 36. Circulate and correct students as necessary. Note down any common problems, and deal with them at the end of the activity.

**Exercise 4: alternative suggestions**

*If your students are all from the same town/city*: you can ask them to imagine they are in a well-known street or square.

*If it is not possible for your students to move around the room*: students can have conversations with as many people as possible sitting near them. Alternatively, choose two students at a time and ask them to come to the front of the class and improvise a short dialogue.

Visit the suggested links to popular radio stations for up-to-date interviews.

## Do you remember? (PAGE 37)

**ANSWERS**
**1** a There's
b Are there
c some
d a
e any
f There's

**2** various answers

**3** a There's a bank **near** the station.
b London's **a** very interesting city.
c There's a post office **on** the left of the bank.
d Excuse me, are there **any** cafés in this street?
e In Paris there are **some** very good restaurants.
f The cinema is on the right **of** the supermarket.
g We're in a café **in** Baker Street.

**4** a small
b interesting
c quiet
d nice
e busy
f famous
g beautiful

**5**

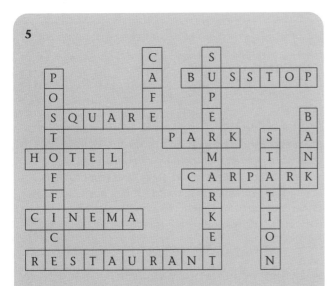

# Consolidation modules 1–4

**A**
- a are
- b 're/are
- c 's/is
- d isn't
- e are
- f are
- g aren't
- h are
- i isn't
- j 's/is
- k 'm/am

**B**

**1**
- a What's your name?
- b Where are you from?
- c What's your job?
- d How old are you?
- e Are you married?
- f What's your address?
- g What's your phone number?
- h Is there a university in your city?

**2**
- 1 c
- 2 f
- 3 e
- 4 g
- 5 a
- 6 h
- 7 d
- 8 b

**C**

**1**
- a milk
- b Spanish
- c a school
- d a town
- e a tree
- f cheese
- g a station
- h awful

**D**

- 1 a
- 2 a
- 3 c
- 4 c
- 5 b
- 6 c
- 7 b
- 8 c

**E**

**1**
- a fish
- b actor
- c write
- d phone
- e single
- f don't
- g baby
- h American
- i women
- j fifty
- k look
- l much

**2** The hidden question is **How old are you?**

**F**

**1**
- yes – no
- stop – go
- hello – goodbye
- high – low

**3** You say yes, I say no.
You say stop and I say go go go. Oh no!

**Chorus**
You say goodbye and I say hello. Hello hello.
I don't know why, you say goodbye, I say hello. Hello hello.
I don't know why, you say goodbye, I say hello. Hello hello.

I say high, you say low.
You say why and I say I don't know. Oh no!

**Chorus x2**
You say yes, I say no.
You say stop and I say go go go. Oh no!

# module 5

## Focus 1 (PAGES 40–41)

Vocabulary: family

**1** Focus the class on the pictures on page 40. Students work individually or in pairs and match the words in a)–f) with the pictures. Check the answers with the whole class, or allow students to check their answers in the *Vocabulary book* on page 22. Also check that students know the singular forms of *(grand)parents* and *(grand)children*.

> **ANSWERS**
> **a** 2 and 5  **b** 4  **c** 1  **d** 1 and 4  **e** 3 and 2  **f** 2

**Exercise 1: additional suggestion**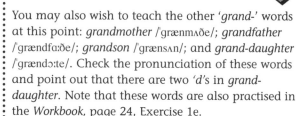

You may also wish to teach the other *'grand-'* words at this point: *grandmother* /'grænmʌðe/; *grandfather* /'grændfɑːðe/; *grandson* /'grænsʌn/; and *grand-daughter* /'grændɔːte/. Check the pronunciation of these words and point out that there are two *'d's* in *grand-daughter*. Note that these words are also practised in the *Workbook,* page 24, Exercise 1e.

**2** **board** 🔲 [5.1] Play the recording, pausing after each word or phrase for students to repeat chorally and individually. Pay particular attention to the pronunciation of *parents* /'peərənts/; *brother* /'brʌðə/; *father* /'fɑːðə/; *mother* /'mʌðə/; *daughter* /'dɔːtə/; *husband* /'hʌzbənd/; *son* /sʌn/. Write the words on the board and mark the stress, which is on the first syllable of each word.

**Exercise 2: alternative suggestion**

**board** Write the words on the board, then ask your students to work in pairs and decide where the stress on each word is. Play the recording for students to check their answers, then drill the words as above.

**3** Students do the exercise individually. Allow students to compare answers in pairs before checking with the whole class. Encourage students to give reasons for their answers where possible.

> **ANSWERS**
> **a** parent  **b** child  **c** grandparent  **d** wife
> **e** children  **f** sister

Possessive *'s*

**4** **a)** Focus students on the picture on page 41, and check they know who Tony and Rosa are. Students work out who the other people are from the information provided and write their names on the picture. Check the answers with the whole class.

> **ANSWERS**
> **a** Carlos  **b** Luis  **c** Marta  **d** Laura  **e** Carmen

LANGUAGE NOTE:

Students might ask why *is* isn't contracted in these sentences. We felt that too many *'s* on the page would be confusing for students at this stage, and that having two *'s* in one short sentence (e.g. *Laura's Tony's husband.*) looks rather unnatural. You might like to point out, however, that we would usually contract the *is* in these sentences in spoken English.

**b)** Students work individually and write the correct family word in the gaps by referring to the picture and the information in Exercise 4a. Early finishers can check in pairs or small groups

**Exercise 4: alternative suggestion**

After doing Exercise 4a, you might prefer to ask the students to draw a family tree of the people in the picture before doing Exercise 4b. This can also be drawn on the board if necessary:

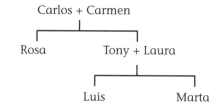

**5** 🔲 [5.2] Play the recording and allow students to check their answers.

> **ANSWERS**
> **a** mother  **b** son  **c** wife  **d** parents
> **e** brother  **f** grandparents  **g** children (*or* son and daughter)

## Grammar

**board** Write *Laura is Tony wife.* and *Marta is Tony and Laura daughter.* on the board, then ask the class what is missing (the possessive *'s*). Alternatively, write *Laura is the wife of Tony.* on the board, then put a line through it and ask students the correct way to say it. Ask students to give you some more examples and write them on the board.

Highlight:

● we use *'s* for family relationships.

● using *of* (e.g. *the wife of Tony*) is incorrect.

● we say *Tony and Laura's daughter*, not ~~*Tony's and Laura's daughter*~~.

Refer students to *Language summary* 5A on page 115 of the *Students' Book*.

LANGUAGE NOTE:
You may want to remind students that *'s* can be either possessive or a contracted form of *is*. Write *Tony is Marta's father*. and *Rosa's a student*. on the board and ask the class to tell you the difference between the two *'s*. Note that this point is practised in the *Workbook*, Exercise 3 on page 25.

# Pronunciation

[5.3] Play the recording and focus students on the linking between words. Play the recording again, pausing after each phrase for students to repeat. Highlight the extra syllable in Luis's /luːɪsɪz/, and explain that after names ending in an /s/ sound the *'s* is pronounced /ɪz/. (for example, *Carlos's, Chris's, Marcos's*).
Note: This recording is an example of 'backchaining', which is a drilling technique designed to help students with linking and sentence stress. If you feel this works with your students, try using this technique in future lessons.

6 **board** Students write their sentences individually before comparing answers in pairs. Check the answers with the whole group on the board.

> **ANSWERS**
> **a** Tony is Marta's father.
> **b** Rosa is Carlos's daughter.
> **c** Carlos is Carmen's husband.
> **d** Tony is Carlos's son.
> **e** Laura is Marta and Luis's mother.
> **f** Laura and Tony are Marta's parents.
> **g** Rosa is Tony's sister.

**Exercise 6: additional suggestion**

Activity 5A *Bob's family* on pages 121 and 122 of the Resource bank (instructions on page 93) provides further practice of relationship vocabulary and *'s*.

# Speaking task

**1** Students work alone and write down the names of four members of their family. If you feel this is inappropriate for your students, tell them to write down friends' names instead.

**2** Draw students' attention to the language in the *Don't forget!* box, and highlight the fact that the *'s* in these sentences are contractions of *is*. Students work in pairs and tell their partners about the people they have written down in Exercise 1. Encourage students to say as much as possible about each person, for example

their age, job, where they live, etc. Move around the room and help students where necessary, noting down any common problems. These can be written on the board for correction work at the end of the task.

**Speaking task: alternative suggestion**

*If you have a class of false beginners*: ask the students to draw a family tree for their own family. Students can then work in pairs and tell their partners about all the people in their family.

## ADDITIONAL PRACTICE

**Workbook:** Family vocabulary, page 24; Possessive *'s*, page 25; *'s = is* or possessive?, page 25

**RB** **Resource bank:** 5A *Bob's family*, pages 121 and 122 (instructions on page 93)

## Focus 2 (PAGES 42–43)
Vocabulary and reading

1 **board** Teach the verbs *live, have, work* and *study* via the examples in the diagrams. Also check the following new vocabulary: *the centre of the city; a lot; alone*. Students then do the exercise alone or in pairs, referring to the *Vocabulary book* on page 23 if necessary. Write the diagrams on the board and check the answers with the whole class. Highlight the prepositions in the following phrases: *in the centre of the city / London / a flat; **for** a big company; **with** computers / your parents*. Drill the expressions chorally and individually, paying attention to the pronunciation of *work* /wɜːk/; *computers* /kəmˈpjuːtəz/; *London* /ˈlʌndən/; *company* /ˈkʌmpəniː/; *garden* /ˈgɑːdən/; *languages* /ˈlæŋgwɪdʒɪz/.

> **ANSWERS**
> **a** with your parents  **b** in a flat
> **c and d** a garden; a cat
> **e** with computers  **f** languages

LANGUAGE NOTE:
You may also want to teach the American word *apartment* /əˈpɑːtmənt/ as an alternative to *flat*.

**Exercise 1: additional suggestions**

The following activities might help students remember these verb–noun collocations.

**a** **board** Write the diagrams from Exercise 1 on the board. Tell the class to shut their eyes, then rub out three of the nouns at random. Ask students to open their eyes again and tell you which words you have rubbed out (alternatively students can write the words down). Continue rubbing out two or three words at a time, checking *all* the words that are missing each time. When all the words have been removed, see if the students can draw the diagrams again from memory.

b  Put students into pairs. Student A says one of the expressions (e.g. *three children*) and Student B says the verb *and* the expression (e.g. *have three children*).

c  Write all the nouns on cards and give one set of cards to each pair. Students divide the cards equally, then play snap. Each student puts one card down at the same time. If the nouns on the cards both take the same verb, the first student to shout out the verb takes all the cards in front of them. If the words don't match, each student puts down another card. The student who has the most cards at the end of the game is the winner.

**2**  [5.4] Focus students on the pictures on pages 42 and 43 and ask them to read the captions. Play the recording and allow students to listen and read. Students match the texts with the pictures.

**ANSWERS**
**a** 2    **b** 3    **c** 1

TEACHER'S NOTE:
We believe it is sometimes very useful for students to listen and read at the same time, to help them make sense of their reading and to see the relationship between sounds and spelling. However, this exercise could also be used to give 'pure' reading practice, and the recorded version could be used to check their answers later in the lesson.

### Present Simple with *I*

**3**  Go through the example with the class before allowing students to do the exercise on their own. Early finishers can compare answers in pairs.

**4**  [5.5] Play the recording so that students can check their answers.

**ANSWERS**
| | | |
|---|---|---|
| **a** Gabor | **b** Louise | **c** Carolina |
| **d** Louise | **e** Carolina | **f** Gabor |
| **g** Gabor | **h** Carolina | |

## Grammar

**board**  Draw two columns on the board headed *positive* and *negative*. Write the two examples from the *Grammar* box on the board, and ask your students to give you one or two more examples from Exercise 3 for each column.

Highlight:
- the name of the tense.
- we use *don't* in negative sentences, which is a contraction of *do not*.
- the *you*, *we* and *they* forms are grammatically the same as the *I* form.

Refer students to *Language summary* 5B on page 115 of the *Students' Book*.

LANGUAGE NOTE:
Auxiliary verbs in English (e.g. *do* in the Present Simple) can cause students a lot of problems, often because they wonder where this new verb has suddenly appeared from! If you have a monolingual class and speak your students' language, you might like to explain that English uses auxiliary verbs to make negatives and questions, and that their use is purely grammatical; they have no meaning on their own. If you have a multilingual class, it is best to teach each use of auxiliary verbs on a case-by-case basis and highlight their grammatical function clearly on the board.

**5**  Students work individually and underline all the verbs in the Present Simple they can find in the three texts on page 42. Put students into small groups to compare answers. Check the answers with the whole class and write some of them on the board if necessary.

LANGUAGE NOTE:
Students might also underline the parts of *be* in the texts. This is a good opportunity to underline the fact that *be* works differently to all other verbs in English. Therefore we suggest you write any examples with *am*, *is* and *are* from the text in a separate column or box on the board.

**6**  Go through the example with the class, then allow students to do the exercise individually. Put students into pairs or small groups and ask them to compare their sentences. Students can share their most interesting sentences with the whole class.

**Exercise 6: additional suggestion**

*Practice with 'you'*: Put students in pairs, if possible with students they don't know very well or don't usually work with. Students write down six or eight sentences about their partner that they <u>think</u> are true, but they are not allowed to ask their partner any questions. For example: *You live in a flat.*; *You don't have any children.* Students then work in pairs and say their sentences to their partner, who must say whether they are true or false.

## Pronunciation

[recording icon] [5.6] Play the recording and ask students to read and listen to the sentence stress. Play the recording again, pausing after each phrase or sentence for students to repeat. Drill the sentences chorally and individually.

LANGUAGE NOTES:
a) Students whose languages do not have similar stress patterns to English can often find it difficult to 'tune in' and hear which words are stressed. Don't expect perfection at this early stage, but do use every opportunity to work on sentence stress with the class through awareness exercises and drilling.

b) With a strong class you might like to point out which words are stressed in these sentences (i.e. verbs in positive sentences; *don't* in negative sentences, nouns), and which words are not stressed (i.e. pronouns, prepositions, articles, possessive adjectives).

## Writing task

1 Go through the sentence stems in the box and the example with the whole class. Students work on their own and write four sentences about themselves **on a separate piece of paper**. (You might like to bring some small sheets of paper into class for this activity.) Students should **not** write their name on the paper.

2 Collect in all the pieces of paper, shuffle them, then redistribute them to the class. Allow students a few moments to read the sentences they have been given, and help students with any problems. Students take it in turns to read out the sentences, and the rest of the class must guess who the person is. Continue until all the students have been identified.

### Writing task: alternative suggestion

*If you have a large class*: put the students in groups of six or eight. Collect in each group's papers, shuffle them, then give them back to the same group. Students read the paragraphs to the other members of their group, who have to guess which person it is.

### ADDITIONAL PRACTICE

**Workbook:** Verbs, page 25; Present Simple, Exercise 5, page 25

## Focus 3  (PAGES 44–45)

Present Simple questions

1 Focus students on the questionnaire at the bottom of page 44 and use the pictures to teach *pet*. Students read the questionnaire and answer the questions individually. (Note that you don't need to teach the

grammar of Present Simple questions before doing this exercise, as students should be able to understand them from the context.)

LANGUAGE NOTE:
You may be asked to explain the difference between *house* and *home* at this point. Explain that *a house* is a type of building, whereas *home* is the place where you live.

2 Students do the exercise in pairs. Circulate and deal with any problems students may have. You can check their answers by asking students to raise their hands if they live in the centre of town/have a garden, etc. (Don't ask students to tell you about the person they have just interviewed, as this would require third person forms, which they haven't done yet!)

### Exercise 2: alternative suggestion

*If you have a small class*: allocate one question to each student. They must find out how many students in the class live in the centre of town / have any pets, etc. Students move around the room and ask everybody in the class their question. When they have finished, each student tells the class their answer. For example: *Six people live in the centre of town*.

## Grammar

board Write: *Where ... you live?* and *... you live in a flat?* on the board and ask the students to complete the questions. Ask students for other questions from the quiz and write them on the board. To help students see the underlying structure, it is useful to write the corresponding words directly below each other (i.e. all the *do's*, *you's*, etc.). See the *Language summary* for one way to organise this. Put a tick and a cross next to *Do you live in a flat?* and ask students for the answers. Write *Yes, I do*. and *No, I don't*. next to the tick and cross.

Highlight:

- *do* is used to make Present Simple questions with *you*.
- the word order: (question word) + *do* + *you* + verb.
- the answers ~~Yes, I like~~. and ~~No, I don't like~~. are incorrect.

Refer students to *Language summary* 5C and 5D on page 115 of the *Students' Book*.

LANGUAGE NOTES:
a) Depending on your class, you may wish to identify *you* in the above questions as the *subject*. Although we need to be aware of overloading students with terminology, the words *subject* and *object* often help students understand grammatical structures. A simple sentence like *I have a dog*. could be used to explain the difference between a subject and object quickly and clearly.

b) You may also wish to tell students that the *I*, *we* and *they* question form is grammatically the same as the *you* form.

3 Students work individually and make questions with *you*. Depending on your class, you may want students to write all the questions in their notebooks, or simply put *Do you ...?* in front of the prompts in the *Students' Book*.

## Pronunciation

1 📼 [5.7] Play the recording to allow students to check their answers to Exercise 3. Highlight the weak form of *Do you* /dəˈjuː/ in the questions.
2 Play the recording again (or model the sentences yourself), pausing after each question for students to repeat chorally and individually. Focus on natural rhythm when drilling, and encourage students to stress the verbs, adjectives and nouns.

TEACHER'S NOTE:

We feel it is important to raise students' awareness of weak forms as early as possible, as this will help students understand spoken English better and sound more natural when they are speaking. In future lessons focus on weak forms and sentence stress when it is useful for your students to do so.

4 Check that students remember the short answers *Yes, I do.* and *No, I don't.* by focusing on the speech balloons. Students move around the room and ask three other students four (or more) questions from Exercise 3. If your students aren't able to move around the room, they can do the activity in groups.

Exercise 4: additional suggestion

Use activity 5B *Present Simple dominoes* on page 123 of the Resource bank (instructions on page 93), which gives practice of Present Simple statements, questions and negatives.

## ADDITIONAL PRACTICE

**Workbook:** Present Simple, Exercises 6 and 7, pages 25 and 26; Question words, page 26

**RB** Resource bank: 5B *Present Simple dominoes*, page 123 (instructions on page 93)

## Vocabulary: personal possessions

5 a) Focus students on the pictures on page 45. Students work in pairs or individually and match the words in the box with the pictures. Check the answers with the whole group, or allow students to check their answers in the *Vocabulary book* on page 24.

**ANSWERS**
**1** a camera  **2** a credit card  **3** a wallet  **4** glasses
**5** a watch  **6** a mobil phone  **7** a magazine
**8** a purse  **9** money  **10** a CD  **11** a radio
**12** a passport

b) **board** 📼 [5.8] Play the recording (or model the sentences yourself) and ask students to repeat the words. Pay particular attention to the pronunciation of *money* /ˈmʌni/; *purse* /pɜːs/ and *radio* /ˈreɪdiəʊ/. Write the words on the board and mark the stress, as below (note that *watch* and *purse* are one-syllable words).

a credit card     a passport     a radio     a CD     a magazine
glasses     a camera     a mobile phone     money     a wallet

Exercise 5b: alternative suggestion

**board** Students work in pairs and mark the stress on the words in Exercise 5a. Write the words on the board and ask students where the stress is. Students can also come up to the board and mark the stress themselves.

6 **board** Write the speech balloons on the board to remind students of the *Do you ...?* question form and the short answers. Check they understand *... with you* in the question, and remind them to use *any* in front of plural nouns (i.e. *money* and *glasses*). Students work in new pairs and ask each other about the items in Exercise 5. Finish the activity by asking how many people in the class have particular items.

Exercise 6: additional suggestion

Allocate one of the items in Exercise 5 to each student. Teach a few extra items (e.g. *a dictionary, a calculator, a phone card, an address book, a newspaper, any stamps*) if necessary. Students must move around the room and find out how many people have that item with them by asking *Do you have ...?* questions. Each student then tells the whole class their answer, for example: *Seven students have a credit card with them.*

7 a) Focus students on the pictures of Maggie, Richard and Ellen on page 45, and check students understand the relationship between them. Students work individually and match the items at the top of the page with the people.

LANGUAGE NOTE:
You may wish to point out that we also use *'s* for things we own (e.g. *It's Ellen's mobile phone.*), as well as for family relationships.

**b)** Focus students on the speech balloons and use them to teach *I think* … . Students work in pairs and compare answers. Encourage students to give reasons for their answers where possible.

**c)** ▭ [5.9] Play the recording and allow students to check their answers. Play the recording again if necessary. Ask students to count up how many they got right, and see which student has the most correct answers.

> **ANSWERS**
> **Maggie's possessions:** passport, glasses, money, purse, CD
> **Richard's possessions:** credit card, watch, magazine, camera
> **Ellen's possessions:** radio, mobile phone, wallet

## ADDITIONAL PRACTICE

**Workbook:** Personal possessions, page 26

## Listening (PAGE 46)

**1** ▭ [5.10] Pre-teach the following items of vocabulary: *a TV*; *a DVD player*; *a PlayStation*; *a video*; *a CD player*. Check the pronunciation of *video* /ˈvɪdɪˌəʊ/ and drill the other new vocabulary if necessary. Focus students on the picture on page 46 and check they understand the situation. (Andy is being asked questions by a market researcher.) Go through the form with the class and check they understand all the words. Play the recording and ask students to complete the form. Play the recording again if necessary. Students compare answers in pairs before checking with the whole class.

> **ANSWERS**
> See tapescript Module 5, recording 10 on page 122 of the *Students' Book*.

**LANGUAGE NOTE:**
In American English, *a video* is usually called *a VCR* (short for Video Cassette Recorder). *A PlayStation* is a computer games console manufactured by Sony.

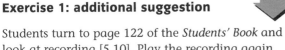

> **Exercise 1: additional suggestion**
>
> Students turn to page 122 of the *Students' Book* and look at recording [5.10]. Play the recording again, allowing students to listen and read. This will help prepare them for Exercise 2.

**2** Ask the class what questions the woman asked Andy in order to fill in the form. Write these on the board if necessary. Put students into pairs, where one student is Andy and the other is the interviewer. Students roleplay the interview in their pairs. When they have finished, ask them to swap roles. Note that the interview does not have to be exactly the same as the tapescript.

> **Exercise 2: additional suggestions**
>
> a Students can do the roleplay again, this time giving their own answers to the questions.
> b You can use the *Vocabulary booster*: *Rooms in a house* on page 124 of the Resource bank (instructions on page 93) any time after Exercise 6.

## ADDITIONAL PRACTICE

**RB** **Resource bank:** *Vocabulary booster*: *Rooms in a house*, page124 (instructions on page 93)

## Real life (PAGES 46–47)

In a shop

**1** board Focus students on the picture on page 47 and ask them to find some of the items in the box. Students may refer to page 25 of the *Vocabulary book* if necessary. Check the answers with the class.

> **ANSWERS**
> In the picture there are newspapers, magazines, cigarettes, postcards and tissues (in the top right-hand corner).

Drill the words chorally and individually. Pay particular attention to the pronunciation of *tissues* /ˈtɪʃuːz/ and *stamps* /stæmps/. Write the words on the board and mark the stress:

a **post**card  a **news**paper  a **mag**azine  **tiss**ues
a **phone** card  **cig**arettes  a **light**er

Note that *cigarettes* and *magazine* can also be pronounced with the stress on the first syllable.

**2** ▭ [5.11] Teach *shop assistant* /ʃɒp əˈsɪstənt/ using the picture. Play the recording and tell students to tick the things Silvia buys in the vocabulary box in Exercise 1. Check the answers with the whole class.

> **ANSWERS**
> Sylvia buys two £5 phone cards and some postcards.

**3** **a)** Focus students on the sentences in A and B. Check students understand that Silvia's sentences are in the correct order, then allow students to do the exercise individually.

**b)** Play recording [5.11] again and allow students to check their answers. Play the recording a final time, pausing after each sentence for students to repeat. Encourage students to sound polite and interested, particularly when repeating Silvia's sentences. Students work in pairs and practise the conversations with their partners. Students can look at their books, but encourage them to practise until they can say the dialogue from memory. You may wish a few pairs to perform the conversation in front of the class before or after they work in pairs (students do not have to leave their seats).

**ANSWERS**
**1** d  **2** e  **3** c  **4** b  **5** a

**4** Put students in new pairs. Student A in each pair should turn to page 108 in the *Students' Book*, and Student B should turn to page 110. Teach the words *customer* /ˈkʌstəmə/ and *shopkeeper* /ˈʃɒpˌkiːpə/, and allow students a few moments to read through the activity and check they understand what to do. Also draw students' attention to the *Useful language* boxes below the pictures for the roleplay, and go through these with the whole class if necessary. Students do the first roleplay, where Student A is the customer and Student B is the shopkeeper. Circulate and help students with language as necessary. When they have finished, students change roles, so that Student A is the shopkeeper and Student B is the customer, and do the second roleplay. Early finishers can find new partners and repeat the activity.

**Exercise 4: additional suggestions**

a At the end of the activity ask one pair to come to the front of the class and act out their roleplay. Repeat this with one or two different pairs.

b If you have a small class, you might like to ask the students to record their conversations onto a cassette. This technique often motivates students to do the roleplays as well as possible, and the recordings can be use for correction work.

 Use the downloadable activities with your students.

## Do you remember? (PAGE 47)

**ANSWERS**

**1** a in  
  b in  
  c with  
  d in  
  e for  

**2** a camera  
  b mobile phone  
  c wallet  
  d glasses  
  e radio  
  f credit card  

**3**

| 👤 | 👤 | 👤👤 |
|---|---|---|
| son | mother | grandchild |
| husband | wife | child |
| father | sister | grandparent |
| brother | daughter | parent |

**4** 1 d  
  2 c  
  3 e  
  4 a  
  5 f  
  6 b

# module 6

## Focus 1 (PAGES 48–49)

### Vocabulary: likes and dislikes

**1** **a)** Focus students on the pictures on page 48. Students work in pairs or small groups and match the words in the box with the pictures, referring to the *Vocabulary book* on page 27 if necessary. Check the meaning of all the words in the box (not just those in the pictures).

**b)** 🔊 [6.1] Play the recording, pausing after each word for students to repeat chorally and individually.

**2** **a)** board Students work alone or in pairs and put the phrases on the line. Draw the line on the board and check the answers with the whole class. Point out that *okay* is often written *OK*. Check students can pronounce the new verbs correctly, particularly *love* /lʌv/ and the /h/ in *hate* /heɪt/.

**b)** Use the speech balloons to point out that the thing or person you are talking about comes after *I like …*, etc., but before *… is/are okay*. Students work in pairs and make sentences about the items in the vocabulary box in Exercise 1. At the end of the activity ask each student to tell the whole class one of their sentences.

**LANGUAGE NOTE:**
If you have a strong class, you may like to point out that we use the gerund (i.e. the *-ing* form of the verb) after *like, love* and *hate*, not the base verb (e.g. I like read.).

### Object pronouns: *him/her/it*

**3** board Check that students remember how to make questions in the Present Simple by writing … *like Brad Pitt?* on the board and asking the class to complete the question. Go through the example with the class, then allow students to do the exercise individually. Students can compare answers in pairs before checking with the whole class. Write the new expressions *I really like …* and *… is/are great!* on the love/hate line on the board.

> **ANSWERS**
> **1** a, f   **2** d, h   **3** c, g   **4** b, e

**LANGUAGE NOTES:**
**a)** While *Yes, I do.* and *No, I don't.* are also correct answers to *Do you like …?* questions, these are not as common among native speakers as you might expect. In Exercise 1 we have therefore provided students with a variety of common answers, which will help them respond more naturally to these questions.
**b)** You may like to point out that when we say we like or hate a famous person, we are usually referring to their music, acting, singing, etc., and not the person themselves!

## Grammar

board Draw two columns on the board headed *subject pronouns* and *object pronouns*. Write *Brad Pitt's okay*; *Madonna's great*; *Cooking's okay*; *Cartoons are great.* in the first column, and *I really like Brad Pitt*; *I love Madonna*; *I like cooking*; *I hate cartoons.* in the second column. Ask the students to replace the nouns in each column with the correct pronoun. As they give you the answers, cross out the noun and write the pronoun above it. Point out that subject pronouns go **before** the verb and object pronouns go **after** the verb.

Refer students to *Language summary* 6D on page 115 of the *Students' Book*. You may also wish to teach the object pronouns *me, us* and *you* at this point.

**LANGUAGE NOTES:**
**a)** If you think your students will have problems with the words *subject* and *object*, teach these before dealing with the language in the *Grammar* box. Write a few simple sentences on the board (e.g. *I have a brother. I love cooking.*) and ask students to identify the subject and object. Check that they understand that in positive sentences the subject comes *before* the verb, and the object comes *after* the verb.
**b)** Depending on your students' native language, it may be worth underlining that all English verbs must have a subject (either a noun or a pronoun). This might avoid common mistakes such as Is great instead of *It's great*.

**4** **a)** Students do the exercise individually. Early finishers can check their answers in pairs or write their own answers to the questions.

> **ANSWERS**
> **a** it   **b** them   **c** It's   **d** him   **e** her   **f** it

**b)** 🔊 [6.2] Play the recording and allow students to check their answers. Play the recording again, pausing after each sentence for students to repeat. Students can then ask the questions in pairs and give their own answers.

**5** Check that students know the vocabulary in the box, and who Jennifer Lopez and Elton John are. Demonstrate the activity by doing a few examples with the whole class, making sure that students use a pronoun in their answers. Students then work in small groups and ask each other questions with *Do you like …?* .

**LANGUAGE NOTE:**
This is a good point in the lesson to highlight that we use the plural form for most nouns (e.g. *dogs, babies, vegetables*) with *like, love* and *hate* because we are talking about these things in general. Depending on your students' language(s), you may also wish to point out that we don't use *the* when talking generally: (e.g. I like the babies). If

students ask why we don't say ~~Do you like musics?~~, you can simply answer that some nouns don't have a plural form. We feel that this will be enough explanation without introducing the terms *countable noun* and *uncountable noun*, which might overload students.

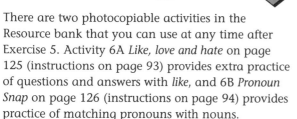

: **Exercise 5: additional suggestions**
:
: There are two photocopiable activities in the
: Resource bank that you can use at any time after
: Exercise 5. Activity 6A *Like, love and hate* on page
: 125 (instructions on page 93) provides extra practice
: of questions and answers with *like*, and 6B *Pronoun
: Snap* on page 126 (instructions on page 94) provides
: practice of matching pronouns with nouns.

## Speaking task

**1** Use the speech balloons to teach the phrase *Me, too.* Draw students' attention to the questions in the *Don't forget!* box, then put students in new pairs and ask them to find six things they both like. They can ask about any of the vocabulary from the exercises on pages 48 and 49, or use their own ideas. Students should make a note of the things they both like while they are talking. Circulate and help students where necessary, noting down errors for later correction work on the board.

**2** Use the speech balloon to teach *both* /bəʊθ/. Each pair tells the class two things they both like.

## ADDITIONAL PRACTICE

**Workbook:** Vocabulary: likes and dislikes, page 29; object pronouns, page 29

**RB** **Resource bank:** 6A *Like, love and hate,* page 125 (instructions on page 93); 6B *Pronoun Snap,* page 126 (instructions on page 94)

## Focus 2   (PAGES 50–51)

### Vocabulary and listening

**1** **board** Focus students on the four diagrams. Use these nouns (which students have already met) to teach the corresponding verbs. Check the pronunciation of *use* /juːz/. Students then work individually or in pairs and match the nouns in the box with the correct verb, referring to the *Vocabulary book* on page 28 if necessary. Draw the diagrams on the board and ask students to complete them with the new vocabulary. Drill the new words, paying attention to the pronunciation of *video* /ˈvɪdiəʊ/, and the stress on *newspaper* /ˈnjuːspeɪpə/.

**ANSWERS**
**watch** a video   **use** the Internet
**read** a newspaper   **play** a computer game

: **Exercise 1: additional suggestions**
:
: a  *If you have a class of false beginners:* you may wish
:    to add more collocations to the diagrams, e.g.
:    *watch a football match / a film on TV; use
:    somebody's phone; read a magazine / a novel; play
:    tennis / basketball / volleyball / golf.*
: b  *To help students memorise the collocations:* put
:    students in pairs and ask one student to say a
:    noun (e.g. *a book*). His/her partner says the
:    matching verb and the noun (e.g. *read a book*).
: c  *Vocabulary booster:* you may use the *Vocabulary
:    booster: Sports* on page 127 of the Resource bank
:    (instructions on page 94) at any time after this
:    exercise.

**2**  **a)** Focus students on the table on page 50. Teach the meaning of *most* and check that students understand *every day* in sentence c). Students read sentences a)–h) and write **T** (true), **F** (false) or **?** (don't know) in the first column of the table.

**b)** Put students into pairs or groups and ask them to compare answers. Encourage students to give reasons for their answers where possible. Discuss their answers with the whole class.

**3**  **a)** 🔲 [6.3] Use the pictures of Emma and Simon to introduce the listening activity. Pre-teach the verb *eat* and the expression *I'm not sure*, both of which appear in the listening texts. Play the recording and ask the students to circle the sentences a)–h) that Emma and Simon talk about. Check the answers with the whole class.

**ANSWERS**
They talk about sentences **a, b, c, d, e** and **g**.

**b)** Play the recording again and ask students to put **T, F** or **?** in the second and third columns in the table. Play the recording again if necessary. Students compare answers in pairs before checking with the whole group. Refer back to the recording if there are any disagreements within the class.

**ANSWERS**

|   |       |   |       |   |
|---|-------|---|-------|---|
| **a** | Emma | T | Simon | ? |
| **b** | Emma | F | Simon | T |
| **c** | Emma | T | Simon | T |
| **d** | Emma | F | Simon | F |
| **e** | Emma | ? | Simon | ? |
| **g** | Emma | F | Simon | F |

## Present Simple: *he* and *she*

**4** 🔲 [6.4] Students work individually and circle the answers they think are correct. Play the recording and allow them to check their answers.

## Grammar

**board** Write *He like shopping.*, *She play computer games a lot.*, *My son watch a lot of TV.* on the board. Ask students what is missing from these sentences, and add the *-s* and *-es* to the verbs (in a different colour pen if possible). Alternatively, use sentences b)–e) from Exercise 4 as examples.

Write *My daughter ... a mobile phone.* on the board and ask students to complete the sentence using a part of the verb *have*. Finally, write *They love school.* on the board and ask students if you need to add an *-s*.

Highlight:

- we add an *-s* to verbs with *he, she, it,* and names of people or places.
- if the verb ends in *-ch* we add *-es* to the verb.
- the third person form of *have* is *has.*
- verbs in the third person plural (e.g. *They love ...*) do not take an *-s.*

Refer students to *Language summary* 6A and 6B on page 115 of the *Students' Book*.

LANGUAGE NOTES:
a) Verbs ending in *-sh* (e.g. *wash*), *-ss* (e.g. *miss)* and *-zz* (e.g. *buzz*) also add *-es* in the third person singular. However, as students have yet to meet any of these verbs, we have not included this in the *Grammar* box. We suggest you highlight the *-es* ending whenever they meet these verbs in the future.
b) Sometimes students get confused by *-s* on nouns, indicating a plural form, and *-s* on verbs, indicating a third person singular form. If you notice this happening with your class, take a few moments to teach/revise the difference between a verb and a noun, and the meaning of their *-s* endings.

## Pronunciation

**board** 🔲 [6.5] Teach *syllable* by writing some words they know on the board (e.g. *write, doctor, football, computer*) and asking students how many syllables there are in each word. Go through the examples with the class. Play the recording and ask students to write **1** or **2** next to each word. Check the answers with the whole class on the board. Explain that verbs ending in the sounds /s/, /z/, /ʃ/ and /tʃ/ always have an extra syllable (pronounced /ɪz/) with *he, she* and *it*. Play the recording again (or model the words yourself), pausing after each word for students to repeat. Pay particular attention to the /ɪz/ ending on *uses, watches* and *teaches.*

**5** Go through the examples with the class and check they understand how to make sentences from the circles. Students do the exercise individually. They can also make sentences with *love(s), hate(s)* and *use(s)* if they wish, and you might like to write these words on the board. As they are working, move round the class, ticking correct sentences and helping students to correct any mistakes they may have made.

**6** Students do the exercise in pairs, using the sentences they have written in Exercise 5. When they have finished students can share one or two of their sentences with the whole class.

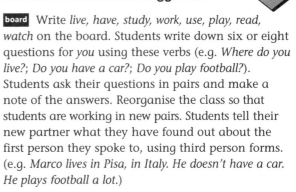

**Exercise 6: additional suggestion**

**board** Write *live, have, study, work, use, play, read, watch* on the board. Students write down six or eight questions for *you* using these verbs (e.g. *Where do you live?*; *Do you have a car?*; *Do you play football?*). Students ask their questions in pairs and make a note of the answers. Reorganise the class so that students are working in new pairs. Students tell their new partner what they have found out about the first person they spoke to, using third person forms. (e.g. *Marco lives in Pisa, in Italy. He doesn't have a car. He plays football a lot.*)

## ADDITIONAL PRACTICE

**Workbook:** Vocabulary: useful nouns, page 30; Present Simple, *he* and *she*, page 30

**RB** **Resource bank:** *Vocabulary booster: Sports,* page 127 (instructions on page 94)

## Focus 3 (PAGES 52–53)

Reading and vocabulary

**1** Teach students the word *couple* (i.e. two people who are either married or going out together). Focus students on the pictures of the six people on pages 52 and 53, but tell them **not** to read the texts. Students work individually or in small groups and try to guess who the couples are. Discuss the possibilities with the whole class, but do not tell them the answers at this stage.

**2** Focus students on the words in bold in sentences a)–g). Either explain the meaning of these yourself or ask the students to check them in the *Vocabulary book* on page 29. Drill the words with the class, paying particular attention to the pronunciation of *theatre* /ˈθɪətə/ and *travelling* /ˈtrævəlɪŋ/, and the extra syllable in *teaches* /ˈtiːtʃɪz/. Students read about the three women and complete the exercise. **Students should not read about the men at this stage.** Early finishers can compare answers in pairs. Check the answers with the whole group.

> **ANSWERS**
> **a** Melanie **b** Isabel **c** Melanie **d** Isabel
> **e** Isabel **f** Nicole **g** Nicole

LANGUAGE NOTE:
Point out that *the theatre*, *the cinema and the Internet* are all fixed expressions with *the*.

### Questions: *he* and *she*

**3** **a)** Students do the exercise individually.

> **ANSWERS**
> **1** Yes, she does.   **2** No, she doesn't.
> **3** We don't know.

**b)** 🔊 [6.6] Play the recording for students to check their answers. Play the recording again, pausing after each sentence for students to repeat chorally and individually. Make sure that students pronounce *does* /dʌz/ and *doesn't* /ˈdʌzənt/ correctly in the short answers.

## Grammar

**board** Write *Melanie likes dancing.* on the board. If possible, use a different colour board pen for the *-s* in *likes*. Ask students to make this sentence into a question, and write *Does Melanie like dancing?* on the board, again using a different colour pen for the *-es* in *Does*. Use these sentences to show students that the *-(e)s* moves from the main verb to the auxiliary verb.

Draw a tick and a cross on the board next to the question and ask students what the answers are. Write *Yes, she does.* and *No, she doesn't.* next to the tick and cross. You may also wish to write one or two questions with *you* and *they* so students can contrast *do* and *does*.

Highlight:

● *does* is used to make questions for *he, she, it* and names of people or places.

● the word order: (question word) + *does* + *he/she* + verb.

● there is no *-s* on the main verb in the question form.

● the answers ~~Yes, she likes.~~ and ~~No, she doesn't like.~~ are incorrect.

Refer students to *Language summary* 6C on page 115 of the *Students' Book*.

**4** Students work individually and write the questions. Check these orally or on the board, and remind students of the answers *Yes, she does.* and *No, she doesn't.* Students ask and answer the questions in pairs.

> **ANSWERS**
> **a** Does Melanie like computer games?
> **b** Does Isabel read a lot?

**c** Does Nicole like cooking?
**d** Does Isabel work with children?
**e** Does Nicole play computer games?

**5** Teach students the new words *drama* /ˈdrɑːmə/ and *secondary school* /ˈsekəndəri skuːl/ (secondary school in the UK is from 11 to 18 years old). Students read about the men, then work in pairs and ask each other questions based on the prompts. Encourage them to ask questions about all three men, and to use *Yes, he does.* and *No, he doesn't.* when answering.

### Negative: *he* and *she*

## Grammar

**board** Write *Oliver … like football.* on the board and ask the students to complete the sentence. If possible, write the *-es* in *doesn't* in a different colour pen. Add one or two more negative examples with other verbs (e.g. *Melanie doesn't play computer games.*; *Isabel doesn't eat meat.*). You may also want to write up one or two negative sentences with *you* and *they* so that students can contrast *don't* and *doesn't*.

Highlight:

● *doesn't* is used in negative sentences for *he, she, it* and names of people or places.

● there is no *-s* on the main verb (e.g. ~~doesn't likes~~).

Refer students to *Language summary* 6A on page 115 of the *Students' Book*.

**6** Students do the exercise individually. Early finishers can check their answers in pairs.

> **ANSWERS**
> **b** correct
> **c** correct
> **d** Oliver doesn't have a job.
> **e** Oliver doesn't like football.

**7** Students do the exercise individually before checking their answers in pairs. Ask a few students to tell the class one or two of their sentences.

**Exercise 7: alternative suggestion**

Students work individually and write six sentences about the men (and women), using both the positive and negative forms of the Present Simple. Three of these sentences should be true, and three should be false. Students work in pairs and say the sentences to each other. They must say if their partner's sentences are true or false without looking at the *Students' Book*.

**8** Students work in groups and discuss who they think the couples are. Encourage students to give reasons for their answers. Discuss the answers with the whole class, again asking students to give reasons. Tell the class to turn to page 109 of the *Students' Book* to check their answers.

> **ANSWERS**
> The couples are: Isabel and Antony; Melanie and Oliver; Nicole and Grant

**9** Use the example to teach *but*. Students work in pairs and find three differences between each couple. Depending on your class, you may want students to write the sentences or just discuss them in their pairs. Check their answers with the whole class. Students can then discuss whether the people make good couples in groups or with the whole class, giving reasons for their answers.

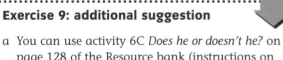

**Exercise 9: alternative suggestions**

a **board** If you feel students need more support, ask the whole class to give you some differences between Antony and Isabel, and write them on the board. As you are writing them up, highlight the use of *doesn't, but* and object pronouns in the sentences. Examples you could use are: *Isabel works in a university, but Antony works in a secondary school. Isabel loves jazz, but Antony hates it. Isabel loves shopping, but Antony doesn't like it.* Students then work in pairs and write three similar sentences for the other two couples.

b Students work in pairs and find as many similarities between the couples as possible. For example: *Isabel and Antony both love reading. Nicole and Grant both use the Internet a lot. Melanie and Oliver both like rock music.*

**Exercise 9: additional suggestion**

a You can use activity 6C *Does he or doesn't he?* on page 128 of the Resource bank (instructions on page 94) at any time after this exercise. If you have a class where students are not able to leave their seats, this activity may also be a good alternative to the following speaking task.

## Speaking task

**1** Check the meaning and pronunciation of *foreign languages* /ˈlæŋgwɪdʒɪz/ and allow students a few moments to read the prompts. Demonstrate the activity yourself by walking around and asking questions with *Do you ...?*. When you find a person who fits the description, show the class that you are

writing their name in the appropriate space in the *Students' Book*. Draw students' attention to the language in the *Don't forget!* box, and teach *Yes, I do.* and *No, I don't.* if necessary. Also check your students can make *Do you ...?* questions for all the prompts. (If you have a weak class, ask them to write the questions down at this stage.) Students then move around the room and try to find one person for each prompt. If your students are not able to move around the room, they can ask as many people as possible from their seats.

**2** Each student tells the class one or two things they have found out. You may need to teach *no one (or nobody)* using the example in the speech balloon. Alternatively, students work in pairs and tell each other what they have found out, using the appropriate *he/she* forms. This can then be followed by a discussion with the whole class.

## ADDITIONAL PRACTICE

**Workbook:** Present Simple questions, page 31; Negatives, page 32, All forms, page 32

**RB** **Resource bank:** 6C *Does he or doesn't he?*, page 128 (instructions on page 94)

 In the Resources section for this module you'll find an online quiz.

## Real life (PAGES 54–55)

Telling the time (1)

**1**  [6.7] Play the recording (or say the times yourself) and focus students on the clocks. Drill the times chorally and individually, paying attention to the pronunciation of *o'clock* /əˈklɒk/, *quarter* /ˈkwɔːtə/ and *half* /hɑːf/. Also point out the weak form of *to* /tə/ in *quarter to five* /ˈkwɔːtə tə faɪv/. (Note that *ten past, twenty to*, etc. is covered in Module 7.)

**Exercise 1: alternative suggestion**

*If you have a class of false beginners:* ask them to write down the times shown on the clocks before playing the recording, to see what they know. They can then listen to the tape to check their answers.

LANGUAGE NOTES:
a) There is of course another way to express time in English, for example: *four fifteen, three thirty, four forty-five.* We believe that most students acquire this 'formula' naturally, and therefore have chosen to focus on the 'harder' version, which is particularly important for students' receptive skills. You may wish to introduce both ways of saying the time to your students.

b) *Quarter past four* and *quarter to five* are also commonly expressed with the indefinite article; i.e. *a quarter past four* and *a quarter to five*.

**2** a) `board` 🔲 [6.8] Ask students to draw ten blank clock faces in their notebooks. Play the recording and ask students to draw the times on the clock faces. Check the answers with the whole class on the board. You could ask students to come up to the board and draw the times themselves.

> **ANSWERS**
> **a** seven o'clock  **b** ten o'clock  **c** twelve o'clock
> **d** half past six  **e** quarter past six  **f** quarter to seven
> **g** quarter to nine  **h** quarter past nine  **i** half past one
> **j** half past twelve

b) Use the speech balloons to teach the question *What time is it?*, and the use of *It's …* in the answer. Drill the question chorally and individually.  Students do the exercise in pairs.

LANGUAGE NOTE:
You may also wish to teach the students the alternative question: *What's the time?*.

**3** Check students know the meaning of *start, finish, open* and *close*. Also highlight the use of *at* with times, as in the example. Students do the exercise individually before checking the answers in pairs or with the whole class.

**4** 🔲 [6.9] Focus students on the illustrations on page 55 and the times listed below. Play the recording and ask students to circle the times they hear. Before you begin, explain to the class that they will not understand everything on the tape, and that they should only listen for the times. Play the recording again if necessary, then check the answers with the whole class.

> **ANSWERS**
> **a** seven o'clock  **b** quarter past eight
> **c** quarter to six  **d** half past three

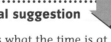

**Telling the time: additional suggestion**

In future classes, ask students what the time is at appropriate moments, for example at the end of a speaking activity, or before and after a break.

## Do you remember?  (PAGE 55)

> **ANSWERS**
> **1**  a  Tim really like**s** classical music.
>    b  The sentence is correct.
>    c  His brother watch**es** videos a lot.
>    d  The sentence is correct.
>    e  She read**s** the newspaper every day.
>    f  Frank teach**es** English at university.
>
> **2a**  a  Do
>    b  Do
>    c  Does
>    d  Do
>    e  Do
>    f  Does
>
> **3**  a  in a school
>    b  football on TV
>    c  tennis
>    d  a book
>    e  a computer
>    f  in a flat
>
> **4**  open ≠ close
>    hate ≠ love
>    expensive ≠ cheap
>    small ≠ big
>    hot ≠ cold
>    start ≠ finish
>    left ≠ right

# module 7

## Focus 1 (PAGES 56–57)

### Vocabulary: daily routines

**1 a)** Focus students on the pictures on page 56, and use the pictures to teach the expression *daily routine* /ˈdeɪli ruːˈtiːn/. Students work in pairs and match the pictures with the expressions in the box. Students may refer to the *Vocabulary book* on page 32 as necessary. Alternatively, teach the daily routine vocabulary yourself first by miming your day for the whole class, then allow students to do Exercise 1 in pairs.

**b)** 📼 [7.1] Play the recording for students to check their answers. Play the recording again, pausing after each expression for students to repeat chorally and individually. Pay particular attention to the pronunciation of *work* /wɜːk/; *breakfast* /ˈbrekfəst/; *lunch* /lʌntʃ/; the stress on *up* in *get up*, and the weak form of *to* /tə/ in *go to work* and *go to bed*.

> **ANSWERS**
> **1** get up  **2** have breakfast  **3** go to work
> **4** start work  **5** have lunch  **6** finish work
> **7** get home  **8** have dinner  **9** go to bed  **10** sleep

LANGUAGE NOTES:
a) We have chosen to teach *get home* rather than *arrive home* here, as it is much more common in spoken English. You may choose to teach your students both expressions. You may also like to point out that *work* is a noun here, not a verb.
b) This is the first time students have met a phrasal verb (*get up*), and the concept of having two-word verbs may be confusing for some students. We suggest you simply say that some verbs in English are two words rather than one. Students at this level are usually happy to learn them as individual vocabulary items.

**Exercise 1: additional suggestion**

Write the ten expressions on cards, and have one set of cards for each group of three students. Shuffle the cards and give each group a set. Students should arrange them **face down** without looking at them first. Students take it in turns to pick up a card until one of them picks up *get up*. The aim of the activity is for students to pick up the rest of the cards **in order** (i.e. the order of the pictures on page 56 of the *Students' Book*). If a student picks up the correct card, he/she keeps it and has another go. If a student picks up the wrong card, he/she must put it back **in the same place** and the turn passes to the next student. The student who has the most cards at the end is the winner.

**2** Teach these 'parts of the day' expressions via times (e.g. 6 a.m. to 12 a.m. = *in the morning*). Drill these expressions chorally and individually, paying attention to

the pronunciation of *morning* /ˈmɔːnɪŋ/; *night* /naɪt/ and the word stress of *afternoon* /ɑːftəˈnuːn/. Also highlight the irregular preposition in *at night*. Students do the exercise in pairs, focusing on when people **usually** do these things. (You may need to pre-teach *usually* /ˈjuːʒuəli/ before they begin the exercise.) Check the answers with the whole class, and discuss any disagreements they may have.

> **ANSWERS**
> **in the morning**: get up, have breakfast, leave home, start work
> **in the afternoon**: have lunch, finish work, (get home)
> **in the evening**: (get home); have dinner, (go to bed)
> **at night**: (go to bed), sleep

LANGUAGE NOTE:
What constitutes afternoon, evening and night often varies between cultures, and there is obviously some overlap between these words. Most people consider sunrise to be the start of morning, and sunset to be the end of the afternoon. You may also wish to teach the expression *at lunchtime,* as many people consider their afternoon doesn't begin until they have had lunch!

### Reading

**3** Focus students on the pictures of Susannah and Marcus on page 57, and allow them time to read the captions. Check students understand what the people's jobs are, and the word *club* /klʌb/. You may also like to teach the more general word *musician* /mjuːˈzɪʃən/ to describe Susannah's job.

LANGUAGE NOTE:
*DJ* is short for *disc jockey*, although the full expression is rarely used nowadays. DJs play music in clubs and on the radio.

**4** Students read the text and decide who is talking (Marcus). Check the answer with the whole group, and ask students to give reasons for their choice. The following words in the text may be new to your students: *late*; *buy*; *records*; *enjoy*; *dance*; *tired*; *best*. We suggest that you don't pre-teach these, as most will be clear from the context and are not required for the tasks. However, you may wish to focus on them after students have finished Exercise 5.

**5** 📼 [7.2] Play the recording and allow students to listen and read. (This exercise will help them make connections between written and spoken English, and improve their listening skills.) Check that students understand *a.m.* and *p.m.*, and use the example to remind students of the third person singular *-s* with *he* and *she*. Students do the rest of the exercise individually. You may wish to ask students to write the times as words rather than numbers. Early finishers can compare their answers in pairs. Check the answers with the whole group.

**ANSWERS**
**a** He sleeps in the morning.
**b** He gets up at one o'clock (in the afternoon).
**c** He has breakfast at half past one.
**d** He goes shopping in the afternoon.
**e** He leaves home at half past nine (in the evening).
**f** He starts work at half past ten (at night).
**g** He gets home at quarter past four.
**h** He goes to bed at five o'clock (in the morning).

6 [7.3] Pre-teach the word *concert* /ˈkɒnsət/ by referring students back to the picture of Susannah. Students do the exercise individually. Early finishers can again check in pairs. When everyone has finished, play the recording and allow students to check their answers. You may like to conclude by asking the class which person's job they would like most, and why.

**ANSWERS**
The correct order is: **b, e, g, d, a, c, f**

**Exercise 6: additional suggestion**

You can use activity 7A *A footballer's day* on page 129 and 130 of the Resource bank (instructions on page 94) at any point after Exercise 6. The activity provides extra practice of daily routine vocabulary and Present Simple questions with *he*.

## Speaking task

**1** Focus students on the pictures on page 56. Students make a note of the time they do these things under each picture or in their notebooks. If you have a young class you might wish your students to use the expressions *start, finish* and *go to school/university* instead of *start, finish* and *go to work*.

**2** Use the speech balloons to introduce *What time do you ...?* and drill the question with the class. If you have a class of real beginners, you may wish to practise all the questions students will need before they work in pairs. Also highlight the use of *at* with times in the answer, and the question *And you?*. (You might also like to teach *about* in the *Don't forget!* box at this point.) Students then do the activity in pairs, noting down their partner's answers in their books. At the end of the activity, each student can tell the class one or two things about their partner.

**Speaking task: alternative suggestion**

Teach the meaning of *before* and *after*, for example by comparing two times when different students have dinner. Students work in new pairs, and must try to find two things they do before their partner, and two things that they do after him/her. At the end of the activity they can then share their answers with the whole class.

## ADDITIONAL PRACTICE

**Workbook:** Daily routines, page 34; Present Simple, page 34

RB **Resource bank:** 7A *A footballer's day*, pages 129 and 130 (instructions on page 94)

## Focus 2 (PAGES 58–59)

Vocabulary: days of the week

**1 a)** [7.4] Students do the exercise in pairs. Play the recording for students to check their answers.

**b)** board Play the recording again, pausing after each word for students to mark the stress on the days. Check the answers on the board, and point out that we use capital letters for days in English. Drill the words chorally and individually. Days that are often hard to pronounce are *Tuesday* /ˈtjuːzdi/, *Thursday* /ˈθɜːzdi/, and *Wednesday* /ˈwenzdi/, which has only two syllables.

**ANSWERS**
Monday   Tuesday   Wednesday   Thursday
Friday   Saturday   Sunday

**2** [7.5] Play the recording, pausing where appropriate to allow the students to say the next two days. Students can then do the same activity in pairs.

**Exercise 2: additional suggestion**

Teach the students *today, tomorrow* and the *day after tomorrow*, and drill these phrases with the class. For the next few lessons you can then begin the class by asking *What day is it today/tomorrow/the day after tomorrow?*

## Adverbs of frequency

**3 a)** board Focus students on the line in the *Students' Book* and ask them to put *usually* and *not usually* in the correct places. Check the answers by drawing the line on the board, and mark the stress on the adverbs (the stress is on the first syllable of each word). Model the words for your class and ask them to repeat them chorally and individually. Students often have problems pronouncing *always* /ˈɔːlweɪz/ and *usually* /ˈjuːʒuəliː/.

**b)** Students do the exercise individually. Do not check in pairs at this stage.

**LANGUAGE NOTE:**
You may wish to point out that the plural form of *Saturdays* and *Sundays* in sentences d) and e) is used to mean every Saturday or Sunday.

**4** Students change the adverbs in any sentences in Exercise 3b to make them true for their countries. If you have a monolingual group, check the answers in pairs or with the whole class. If you have a multilingual group, students can compare answers in different nationality groups before discussing them with the whole class. Remind students to use *in* with countries (as shown in the speech balloon) before they begin.

# Grammar

**board** Write the examples with *always, usually, sometimes* and *never* from Exercise 3b on the board, or ask students for examples about their country. Highlight the word order of **subject + adverb + verb**. It is useful to write the sentences so that similar words are under each other, to help students see the grammatical pattern in the sentences (see the *Language summary* on page 116).

Write the example with *don't usually* on the board, and highlight the word order of **subject + don't + usually + verb**. You may also wish to write a similar sentence using *doesn't*, for example: *My sister doesn't usually get up early*.

Refer students to *Language summary* 7A and 7B on page 116 of the *Students' Book*.

**LANGUAGE NOTE:**
There is a lot of flexibility regarding the position of these adverbs in a sentence, which can vary from adverb to adverb (for example, *sometimes* can go at the beginning of a sentence, but *always* can't). At this level, however, we feel this simple rule is appropriate for students, and any more information will confuse them.

........................................................
**Exercise 4: additional activity**

You can use activity 7B *Adverb partners* in the Resource bank on page 131 (instructions on page 95) at any time after the covering the language in the *Grammar* box.
........................................................

## Listening

**5** **a)** Focus students on the sentences and pictures in the 'In my country …' box at the bottom of page 59. Teach the following new vocabulary: *wear* /weə/; *shoes* /ʃuːz/; *kiss* /kɪs/; *meet* /miːt/, and drill the new words with the class. Students do the exercise individually.

**b)** Put students in small groups to compare their answers. If you have a multilingual group, ask students from different countries to work together. Discuss the answers with the whole class.

**6** **a)** 🔊 [7.6] Focus students on the pictures of Mansoor and Justine, and check students know where Dubai is (in the Middle East). Play the recording and allow students to do the exercise. Play the recording again if necessary. Students can compare answers in small groups. Finally, check the answers with the whole class, playing sections of the recording again if necessary to resolve any problems. You may wish to write the answers on the board in two columns, in preparation for Exercise 6b.

**ANSWERS**
Mansoor talks about sentences **a**, **b**, **c**, **d** and **f**
Justine talks about sentences, **a**, **e**, **c**, **d** and **f**

**b)** **board** Draw two columns on the board headed *Mansoor* and *Justine*, and ask the students to copy it into their notebooks. Play the first part of the recording, pause the tape, and put a) *sometimes* beneath Mansoor. Play the rest of the recording, pausing after each sentence to allow students time to write. You may find it helpful to do the first sentence with the whole class. Students compare their answers in pairs or groups. Encourage students to make complete sentences as they compare answers. Finally, check the answers with the whole class.

**ANSWERS**

| Mansoor | Justine |
|---|---|
| **a** sometimes | sometimes |
| **b** never | – |
| **c** usually | usually |
| **d** usually | don't usually |
| **e** – | always |
| **f** don't usually | don't usually |

**7** Students do the exercise individually. As they are working, move around the room and correct any mistakes you see. Put the students into new pairs to say their sentences to each other and decide if their partner's sentences are true or false.

**8** Students work individually and write sentences for themselves. Alternatively, they can simply write the appropriate adverb next to each prompt. Put students in pairs or groups to compare their sentences. Students can share any surprising or interesting things they found out about their partner(s) with the whole class.

........................................................
**Exercise 8: alternative suggestion**

When students are comparing sentences in pairs, they should note down how many of their sentences have the same adverb. Remind students of the expression *Me too!* before they begin. Students can then tell the class what they have in common: e.g. *Paolo and I never get up early on Sundays*.
........................................................

## ADDITIONAL PRACTICE

**Workbook:** Vocabulary: days of the week, page 35; Adverbs of frequency, page 35; Word order with adverbs, page 35

RB **Resource bank:** 7B *Adverb partners,* page 131 (instructions on page 95)

# Focus 3 (PAGES 60–61)

## Reading and speaking

1 [7.7] Students do the exercise individually or in pairs. Play the recording for students to check their answers. Check the meaning of any new words or phrases. Drill the vocabulary with the class, paying particular attention to the pronunciation of *homework* /ˈhəʊmwɜːk/; *cinema* /ˈsɪnəmə/; *listen* /ˈlɪsən/ and the weak form of *to* /tə/ in *go to the cinema* and *listen to music.* Also highlight the use of the article *the* in *go to the cinema* and *clean the house.*

> **ANSWERS**
> **meet** friends   **go to** the cinema   **read** a book
> **do** your homework   **stay** in   **watch** TV
> **listen to** music   **clean** the house

LANGUAGE NOTE:
You may also wish to teach *go out* as a general opposite of *stay in.*

> **Exercise 1: additional suggestions**
>
> a *If you have a strong class:* write the verbs from Exercise 1 on the board and ask students to work in pairs and think of one other noun or expression that goes with each verb. Write the students' ideas on the board for all the class to copy. Some suggestions are: *meet my classmates / my sister; go to a club / the theatre / a concert; read a magazine; do some work; stay at home; watch a film on TV / a football match; listen to CDs / the radio; clean my room / my car.*
>
> b Write the vocabulary in Exercise 1 on cards, making 16 cards in total (for example, *meet* and *friends* should be on separate cards). You will need one set of cards for each group of three students. Give a set of cards to each student and ask them to put them on the table face down. Each student takes it in turns to turn over two cards. If the cards match, the student keeps the card and has another go. If they do not match, he/she should put them back in the same place, and the turn passes to the next student. The student who gets the most pairs is the winner.

2 You may wish to pre-teach the following new items of vocabulary before they do the quiz: *hungry* /ˈhʌŋgri/; *tired* /ˈtaɪəd/; *to buy; to go shopping; half an hour.* Drill these

new words as necessary. Students then do the quiz on their own. Encourage students to choose the answer that is the closest for them, even if it is not exactly correct, rather than leaving an answer blank.

3 **a)** Students work in pairs and take it in turns to ask each other the questions in the quiz. They must make a note of their partner's answers in their books during the activity, so that they have the information to do Exercise 3b. You may wish to teach the expression *What about you?* before they begin, to avoid students repeating the questions.

**b)** Ask each student to count how many a's, b's and c's their partner has, then turn to page 112 in the *Students' Book.* Students should then read out the entry which matches their partner's answers. Alternatively, you may wish to go through the Answer key on page 112 with the whole class, explaining any new words or expressions where necessary. Finally, ask how many of the class agree with the descriptions of how they spend their free time.

## Time expressions

4 board Focus students on the examples in the diagrams before allowing students to do the exercise individually or in pairs. Encourage them to look back at the quiz on page 60 for examples of the time expressions if necessary. Check the answers on the board with the whole class. Use these to highlight the following general rules: *on* **+ days;** *in* **+ parts of days;** *at* **+ times,** and check students understand the meaning of *every.* Also highlight the use of *at* in the expressions *at the weekend* and *at night.* Refer students to *Language summary* 7C on page 116 of the *Students' Book* for a summary of these time expressions.

> **ANSWERS**
> **on** Saturday; Wednesday; Sunday
> **in** the morning; the afternoon; the evening
> **at** half past ten; quarter past four; two o'clock
> **every** weekend; day; week

5 Students work in pairs. One student says a time expression without the preposition, and his/her partner should say the complete expression. Demonstrate this with the class before you begin. Students should swap roles after a minute or two.

6 **a)** Students do the exercise on their own. Early finishers can compare answers in pairs. Check the answers with the whole class.

> **ANSWERS**
> **a** every   **b** at; in   **c** every   **d** at   **e** every
> **f** on   **g** at; in

**b)** Students work in new pairs and ask each other the questions. Encourage students to give extra information in their answers where possible. For example: *No, I study English on Tuesday and Thursday.* for question a).

### Exercise 6: additional suggestion

Activity 7C *A classroom survey* on page 132 of the Resource bank (instructions on page 95) provides extra practice of time expressions and Present Simple questions.

## Speaking task

1  Students work in pairs and write six questions to ask you. Draw students' attention to the language in the *Don't forget!* box before they begin. Early finishers can write two or three more questions.

2  Students take it in turns to ask you their questions. Try to give honest answers where possible!

### Speaking task: alternative suggestion

*If it is not appropriate for students to ask you personal questions*: students can work in pairs and write six (or more) questions to ask another student. When they are ready, rearrange the class so that each student is working with a new partner. Students ask their new partner their questions and make a note of the answers. Finally, students return to their original partner and tell him/her what they have found out, for example: *Tomas usually meets friends on Friday evenings.* This final stage provides valuable practice of *he/she* verb forms.

### Writing

7  **a)** Focus students on the example paragraph, and allow students time to read. Students then do the exercise individually. Remind students **not** to write their name on the paper. Also ensure that students write their paragraph on a clean piece of paper, not in their notebooks. (You may like to bring in some paper for them to write on.) Circulate and help students with expressions and ideas as they are writing.

**b)** Collect in all the papers and redistribute them to different students. Each student reads his/her paragraph and decides who they think wrote it. Students then move around the room and ask questions to find the person who wrote their paragraph. If your students cannot move around the room, this final stage can be done by students reading out the paragraphs to the whole class.

### Exercise 7b: alternative suggestions

a  *If you have a small class*: students can take it in turns to read out the paragraphs instead of walking round the room. The whole class then tries to guess who each person is.

b  Write a number on each paragraph students give you and stick them round the classroom. Students move around the room in pairs and try to decide who wrote each paragraph. They can make a note of their ideas using the numbers on each paper, e.g. 1 – *Adriana*, etc. Students then compare answers with the whole class and find out how many they guessed correctly.

### Vocabulary: additional suggestion

You can use the *Vocabulary booster: Verbs and nouns* on page 133 of the Resource bank (instructions on page 95) at any time after Exercise 7.

### ADDITIONAL PRACTICE

**Workbook:** Verbs and nouns, page 36; Time expressions, page 36

**RB Resource bank:** 7C *A classroom survey*, page 132 (instructions on page 95); *Vocabulary booster: Verbs and nouns*, page 133 (instructions on page 95)

## Real life  (PAGES 62–63)

### Telling the time (2)

1  **a)** **board** Draw the clocks for a) and e) on the board (i.e. five past eight and twenty-five to one), and ask students to tell you what the times are. Write the times in words under the clocks. Students can then do the exercise individually, using the examples a) and e) to complete the rest of the times.

**b)** [7.8] Play the recording for students to check the answers. Check they understand the meaning of *past* and *to* in the times. Play the recording again (or model the sentences yourself) for students to repeat chorally and individually. Highlight the pronunciation of *past* /pɑːs/ and *to* /tə/ in the times.

> LANGUAGE NOTE:
> There is of course another way to express these times in English, for example: *six twenty, eight fifty,* etc. As with the times in Module 6, we believe that most students acquire this 'formula' naturally, and therefore we have again focused on the 'harder' version, which is particularly important for students' receptive skills. You may wish to introduce both ways of saying the time to your students.

2  **a)** [7.9] Play the recording and allow students to do the exercise on their own. Tell students that they do not have to understand everything that is said, and should

listen only for the times. Play the recording again if necessary, then check the answers with the whole class.

**ANSWERS**
**a** 4.20  **b** 2.10  **c** 9.55  **d** 7.35  **e** 6.20
**f** 9.25  **g** 2.50

**b)** Students do the exercise in pairs. Encourage students to use all the times in Exercise 2a, not just those that were the correct answers.

**Exercise 2b: additional suggestion**

Tell each student to draw eight blank clock faces on a piece of paper, and write eight different times at the bottom of the paper (**not** on the clock faces). Students work in pairs and say their times to their partner, who must draw the times on the blank clocks. When they have both completed all their clocks students should compare answers.

3  [7.10] Teach your students *programme* /ˈprəʊɡræm/ and *The News* /ðə njuːz/. If necessary, check they know that *Titanic* and *Casablanca* are famous films, and that George Michael is a famous singer. Play the recording and ask students to write the times in the table. Play the recording again if necessary. Students can compare answers in pairs before checking with the whole class.

**ANSWERS**

| Programme | Time |
| --- | --- |
| The News | 7.00 |
| George Michael in Concert | 7.10 |
| *Titanic* | 7.50 |
| *Casablanca* | 8.55 |
| Football Night | 9.30 |

LANGUAGE NOTE:
You may wish to point out that *The News* is actually singular (for example: *The News is on BBC1 at ten o'clock.*), and is used with the definite article *the* when referring to a TV programme.

4 Teach the word *channel* /ˈtʃænəl/ via the TV Guide, and use the speech balloons to introduce the question: *What time does (House and Garden) start?*. Drill the question with the whole class for a few different programmes (e.g. those in the table in Exercise 3). Put the students into pairs. Student B should turn to page 111 in the *Students' Book*, and Student A should look at the TV Guide on page 63. Students ask each other what time the programmes start, and write the times in their version of the TV Guide. **Students should not look at each other's books during the activity**. When they have all the times they should then look at each other's books and compare answers.

LANGUAGE NOTE:
It is useful to highlight the preposition *on* in expressions such as *on TV, on BBC1* and *It's on at ten.* If you have a strong class you may wish to teach the alternative question *What time is House and Garden on?* before they begin the pairwork in Exercise 4.

## ADDITIONAL PRACTICE

**Workbook:** Telling the time, page 36

Use the activities relating to British TV to learn more about life in the UK.

# Do you remember? (PAGE 63)

**ANSWERS**
**1** a have
   b go to
   c gets
   d get up
   e start
   f leave

**2** a I usually get up before eight o'clock.
   b I don't usually have breakfast.
   c I sometimes go shopping on Sunday.
   d I always watch sport on TV at the weekend.
   e I never leave home before nine o'clock.

**3** various answers

**4** a five past ten
   b twenty past ten
   c ten past five
   d ten to five
   e twenty-five to five
   f five to ten

# module 8

## Focus 1 (PAGES 64–65)

*can* and *can't*

**1** Students work individually and check the words in bold in the *Vocabulary book* on page 37. Alternatively, teach the words yourself through miming the actions in front of the class. Drill the words chorally and individually, paying particular attention to the pronunciation of *guitar* /gɪˈtɑː/ and *walk* /wɔːk/.

LANGUAGE NOTE:
You may wish to point out the use of *the* when we talk about playing a musical instrument (e.g.: *play the guitar*, *play the violin*), compared to playing a game or sport (e.g.: *play chess, play football*).

**2** Focus students on the pictures on page 64. Students match the pictures with the sentences. Check the answers with the whole group. You may also wish to teach the meaning of *well* /wel/ and *brilliantly* /ˈbrɪljəntli/ in sentences c) and d) at this point.

**ANSWERS**
**a** 2  **b** 4  **c** 3  **d** 1

## Grammar

board Draw two columns on the board headed *positive* and *negative*. Write: *She … swim.* in the first column and *He … read music.* in the second column, and ask students to complete the sentences. Ask students for one or two other sentences with *can* and *can't* about the people in the pictures, and write them on the board in the correct columns.

Highlight:

- the word order: subject + *can/can't* + verb.
- *can* is the same for every subject (*I/you/he/she/we/they*), and there is no -*s* with *he* and *she*: ~~He / She cans swim.~~
- there is no *to* after can: ~~I can to swim.~~
- there is no *don't* in the negative form: ~~I don't can swim.~~

You may choose to refer students to *Language summary* 8A on page 116 of the *Students' Book* when you have covered question forms with *can* on page 65.

LANGUAGE NOTE:
In this module a few adverbs are introduced to encourage natural communication (e.g. *well, brilliantly, fast*). We feel it is enough at this level for students to learn these as single vocabulary items, without involving them in the grammatical rules of adverbs.

## Pronunciation

**1** [8.1] Play the recording and focus students on the pronunciation of *can* /kæn/ and *can't* /kɑːnt/ in the examples. Point out that in positive sentences we use the weak (unstressed) form of *can* /kən/, and the verb (*run*) is stressed. Also point out that in negative sentences *can't* and the verb are both stressed. Drill the sentences chorally and individually.

**2** [8.2] Play the recording, pausing after each sentence to allow students to write. Play the recording again if necessary. Students check their answers against the recording. Drill the sentences with the class, focusing on sentence stress and the pronunciation of *can* and *can't*.

**ANSWERS**
**a** She can't cook very well.
**b** We can play chess.
**c** He can speak Chinese.
**d** My parents can't speak English.
**e** My grandmother can't swim very well.

LANGUAGE NOTE:
It is important to encourage students to use the weak form of *can* in positive sentences, as the strong form /kæn/ often sounds very much like *can't*, which can result in confusion and communication breakdown. One way to encourage the use of the weak form of *can* /kən/ is to make students 'overstress' the verb when drilling positive sentences. Note also that in American English *can't* is pronounced /kænt/.

**3** **a)** Focus students on the pictures on page 65 and the verbs below them. Students work individually and check the verbs in the *Vocabulary book* on page 37. The following words may be new to students: *see; hear; sit; stand; talk; ride a bicycle.* You may wish to drill some of these words, particularly *hear* /hɪə/, *talk* /tɔːk/ and *bicycle* /ˈbaɪsɪkəl/.

**b)** Draw students' attention to the use of *can* and *can't* in the examples. Students then do the exercise in pairs. Depending on your class, you may want students to write the sentences, or simply to say them to each other. Discuss the students' ideas with the whole class.

**ANSWERS**
[Note: these are suggested answers only.]
**A new baby**: can see, can hear, can't sit, can't stand, can't eat food
**A three-year-old child**: can walk, can talk, can run, can't read, can't write
**A seven-year-old child**: can swim, can ride a bicycle, can use a computer, can't play chess

### Questions with *can*

4 Teach students the meaning of *well* and *fast*, using the pictures on page 64 or your own ideas. Also check they understand the other new words: *cook* /kʊk/, *swim* and *your left hand*. Students then do the exercise individually.

## Grammar

**board** Write *... you drive?* on the board and ask students to complete the question. Elicit two or three more questions beginning with *Can ... ?* and write them on the board. Write a tick and a cross next to the questions, and ask students for the answers. Write *Yes, I can.* and *No, I can't.* on the board.

Highlight:

- the word order: *Can* + subject + verb.
- the question is the same for every subject (*I/you/he/she/we/they*).
- there is no *do* or *does* in questions with *can*: ~~Do you can swim?~~
- the verb is not repeated in the short answer: ~~Yes, I can drive.~~

Refer students to *Language summary* 8A on page 116 of the *Students' Book*.

LANGUAGE NOTE:
*Can* can be pronounced either /kən/ or /kæn/ in questions. Unlike *can* in positive sentences, however, there is little chance of confusion if the strong form is used.

5 Drill the questions in the speech balloons with the whole class. Students work in pairs and ask each other questions based on the prompts in Exercise 4. Encourage students to use the correct short answers when responding.

LANGUAGE NOTE:
If you have a class of false beginners, you may wish to teach one or two other common responses to *Can ...?* questions, such as: *Yes, but not very well.* and *No, not at all.*

**Exercise 5: additional suggestion**

When students have finished Exercise 5, they can work with a new partner and tell him/her about the first person they spoke to. For example: *Dmitri can't run fast, but he can play chess well.*

6 [8.3] Introduce the listening by saying that two English people, Ben and Karis, are asking each other about the topics that students have just discussed. Play the recording and ask students to write down what Ben and Karis can do, in their notebooks. (Alternatively, students can

simply write **B** and **K** next to the phrases in Exercise 4.) Play the recording again if necessary. Students can compare answers in pairs before checking them with the whole group.

**ANSWERS**
**Ben** can: drive, swim100 metres, speak Spanish
**Karis** can: drive, ride a bicycle, swim 100 metres, speak French, play the violin

## Speaking task

1 If possible, put students into new pairs before they begin this exercise. They should ask about the phrases in Exercises 1 and 4 and the *Don't forget!* box, or their own ideas. During the activity students should write down anything they can do but their partner can't. While they are working, circulate and help students with vocabulary and pronunciation.

2 Draw students' attention to the sentence in the speech balloon, particularly the use of *but* and the fact that we don't repeat the main verb at the end of the sentence. Students take it in turns to tell the class the things they can do but their partner can't.

**Speaking task: additional suggestion**

a You can use activity 8A *What can you do?* on pages 134 and 135 of the Resource bank (instructions on page 96) at any time after Exercise 5.

b Students write down four things they can do. They then move around the room and find one person who can also do the things they have written down. They must find a different person for each of the four things on their paper. Finally, students can tell the whole class their answers.

c Students write down the names of three people they know well (either friends or family members). Students work in pairs and ask each other what the people can and can't do. Students must find two things each person can do, and two things they can't do.

## ADDITIONAL PRACTICE

**Workbook:** Action verbs, page 39; *can* and *can't*, page 39; Short answers, page 40

**RB** **Resource bank:** 8A *What can you do?*, pages 134 and 135 (instructions on page 96)

# Focus 2 (PAGES 66–67)

## Vocabulary: the body

**1** Check students understand the verb *to point* and demonstrate the activity if necessary. Students do the exercise in pairs, checking any words they don't know in the *Vocabulary book* on page 38. Check the answers with the whole class, and highlight the irregular plural of *foot*.

**2** [8.4] Play the recording (or model the words yourself), pausing after each word for students to repeat chorally and individually. Pay particular attention to the pronunciation of *foot* /fʊt/, *blood* /blʌd/ and the /h/ sound in *head* and *hand*.

> **Exercises 1 and 2: additional suggestions**
>
> a If you think your students won't know any of the words, teach them to the whole class first and use Exercise 1 as practice.
>
> b *Vocabulary booster*: You may use the *Vocabulary booster: Parts of the body* on page 136 of the Resource bank (instructions on page 96) at any time after Exercise 1.

**3 a)** Students read the sentences on pages 66 and 67 and decide which two of them are false.

**b)** Draw students' attention to the language in the speech balloons and teach the expression *Are you sure?*. Students can then compare answers in pairs or groups. Encourage students to give reasons for their answers where possible.

**4 a)** [8.5] Focus students on the picture of Professor Klein and play the recording. Students listen and check their answers.

> **ANSWERS**
> Sentence **3** is wrong. An adult eats about 500 kg of food every year.
> Sentence **7** is wrong. We can only live without water for five to seven days.

**b)** Ask the class to look at all the sentences again and decide which facts they think are amazing. Discuss their ideas with the whole class.

> **Exercise 4: additional suggestion**
>
> If you need to play the recording a second time, ask students to turn to tapescript 5, Module 8 on page 124 of the *Students' Book*. Play the recording again and allow students to listen and read.

## Vocabulary: *metres, minutes, kilos*

**5 a)** Students do the exercise individually or in pairs, referring to the *Vocabulary book* on page 39 if necessary.

**b)** [8.6] Play the recording for students to check their answers.

> **ANSWERS**
> **1** a second; a minute; an hour; a day
> **2** a centimetre; a metre; a kilometre
> **3** a gram; a kilo
> **4** 1%; 25%; 80%; 100%

## Pronunciation

**board** Play recording [8.6] again, pausing after each word or phrase for students to mark the stress on the words. Check the answers with the whole class on the board. (Note that *kilometre* is also pronounced /kɪˈlɒmɪtə/, and *hour*, *day* and *gram* are one-syllable words.)

> **ANSWERS**
> second   minute   centimetre   metre   kilometre
> kilo   one per cent   twenty-five per cent
> a hundred per cent   eighty per cent

Play the recording again (or model the phrases yourself), pausing after each one for the students to repeat. Pay particular attention to the pronunciation of *minute* /ˈmɪnɪt/, *hour* /aʊə/ and the /ə/ sound in *metre* /ˈmiːtə/.

LANGUAGE NOTE:
These 'quantity words' are similar in most languages, but the pronunciation is often different. If your students already know these words, try to ensure they can pronounce the words in an English way.

### ADDITIONAL PRACTICE

**Workbook:** Vocabulary: parts of the body, page 40; Vocabulary: quantities, page 40

**RB Resource bank:** *Vocabulary booster: Parts of the body*, page 136 (instructions on page 96)

# Focus 3 (PAGES 68–69)

## Reading and listening

**1** Focus students on the pictures on page 68 and allow them time to read the caption about Jack Warren. Check the meaning and pronunciation of *astronaut* /ˈæstrənɔːt/, *space* /speɪs/, *Space Shuttle* /ˈspeɪs ʃʌtl/ and *several* /ˈsevrəl/. Ensure that students understand what his job is before continuing.

**2** Students do the exercise individually. The following words may be new to your students: *Earth* /ɜːθ/; *play cards*; *a spacewalk*; *a bed*; *a sleeping bag*. Early finishers can compare answers in pairs.

**3** ⌨ [8.7] Play the recording and allow students to check their answers. If you need to play the recording again, students may like to read the tapescript on page 124 of the *Students' Book* at the same time.

**ANSWERS**
1 c  2 e  3 f  4 d  5 a  6 b

*Wh-* questions

## Grammar

**1** Students do Exercise 1 individually or in pairs. Check the answers with the whole class, and drill the question words as necessary. You may also wish to teach the word *because* /bɪˈkɒz/, and point out that it is usually used to answer questions with *Why?*.

**ANSWERS**
1 d  2 a  3 b  4 c  5 f  6 e

**2** **board** Write two or three questions with *do* on the board (e.g. *Where do you sleep? Why do you like working in space? Who do you talk to on Earth?*). These questions can be elicited from the class by saying the answer and asking students to give you the question. Write the sentences with similar words above each other, so that students can see the underlying pattern. Highlight the word order: **question word + *do* + subject + verb**. You may also wish to write similar words in different colours, or draw lines between the words as in the *Students' Book*.

Write a question with *can* on the board (e.g. *What can you do in your free time?*), and again highlight the word order: **question word + *can* + subject + verb**.

Finally, write a question with *be* on the board (e.g. *How many astronauts are there?*). Use this to remind students that questions with *be* do not have the auxiliary verb *do*. Also highlight that *How many ...?* is often followed immediately by a noun.

Refer students to *Language summary* 8B on page 116 of the *Students' Book*.

TEACHER'S NOTE:
We suggest you leave the examples on the board while students do Exercises 4 and 5, so that you can refer to them during correction stages.

**4** Refer students back to the pictures of Jack Warren on page 68, and ask the class what they think his life is like when he is not in space. Students can then do the exercise individually. Early finishers can compare answers in pairs. Check the answers with the whole group by asking individual students to read out the questions. Also check that students remember the question *How old ...?*.

**ANSWERS**
1 Where  2 Where  3 Who  4 What
5 What  6 How many  7 How old  8 Why

........................................................
**Exercise 4: additional suggestion**

You may use activity 8B *Question word* quiz on page 137 of the Resource bank (instructions on page 96) at any time after this exercise.
........................................................

**5** Students do the exercise on their own before checking the answers with the whole class. If any students finish early, ask them to write three more questions to ask other students.

**ANSWERS**
**a**  What do you do at the weekend?
**b**  What's your favourite book or film?
**c**  Who's your favourite singer?
**d**  When do you go to bed?
**e**  Where do you go for your holidays?
**f**  How many people are there in your family?
**g**  What's your favourite TV programme?

## Pronunciation

1 ⌨ [8.8] Play the recording and allow students to listen and read sentences a)–e). Use these examples to highlight the fact that we stress important words, like verbs, nouns and adjectives, and don't stress 'little words', like pronouns, possessive adjectives, prepositions or auxiliary verbs. (Depending on your class, you may not want to use too many grammatical terms. Instead, simply pick examples of these from the sentences to highlight the point.)

2 Play the recording again, pausing after each line for the students to repeat chorally and individually. The first line for each example (e.g. *What ... do ... weekend?*) focuses students on the stressed words only. Students should then repeat the second line (e.g. *What do you do at the weekend?*) with the same stress pattern.

LANGUAGE NOTE:
Your students may find this exercise relatively easy or quite challenging, depending on their first language(s). At this level do not expect perfection, particularly if your students speak a language where each word is stressed equally. However, it is important to help students hear and say sentences in English with natural stress and rhythm, and this 'say only the stressed words' technique is one way to encourage this. If you feel this drilling technique works with your class, consider using it where appropriate in future lessons.

**6** Students do the exercise in pairs. When they have finished, ask each student to tell the class one thing they have found out about their partner.

**Exercise 6: alternative suggestion**

Students work individually and write down their own answers to the questions in Exercise 5. Students then move around the room and ask their classmates the questions. The aim of the activity is to find one other student who has the same answer as them for each question. When students find someone who has the same answer, they should write his/her name next to the question. At the end of the activity students can compare answers in pairs or with the whole class.

## ADDITIONAL PRACTICE

**Workbook:** Questions, page 41

RB **Resource bank:** 8B *Question word* quiz, page 137 (instructions on page 96)

# Real life (PAGES 70–71)

## Big numbers

**1** Students do the exercise individually. Check the answers with the whole class. Drill the words with the whole class and individually, paying attention to the /θ/ sound in *thousand* /ˈθaʊzənd/ and the /h/ sound in *hundred* /ˈhʌndrəd/.

**2** board [8.9] Allow students a few moments to read through the exercise before playing the recording. Check the answers with the whole class, and play the recording again if necessary.

Highlight the following on the board:

* The lack of a plural -s in *two hundred, twenty thousand, five million,* etc.
* The use of the indefinite article *a* to mean *one* in *a hundred, a thousand, a million.*
* the use of *and* in big numbers, e.g. *a hundred and fifty.*
* the use of commas when writing big numbers over a thousand, e.g. 20,000; 1,000,000.

**ANSWERS**
**a** a hundred   **b** three hundred   **c** a hundred and fifty   **d** two hundred and seventy-five
**e** a thousand   **f** twenty thousand

**Exercise 2: alternative suggestion**

Students look at the numbers on the left and try to predict the correct answers before listening to the recording. They can then listen to check their answers.

**3** [8.10] Play the recording and ask students to write the numbers. If necessary, pause the tape after each number to allow students time to write. Students can compare answers in pairs before checking them with the whole class.

**ANSWERS**
**1** 7,000,000   **2** 5,000   **3** 800   **4** 1,200   **5** 475
**6** 650,000   **7** 306   **8** 9,999

**Exercise 3: additional suggestion**

Students work individually and write down eight numbers. Put students into pairs. Student A says his/her numbers, and Student B writes them down. When they have finished, Student B says his/her numbers and Student A writes them down. At the end of the activity students compare answers and see how many they got right.

**4 a)** Students do the quiz in groups of three or four. Watch out for students cheating on questions 1 and 7, and deduct points from any team caught looking through the book! You may also wish to give an extra point to the team that finishes first.

**b)** Students check their answers on page 109 of the *Students' Book*. Each group tells the class their score. The group with the most points are the winners.

**ANSWERS**
**1** b   **2** c   **3** c   **4** b   **5** b   **6** b   **7** a

## ADDITIONAL PRACTICE

**Workbook:** Big numbers, page 41

 Use the online activities for this module to help your students with English spelling.

# Do you remember? (PAGE 71)

**ANSWERS**
**1**

| R | O | P | S | E | E | W |
|---|---|---|---|---|---|---|
| E | S | L | S | G | S | A |
| W | W | A | L | K | T | H |
| R | I | Y | R | E | A | D |
| I | M | S | I | T | N | U |
| T | A | L | K | E | D | S |
| E | M | H | E | A | R | E |
| R | U | N | L | T | A | G |

**2**   various answers

**3a**  a  How many
        b  When
        c  What
        d  Who
        e  Where
        f  Why

**4**   a  ear
        b  head
        c  eye
        d  arm
        e  leg
        f  foot
        g  bone
        h  blood
        i  hand

# Consolidation modules 5–8

**A**
**1**  a  loves        h  like
       b  don't        i  doesn't
       c  plays        j  eats
       d  doesn't      k  gets up
       e  get up       l  hate
       f  like         m  love
       g  sends

**2**
Carol says she doesn't like dance music. Eddie says
that she loves dance music.
Carol says she eats meat and Eddie doesn't. Eddie
says that he eats meat and Carol doesn't.
Carol says that Eddie sends her emails every week.
Eddie says that he sends her emails everyday.

**B**
**1**  **Name:** Max
       **Nationality:** English
       **Lives:** in Turkey
       **Job:** teacher
       **Age:** 29
       **Married:** no

**2**  a  True
       b  False
       c  True
       d  False
       e  True
       f  True
       g  False

**C**
**1**  1  b
       2  c
       3  a
       4  b
       5  b
       6  a
       7  a
       8  c

**D**
1  amazing       14  never
2  brother       15  open
3  credit        16  plays
4  dinner        17  quarter
5  evening       18  radio
6  flat          19  sleeps
7  glasses       20  theatre
8  husband       21  usually
9  interesting   22  video
10 jazz          23  wallet
11 kilometres    24  Excuse
12 lunch         25  every
13 million       26  magazines

**E**
**1**  a  Monday (1)
       b  Wednesday (3)
       c  Saturday (6)
       d  Sunday (7)
       e  Tuesday (2)
       f  Thursday (4)
       g  Friday (5)

**2**  love
       Guess
       need
       you
       day
       Always
       say
       all the time
       love
       show
       need
       Guess

# module 9

## Focus 1 (PAGES 74–75)

### Common adjectives

1 Focus students on the photographs on pages 74 and 75. Teach the meaning of *ago* (in the expression *a hundred years ago*) and *now*, and drill these briefly with the class. Students do the exercise in pairs. Discuss their ideas with the whole class.

2 If necessary, check students remember the words *building, road* and *place*. Students then do the exercises in pairs or small groups, checking any words they don't know in the *Vocabulary book* on page 42. Check the answers with the whole class. Note that pronunciation is dealt with in Exercise 3b.

LANGUAGE NOTE:
Use these examples to point out that adjectives usually come before nouns in English. Also point out that adjectives do not have a plural form (e.g. ~~slows cars~~), as in some languages.

3 **a)** Students do the exercise in their same pairs, referring to the *Vocabulary book* on page 42 as necessary.

**b)** 📼 [9.1] Play the recording for students to check the answers. Alternatively, you can check the answers on the board. Play the recording again (or model the sentences yourself), stopping after each word for students to repeat chorally and individually. Words that students often have problems pronouncing are: *beautiful* /ˈbjuːtəfəl/; *dangerous* /ˈdeɪndʒərəs/; *busy* /ˈbɪzi/, *ugly* /ˈʌgli/ and *quiet* /ˈkwaɪət/.

### ANSWERS
young ≠ old
poor ≠ rich
new ≠ old
busy ≠ quiet
happy ≠ unhappy
slow ≠ fast
beautiful ≠ ugly
dangerous ≠ safe

#### Exercise 3: additional suggestion

Students work in pairs. Student A says an adjective, and Student B says the opposite adjective. After a couple of minutes students swap roles.

4 Students do the exercise with a different partner. Use the speech balloons to remind students of *this* and *these* before they begin. Discuss students' opinions with the whole class.

5 **a)** Students work individually and answer the questions. Encourage students to answer as many questions as possible, but it doesn't matter if they miss out one or two. You may wish to set a time limit of five minutes for this activity.

**b)** Students compare their answers in pairs or small groups. Encourage students to make complete sentences when discussing their answers, as shown in the speech balloons. If you have a multilingual class, you may wish to group students from the same country or region together, as they are more likely to know the same towns, famous people, book characters, etc. Finish the activity with a brief class discussion of their ideas.

#### Exercise 5: additional suggestions

a You may use activity 9A *Adjective dominoes* on page 138 of the Resource bank (instructions on page 96) at any time after Exercise 5.

b **board** Students work in pairs. Student A says an adjective–noun combination (e.g. *a beautiful town*). Student B must respond with another adjective for the same noun (e.g. *a busy town*). Student A then says another noun with the same adjective (e.g. *a busy person*). Student B then replaces the adjective again (e.g. *a young person*), and so on. If one of the students repeats a noun or adjective, he/she loses the game. Repeat the activity with Student A changing the adjectives and Student B changing the nouns. This activity is best demonstrated on the board before you begin.

### ADDITIONAL PRACTICE

**Workbook:** Vocabulary: common adjectives, page 44

**RB** **Resource bank:** 9A *Adjective dominoes*, page 138 (instructions on page 96)

## Focus 2 (PAGES 76–77)

### Reading and listening

1 Focus students on the pictures on page 76. Students work in pairs and try to find the words in the box, referring to the *Vocabulary book* on page 43 as necessary. Check students have found pictures of *a servant, a ship* and *the President of the United States*, and check students understand *a housewife* and *a village*. Drill the new words with the whole class. The following words are sometimes hard for students to pronounce: *village* /ˈvɪlɪdʒ/; *ship* /ʃɪp/; *servant* /ˈsɜːvənt/. Also highlight that *President* is usually spelt with a capital letter, and that the plural of *housewife* is *housewives*.

**2 a)** Check students understand that all the sentences refer to life in the year 1900, and that the year itself is pronounced *nineteen hundred*. Students do the exercise individually. The following words may be new to students: *a journey* /ˈdʒɜːni/; *Europe* /ˈjʊərəp/; *a billion* /ə ˈbɪljən/.

LANGUAGE NOTE:
You don't need to teach *was* and *were* before they do this exercise, as the context should be enough to help students understand at this stage. If students ask you what *was* and *were* mean, simply say that they are the past of *be*. The details of when each form is used can then be covered when you deal with the *Grammar* box later in the lesson.

**b)** Students compare answers in pairs or small groups. Draw students' attention to the language in the speech bubbles before they begin.

**3** [9.2] Play the recording for students to check their answers. Ask the class how many they got right and which sentences they think are the most surprising.

**ANSWERS**
The true sentences are **1**, **3**, **5**, **8** and **9**.

*was* and *were*

# Grammar

**board** Write *in 1900* at the top of the board and draw two columns headed *Singular* and *Plural*. Write *St Petersburg ... the capital of Russia.* and *Moscow ... the capital.* in the first column and ask students to complete the sentences. Similarly, write *Most women ... housewives.* and *There ... many women at university.* in the second column and ask students to fill in the gaps. You may wish to add one or two other sentences about life in 1900 to each column.

Highlight:

● *was* and *were* are the past of *be*.

● we use *was* with *he, she, it* and names of people and places.

● we use *were* with *they* and plural nouns.

● the negative contractions *wasn't* and *weren't*.

Refer students to *Language summary* 9 on page 117 of the *Students' Book*. You may also wish to point out the use of *was* and *were* with *I, you* and *we*.

........................................................
**Grammar: additional suggestion**

Ask students to turn to tapescript 2, Module 9 on page 125 of the *Students' Book*. Students underline all the examples of *was/were* and *wasn't/weren't* they can find in the sentences. Play the recording again for students to check. This is also a good opportunity to highlight the weak pronunciation of *was* /wəz/ and *were* /wə/ before students practise these later in the lesson.
........................................................

**4 a)** Focus students on the sentences at the bottom of page 77, and check the class understand that these sentences are also about the year 1900. The following words may be new to your students: *Queen* /kwiːn/; *Tsar* /zɑː/; *well-known* /wel ˈnəʊn/; *train* /treɪn/; *aeroplane* /ˈeərəpleɪn/. Students do the exercise individually. Early finishers can check in pairs.

**b)** [9.3] Play the recording and allow students to check their answers. Discuss any sentences that students think are surprising.

**ANSWERS**
**1** was   **2** was; was   **3** weren't; were; were
**4** were; weren't; wasn't   **5** was; wasn't
**6** were; weren't; was

## Pronunciation

1 [9.4] Play the recording and ask students to listen and read. Highlight the weak forms of *was* /wəz/ and *were* /wə/, and emphasise that this is how *was* and *were* are usually pronounced. Also draw students' attention to the sentence stress. Play the recording again, this time pausing after each sentence for students to repeat chorally and individually.

2 [9.5] Again play the recording while students read the sentences. Highlight the pronunciation of *wasn't* /ˈwɒzənt/ and *weren't* /wɜːnt/, and the fact that these words are stressed because they are negative. Play the recording again and drill the sentences with the class.

TEACHER'S NOTE:
When drilling weak forms such as *was* and *were*, it is easy to stress these words in the process of highlighting them. It is therefore often useful to drill weak forms in conjunction with a stressed word before or after it. For example, drilling the phrases ... *was Queen* /wəz kwiːn/ or *Cars were* ... /kɑːz wə/ from the sentences in the pronunciation box may help your students achieve more natural pronunciation.

### ADDITIONAL PRACTICE

**Workbook:** Past Simple of *be*, page 44; *wasn't/weren't*, page 45

## Focus 3 (PAGES 78–79)
Reading and vocabulary

**1** Focus students on the pictures on page 78, and use them to teach the word *born* /bɔːn/. Ask students to read the captions at the top of the box (**not** the texts) and answer questions a)–d). The following words in the captions may be new to your students: *farmer* /ˈfɑːmə/; *old people's home* /əʊld ˈpiːpəlz həʊm/. You may also wish to teach *farm* /fɑːm/, which appears in the text. Check the answers with the whole class.

## ANSWERS

**a** Toru Mitsui – Japan; Estelle Dupont – France
**b** They were both born in 1900.
**c** They were both a hundred years old.
**d** Toru Mitsui – poor; Estelle Dupont – rich

**2 a)** Focus students on the sentences and ask students to check the words in bold in the *Vocabulary book* on page 44. Alternatively, you can teach the new words yourself to the whole class. You may also wish to drill the new words, particularly *comfortable* /ˈkʌmftəbəl/ and *hungry* /ˈhʌŋgri/. Point out that *died* is the past tense of *die*, and you may also wish to teach *sad* /sæd/ as an alternative to *unhappy*. Students work individually and decide who said the sentences, Toru Mitsu or Estelle Dupont. Students can then compare answers in pairs. Do not check the answers with the whole group at this stage.

LANGUAGE NOTE:
While *better* is obviously the comparative form of *good*, we suggest you teach it simply as an item of vocabulary rather than get involved in a discussion about comparatives.

**b)** Students read the texts and check their answers to Exercise 2a. Check the answers with the whole group.

## ANSWERS

**a** Estelle Dupont
**b** Estelle Dupont
**c** Toru Mitsui
**d** Estelle Dupont
**e** Toru Mitsui
**f** Estelle Dupont

**3** Divide the class into two groups, Group A and Group B. Ask Group A to read the text on Toru Mitsui and Group B to read the text on Estelle Dupont. Both groups should answer the same questions. The following new words also appear in the texts: **Toru Mitsui**: *farm* /fɑːm/; *sad* /sæd/; *It's funny* (meaning 'it's strange'); *childhood* /ˈtʃaɪldhʊd/. **Estelle Dupont**: *chateau* /ˈʃætəʊ/; *bedroom* /ˈbedruːm/; *an only child* (= no brothers or sisters). We do not suggest you pre-teach all these words as most are clear from the context, but be ready to explain them briefly if necessary.

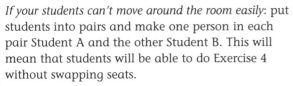

### Exercise 3: alternative suggestions

*If your students can't move around the room easily*: put students into pairs and make one person in each pair Student A and the other Student B. This will mean that students will be able to do Exercise 4 without swapping seats.

*If some students finish early*: ask them to underline any new words they don't know and check their meaning with another student or in a bilingual dictionary.

## Questions with *was* and *were*

# Grammar

**board** Write … *she happy?*; … *his parents rich?* and … *you happy?* on the board. (This can be done while students are doing Exercise 3.) Ask your students to complete the sentences with *was* or *were*. Put a tick and a cross next to each question and ask students to give you the appropriate short answers. Write them on the board. Also write up one or two *Wh-* questions, for example: *What was his job?* and *Where were they from?*. Drill the questions and short answers with the class, focusing on natural rhythm and stress.

Highlight:

- the change in word order in questions: *she was > was she?*
- we also use *was/wasn't* with *I*, e.g. *No, I wasn't.*
- the use of pronouns in short answers.
- *was* and *were* are unstressed in questions (particularly in *Wh-* questions), but are stressed in short answers.

Refer students to *Language summary* 9 on page 117 of the *Students' Book*.

TEACHER'S NOTE:
While it is important to encourage students to use the weak forms of *was* /wəz/ and *were* /wə/, too much focus on this can distract them from more basic problems like getting the words in the correct order. Drilling that focuses on sentence stress, rather than the weak forms, is often more useful in helping students say the sentences correctly. Generally, if the sentence stress is correct, weak forms usually fall into place automatically.

**4 a)** Drill the questions with the whole class, focusing on natural rhythm and stress. Students then work with a partner **from the same group** and ask each other the questions from Exercise 3.

**b)** Rearrange the class so that one student from Group A is working with one student from Group B. Student A then asks Student B about Estelle Dupont, and Student B asks Student A about Toru Mitsui. Encourage students to tell their partners more information about the people where possible.

## ANSWERS

| | Toru Mitsui | Estelle Dupont |
|---|---|---|
| **a** | a farmer | a businessman |
| **b** | in a small village near Hiroshima | ten kilometres from Bordeaux |
| **c** | Yes, it was. | No, it wasn't. |
| **d** | eleven | one |
| **e** | Yes, he was. | No, she wasn't. |

**5** **a)** Students work individually or in pairs and match up the adjectives. Check the meaning of the words with the whole class. Drill the words chorally and individually, paying particular attention to the pronunciation of *noisy* /ˈnɔɪzi/; *quiet* /ˈkwaɪət/; *naughty* /ˈnɔːti/; and *dirty* /ˈdɜːti/. Also point out that *naughty* is only used to describe children.

**ANSWERS**

noisy ≠ quiet;  tall ≠ short;
good ≠ naughty;  dirty ≠ clean

**b)** Tell students that they are going to ask each other about their lives when they were eight years old, and draw students' attention to the prompts. You may wish to pre-teach the following words and expressions: *to be good at something*; *maths* /mæθs/; *to be nice to someone*; *a game*; *a film*; *your best friend*. Check that students know how to make questions based on the prompts, particularly those headed *Favourites* (e.g. *What was your favourite game?*). Students work individually and write questions based on the prompts. Ask students to write at least ten questions. Alternatively, set a time limit of five or ten minutes.

**Speaking task**

**1** Ask students to think about their lives when they were eight years old, and allow them a few minutes to work out how they might answer the questions in Exercise 5b. (Note that this 'thinking time' is important for the success of the speaking task, as it gives students the opportunity to prepare what they are going to say.) Circulate, and help with vocabulary as necessary.

**2** Draw students' attention to the speech balloons and use them to teach *I can't remember!*. Students interview each other in pairs about his/her childhood. While they are working you may want to make notes of any common mistakes you hear, particularly in the use of *was* and *were*. These can be written on the board at the end of the activity for students to correct. Finish the activity by asking the students to share any interesting things they found out about their partner.

## ADDITIONAL PRACTICE

**Workbook:** Questions, page 45; *was/were* and *wasn't/ weren't*, page 45; Short answers, page 46

**RB** **Resource bank:** 9B *Where were you?*, page 139 (instructions on page 97)

Use the suggested links and related activities to read about the past with your students.

## Real life (PAGES 80–81)

### Years and ages

**1** 🔊 [9.6] Focus students on the years in the box. Play the recording and ask students to listen and read. Play the recording again, pausing after each year for students to repeat chorally and individually.

Highlight the following points:

● we say *nineteen hundred*, not ~~nineteen hundreds~~.

● we say *two thousand*, not ~~two thousands~~.

● the *and* in *two thousand and five*.

Also check the word stress, for example:

nineteen hundred; nineteen eighty-four; two thousand and five

You may also wish to point out that other years follow the same pattern; for example, 1742 is said *seventeen forty-two*.

**2** **board** 🔊 [9.7] Play the recording and ask students to write down the dates. Play the recording again if necessary, then ask students to compare answers in pairs. Check the answers with the whole group by stopping the recording after each date and writing the answers on the board. Use d) to highlight that we say 'oh' for zero in dates, for example 1906 = 'nineteen oh six'.

**ANSWERS**
| a 1995 | b 2008 | c 1949 | d 1906 |
|--------|--------|--------|--------|
| e 1899 | f 2020 | g 1918 | h 1980 |

### Exercise 2: additional suggestions

a Students work individually and write down eight different years. Put students into pairs. They take it in turns to say their years to each other, and their partner writes them down. When they have finished, students check their answers by comparing papers.

b If you wish to provide more practice of *ago* (which was introduced in Focus 1), write some years on the board and ask students to tell you how many years ago they were. Alternatively, students can do this exercise in pairs.

**3 a)** Check that the whole class know all the people in the pictures and why they are famous (see below for more information). Also check that students know all the places in the box (Skopje is now the capital of Macedonia in Eastern Europe, and Somalia is a country in North Africa). Students do the exercise individually. Encourage students to guess if they are not sure. Early finishers can compare answers in pairs.

**Walt Disney** was the founder of the Disney entertainment empire, and he also created Mickey Mouse.
**Catherine Zeta-Jones** is an actress, and is married to actor Michael Douglas.
**Mother Teresa** spent her life working with the poor in Calcutta, India.
**Luciano Pavarotti** is an Italian opera singer.
**Iman** was a fashion model, and is now a successful businesswoman. Her husband is David Bowie.
**Al Pacino** is a Hollywood actor, and appeared in *The Godfather* films.
**Nicole Kidman** is an actress, and she grew up in Australia. She was married to actor Tom Cruise.
**Muhammad Ali** was world heavyweight boxing champion in the 1960s and 1970s.

b) **board** 🔲 [9.8] Play the recording for students to check their answers. Write *When ... Walt Disney ... ?* and *Where ... he ...?* on the board, and ask students to complete the questions. Elicit the answers from the students (*He was born in 1901/Chicago.*) and write them on the board.

Highlight the following:

● the word order: **Question word + *was* + person + born**.

● the weak form of *was* /wəz/.

● the use of *in* with years.

Drill the questions and answers chorally and individually, focusing on natural rhythm and stress. Students then work in pairs and ask each other questions about the people on page 80.

**ANSWERS**
**Walt Disney:** Chicago, USA, 1901
**Catherine Zeta-Jones:** Wales, 1969
**Mother Teresa:** Skopje, 1910
**Luciano Pavarotti:** Italy, 1935
**Iman:** Somalia, 1955
**Al Pacino:** New York, 1940
**Nicole Kidman:** Hawaii, 1967
**Muhammad Ali:** Louisville, USA, 1942

LANGUAGE NOTE:
*To be born* is often a problematic verb for students because of its passive structure (in many languages it translates as an active verb). This means that students often leave out *was* or *were*, resulting in mistakes like ~~He born in 1902.~~ Make sure you monitor students' language carefully during practice stages, correcting any errors you hear on the spot.

**4 board** Use the speech balloons to introduce the questions *Where were you born?* and *When were you born?* and write them on the board. Ask one student for his/her answers, and write them next to the questions. Tell the class that short answers to these questions (e.g. *In Rio de Janeiro. In 1980.*) are very common. Drill the questions and answers with the class, paying particular attention to the sentence stress and the weak forms of *was* /wəz/ and *were* /wə/.

Where were you born?
I was born in Rio de Janeiro.
When were you born?
I was born in nineteen eighty.

Students move around the room and ask three (or more) students the questions. If your students are not able to move around the room, they should ask people sitting near them.

### Exercise 4: additional suggestion

When students have finished, they work in pairs and tell their partner about the people they have spoken to. For example: *Carola was born in Spain in 1979.*

## Speaking task

**1 a)** Students do the exercise individually. Ensure that students write their answers on a separate piece of paper. You may wish to bring in some paper and distribute it to the class before they do this exercise.
b) Students write their sentences individually, based on their answer for Exercise 1a. Ensure that students do not write their names on the paper.

**2** a) Collect in all the papers, shuffle them, and then redistribute them randomly to the class. Allow students a minute or two to read the sentences on their new piece of paper.

b) Draw students' attention to the question in the speech balloon on page 81, and check the questions for the other family members if necessary. Students move around the room and ask questions to find out whose paper they have. Encourage students to ask about all the people on their paper to check they have found the right person.

**Speaking task: alternative suggestion**

*If your students are not able to move around the room:* divide them into groups of five or six. Collect the papers from each group and redistribute them randomly. Allow students a minute or two to read the sentences. Students ask questions in their groups to find out whose paper they have. Encourage students to ask about all the people on their paper to check they have found the right person.

**Vocabulary: additional suggestion**

The *Vocabulary booster: Describing people* on page 140 of the Resource bank (instructions on page 97) can be used at any time in the module.

## ADDITIONAL PRACTICE

RB **Resource bank:** 9B *Where were you?*, page 140 (instructions on page 97)

# Do you remember? (PAGE 81)

**ANSWERS**

**1a** a Were
  b Was
  c Were
  d Was
  e Were
  f Were

**2** a was
  b was
  c weren't
  d wasn't
  e were
  f weren't
  g was

**3a and b**
  a poor (≠ rich)
  b safe (≠ dangerous)
  c busy (≠ quiet)
  d ugly (≠ beautiful)
  e short (≠ tall)
  f clean (≠ dirty)
  g slow (≠ fast)

**4** 1 f
  2 d
  3 e
  4 a
  5 b
  6 c

# module 10

## Focus 1 (PAGES 82–83)

### Past Simple: irregular verbs

**TEACHER'S NOTE:**
Traditionally low-level coursebooks introduce regular verbs before irregular ones, but we believe that this approach often leads to rather unnatural examples and texts. As many common verbs in English are irregular, (*have, go, make,* etc.), we feel that it is appropriate to introduce these first. The Past Simple of regular verbs follows in Focus 2.

**1** Focus students on the pictures of the famous people on page 82, and allow them a few moments to read the captions. Use these to teach the meaning of *creative* /kriˈeɪtɪv/ in the heading. Also use the students' knowledge of the four people to teach the following new vocabulary in the captions: *Dutch* /dʌtʃ/; *artist* /ˈɑːtɪst/; *fashion designer* /ˈfæʃən dɪzaɪnə/; *musician* /mjuˈzɪʃən/; *director* /dəˈrektə/. Students work individually and match the sentences a)–h) to the pictures. They should check any words they don't know in the *Vocabulary book* on page 47. Apart from the irregular past tenses, the following new words appear in the sentences: *hat; successful; a band; an album; an art gallery.*

**TEACHER'S NOTE:**
You do not need to pre-teach all the irregular past tenses in this exercise. Students will probably understand most of them from the context, and the verbs are focused on in detail later in the lesson.

**2** [10.1] Play the recording for students to check their answers. Note that there is more information on the tape than in the sentences in Exercise 1.

> **ANSWERS**
> **a** Vincent van Gogh
> **b** Coco Chanel
> **c** Bob Marley
> **d** Charlie Chaplin
> **e** Coco Chanel
> **f** Bob Marley
> **g** Charlie Chaplin
> **h** Vincent van Gogh

### Exercise 2: additional suggestion

Ask students to turn to Module 10, recording 1 on pages 125 and 126 of the *Students' Book*. Play the recording and ask students to listen and read the text at the same time. As mentioned earlier, this kind of activity is often a useful follow-up to listening tasks, as it enables students to make connections between sounds and words.

**3** Draw students' attention to the example before allowing students to do the exercise individually. Check the answers with the whole class. Note that students should also underline *was*, even though it is not included in the *Grammar* box.

## Grammar

Students work individually and write the verbs. If students are not sure of a verb, they should check in the Verb table on page 63 of the *Vocabulary Book*. (Note that the verbs *sell, become* and *make* may also be new to your students.) Highlight that these verbs are in the Past Simple tense, and are all irregular verbs.

You may wish to refer students to *Language summary* 10 on page 117 of the *Students' Book* after you have taught regular Past Simple verbs in Focus 2.

**LANGUAGE NOTE:**
It is important that students become accustomed to the idea of irregular verbs early on in their language development, as so many common verbs in English have irregular past tenses. Whenever you introduce new verbs in future classes, tell the students if it has a regular or irregular past tense, and write the irregular past tenses on the board. This will encourage students to 'collect' past tenses – and hopefully learn them!

**4** board [10.2] Play the recording for students to check their answers. Use the recording (or model the words yourself) and drill all the verbs and past tenses with your students. Write the words on the board for students to check their spelling.

**5** Students do the exercise individually. Early finishers can compare answers in pairs. Check the answers with the whole group. You may wish to pre-teach *perfume* /ˈpɜːfjuːm/ in sentence e).

> **ANSWERS**
> **a** became **b** made **c** left; went **d** had
> **e** made **f** sold **g** met **h** became

 Take your students to the Perfect Partners section of the website and see a selection of Penguin Readers suitable for their level.

**6** a) Focus students on the quiz at the bottom of page 83. Students do the quiz in teams of three or four. Emphasise that there can be more than one answer for some questions. The following new words appear in the quiz: *poetry* /ˈpəʊətri/; *detective story* /dɪˈtektɪv stɔːri/; *blues* (a type of music) and *sang* /sæŋ/, which is the irregular past tense of *sing*. You may wish to teach these before students start the quiz.

**b)** 🔊 [10.3] Play the recording for students to check their answers. Give one point for each correct answer (making 8 points in total) and see which team has the most points.

> **ANSWERS**
> **1** a and b  **2** c  **3** b  **4** a and b  **5** a  **6** c

**7** board Students do the exercise individually or in pairs. Students can write sentences about the people in the box, or other creative people they know. (See below for information about the people in the box.) Write all the verbs from the *Grammar* box on the board as prompts before they start. Circulate and help students with any problems or new vocabulary as they are working. Students can then compare their sentences in pairs. Conclude the activity by asking students to read out some of their sentences for the whole class.

> **ANSWERS**
> **Agatha Christie:** English writer 1890–1976. She wrote detective stories, and created the character Hercule Poirot.
> **Cervantes:** Spanish writer 1547–1616. He wrote *Don Quixote.*
> **Greta Garbo:** Swedish actress 1905–1990. She went to live in the USA and became an actress.
> **Leonardo da Vinci:** Italian artist and scientist 1452–1519. He was a famous painter, and painted *The Last Supper.*
> **Federico Fellini:** Italian film director 1920–1994. He made many famous films, including *La Dolce Vita.*
> **Tolstoy:** Russian writer 1828–1910. He wrote *War and Peace* and *Anna Karenina.*
> **Gianni Versace:** Italian fashion designer 1946–1997. He made clothes for many famous people.
> **Adnan Saygun:** Turkish composer 1907–1991. He wrote symphonies and operas based on traditional Turkish folk music.

> **Exercise 7: alternative suggestions**
>
> a *If your students don't know the people in the box:* you may wish to write some more names on the board so that they have more people to choose from. Here are some suggestions of other 'dead creative people' that students might know: Stanley Kubrick (film director); John Wayne (actor); Jimi Hendrix (musician); Beethoven (composer); Pablo Picasso (artist); Marilyn Monroe (actress); Alfred Hitchcock (film director); Jane Austen (writer); Humphrey Bogart (actor); Vivaldi (composer); Frank Sinatra (singer); Ernest Hemingway (writer); Dostoyevsky (writer); Salvador Dali (artist); Kurt Cobain (singer). Add any other names you think your students might know.

b *If you have a monolingual class:* ask students to think of some creative people from their country and write these names on the board before they begin. Check that all these people are dead, otherwise students may not be practising the past tense!

c *If you have a strong class:* students work in pairs and write three true sentences and three false sentences about creative people. Pairs then work together in groups of four. Each pair reads out their sentences, and the other pair should say if the sentences are true or false. The pair that gets the most correct answers are the winners.

## ADDITIONAL PRACTICE

**Workbook:** Past Simple: irregular verbs, page 49

## Focus 2 (PAGES 84–85)

### Reading

**1** Focus students on the pictures of J.K. Rowling and Harry Potter on page 84. (Note that Rowling is pronounced 'rolling'.) Ask the class who the people are, and ask if they have read any Harry Potter books or seen the film(s). Discuss what they know about Harry Potter with the whole class, and use this opportunity to teach *wizard* /ˈwɪzəd/.

> **Harry Potter**
>
> J.K. Rowling's Harry Potter books have been a publishing phenomenon all over the world. Harry is a wizard, and each book is based on one year of his schooldays at Hogwarts, a school of magic where wizards learn their craft. In the books, Harry (along with his friends Ron and Hermione) battle against the evil wizard Voldemort, and try to discover the secret behind the death of Harry's parents. There are to be seven books in total, and they are equally popular with both children and adults. A film based on the first book, *Harry Potter and the Philosopher's Stone,* was released in November 2001.

> **Exercise 1: alternative suggestion**
>
> Students work in groups and write down as many things as they know about Harry Potter in three minutes. (If you have a monolingual class, you may wish to do this in the students' own language). Students then compare ideas with the rest of the class.

**2** Pre-teach the following vocabulary that appears in the sentences: *to get married*; *unemployed* /ˌʌnɪmˈplɔɪd/. Students read the text and put the sentences in order. Early finishers can check their answers in pairs. The following words in the text may also be new to students: *rabbit*; *secretary*; *train*; *Portugal, Portuguese*; *to return*; *warmer*. We suggest you deal with these words if and when they come up.

3  [10.4] Play the recording and allow students to listen and read. Students check their answers as they are listening. Check the answers with the whole class.

**ANSWERS**
The correct order is: **g, c, f, h, b, e, i, a, d**

### Exercise 3: additional suggestion

Students read the text again and underline three words they would like to know the meaning of. Students then work in small groups and compare words, helping each other with meaning if possible. They can look up their words in bilingual dictionaries in their groups, or you can explain the meanings to the whole class.

## Past Simple: regular verbs

# Grammar

**board** Write *work*, *start*, *live* and *study* on the board and ask students what the Past Simple of these verbs are. Write the endings for each verb on the board, in a different colour pen if possible.

Highlight:

- regular verbs take *-ed* to form the Past Simple.
- verbs ending in *-e* (e.g. *live*) simply add a *-d*.
- with verbs ending in *-y* (e.g. *study*), the *y* changes to *-ied*.

Refer students to *Language summary* 10 on page 117 of the *Students' Book*.

LANGUAGE NOTE:
The rule above for verbs ending in *-y* is a simplification. It would be more accurate to say verbs ending in 'consonant + y' change to *-ied*. Verbs ending in 'vowel + y' (e.g. *play*) simply take the *-ed* ending (e.g. *played*). However, at this level we feel the *y > -ied* rule is enough for students to learn; *played* can simply be taught as an exception.

4 **board** Students do the exercise individually. Check the answers on the board with the whole class, again writing the ending in a different colour if possible. Also point out that there is a table of regular past tenses on page 62 of the *Vocabulary book*.

**ANSWERS**
**a** watched **b** worked **c** started **d** liked
**e** talked **f** returned **g** loved **h** hated **i** married

# Pronunciation

Traditionally, course books have made a distinction between Past Simple forms which end in /t/, /d/ and /ɪd/. In our experience, however, this does not always produce the results that teachers hope for, and the distinction between /t/ and /d/ is confusing for students. We believe the important thing is to focus on when we *don't* say /ɪd/, for example in *talked* /tɔːkt/ or *watched* /wɒtʃt/. We have found the best way to deal with this is to focus on the number of syllables in the Past Simple form, highlighting the verbs that only have one syllable as well as those that add an extra /ɪd/ syllable. Usually the verbs with only one syllable need more drilling practice than those with two syllables, as the groups of consonants at the end of the word are hard for students to pronounce. Note that the /t/, /d/ and /ɪd/ endings are covered in the *Vocabulary book* on page 48.

1 [10.5] Play the recording. Students should write '1' next to the past tense in Exercise 4 if it has only one syllable, and write '2' if it has two syllables. Check the answers with the whole class, using the board. Point out that the verbs which end with the letter 't' (*start* and *hate*) add an <u>extra</u> syllable in the Past Simple. (*Return* and *marry* both have two syllables in the infinitive and past tense forms, and do not add an extra syllable.)

**ANSWERS**
*started, returned, hated* and *married* have two syllables. All the other past tenses have one syllable.

2 Play the recording again (or model the sentences yourself), pausing after each past tense for students to repeat chorally and individually.

LANGUAGE NOTE:
An extra syllable is also pronounced in past tenses of verbs that end with the letter 'd' (e.g. *ended, needed*). This has not been highlighted as students have yet to meet any verbs that end in *-d*.

5 Students do the exercise individually. Point out that some of the verbs are irregular before they begin. Check the answers with the whole group.

**ANSWERS**
**a** liked; wrote; was **b** worked **c** had; started
**d** worked; wrote **e** lived **f** finished

### Exercise 5: additional suggestions

There are three photocopiable activities in the Resource bank that you can use at any time after Exercise 5. We suggest you use these activities for revision in future lessons, as appropriate. The activities are: 10A *Past Simple* quiz on page 141

(instructions on page 97); 10B *Ten things about me* on page 142 (instructions on page 97); 10C *Past Simple bingo* on page 143 (instructions on page 97).

**6** Students do the exercise individually, referring to the Verb tables on pages 62 and 63 of the *Vocabulary book* for the past forms of the verbs where necessary. Check that students know all the past forms of the verbs before moving on to the Speaking task. The following words or expressions may be new to your students: *change schools/ jobs; a partner* /ə ˈpɑːtnəl/; *move house; have a child*. You may wish to pre-teach this vocabulary before students begin the exercise.

LANGUAGE NOTE:
*Partner* is commonly used to mean anyone you are in a relationship with, e.g. your husband, wife, boyfriend or girlfriend.

## Speaking task

**1** board Draw students' attention to the time line and check that students understand what it represents. Alternatively, draw your own time line on the board with various dates and events in your life marked on it. Students work individually and draw their own life line. Allow students about ten minutes for this. Early finishers should add three more events to their line.

**2** Students work in pairs and tell each other about their time lines. You may wish to demonstrate this by talking about your time line on the board first. As they are working, circulate and help students where necessary. You may also wish to note down any common errors you hear. These can be written on the board at the end of the activity for students to correct. Early finishers can swap partners and repeat the activity. At the end of the Speaking task, students can tell the whole class one or two interesting things they found out about their partner.

**Speaking task: additional activity**

Students can write a paragraph about their life for homework.

## ADDITIONAL PRACTICE

**Workbook:** Past Simple: spelling of *-ed* endings, page 49; Past Simple: regular verbs, page 49; Vocabulary: life events, page 50; Sentences in the past, page 50

RB **Resource bank:** 10A *Past Simple* quiz, page 141 (instructions on page 97); 10B *Ten things about me*, page 142 (instructions on page 97); 10C *Past Simple bingo*, page 143 (instructions on page 97)

## Focus 3 (PAGES 86–87)
Reading and vocabulary

TEACHER'S NOTE:
The aim of the activities on pages 86 and 87 is to give students more extensive reading and listening practice. If you have a class that is weak at reading, you may wish to pre-teach some of the new verbs and their past tenses that appear in the text. See the **Exercise 3: additional suggestion** box for ideas on how to do this.

**1** Students do the exercise in groups. Encourage them to look at the pictures if necessary. You may wish to teach the adjectives *Welsh* /welʃ/ and *Scottish* /ˈskɒtɪʃ/, and discuss the question with the whole class. (Arthur was an English king in the sixth century.)

**2** Students work in pairs and find the vocabulary in the pictures. Students can refer to the *Vocabulary book* on page 49 to check any words they don't know. Check the answers with the whole group and drill the words with the class. Words that students may have difficulty pronouncing are: *magic* /ˈmædʒɪk/; *sword* /sɔːd/; *castle* /ˈkɑːsəl/; *soldier* /ˈsəʊldʒəl/; *knight* /naɪt/; *battle* /ˈbætəl/. You may also wish to draw students' attention to the silent letters in *sword, castle* and *knight*.

**3** Students do the exercise individually. Early finishers can compare answers with another student. Check the answers with the whole group. Note that *Guinevere* is pronounced /ˈgwɪnɪvɪəl/.

**ANSWERS**
**1** c **2** f **3** b **4** e **5** d **6** a

**Exercise 3: additional suggestion**

If you think the vocabulary level in the text is too challenging for your students, consider teaching some of the new verbs and their past tenses at the beginning of the lesson. Here are two ways you could do this:

**a** board Write the following verbs on the board: *teach, need, see, give, know, sit, tell, throw, take, disappear*. Check the meaning of any words students don't know with the whole class. Students then work individually or in pairs and find the past tenses in the Verb tables on pages 62 and 63 of the *Vocabulary book* or in the dictionary. (Note that not all these verbs are in the *Vocabulary book* word tables.) Check the answers with the whole class on the board. Drill the new vocabulary with the whole class. Words that students find hard to pronounce include: *taught* /tɔːt/; *saw* /sɔː/; *told* /təʊld/; *throw* /θrəʊ/; *threw* /θruː/.

b   Draw two columns on a worksheet. Write the verbs above in the first column, and their past tenses in a different order in the second column. Photocopy the worksheet and distribute it to the class. Students work individually or in pairs and match the verbs with the past tenses. Drill the words as above. This activity could also be set for homework in the previous lesson to help prepare them for the reading.

## Listening

**4** [10.6] Play the recording and allow students to read the text at the same time. This is useful consolidation at this stage of the lesson, as it helps students connect the words on the page with the sounds they hear, thus improving their listening skills.

**5** **a)** Draw students' attention to the example before allowing them to do the exercise individually. Encourage students to refer to the Verb tables on pages 62 and 63 of the *Vocabulary book* if necessary.

**b)** Students compare answers in pairs. Check the answers with the whole group.

> **ANSWERS**
> **1** **c** Arthur was born in Tintagel Castle.
> **2** **b** He became king when he was fifteen.
> **3** **e** The Lady of the Lake gave a magic sword to Arthur.
> **4** **f** King Arthur lived at Camelot, with his knights.
> **5** **d** He married Guinevere.
> **6** **g** But Guinevere loved Sir Lancelot.
> **7** **a** Arthur died in a terrible battle.

LANGUAGE NOTE:
Students may ask you what the difference is between *marry* and *get married*, which appeared in the J.K. Rowling reading text. The main difference is that *marry* requires an object, whereas *to get married* can be used on its own.

**6** Discuss the question with the class and allow students to share their ideas with the whole group. Encourage students to tell the groups what happened in the story if possible.

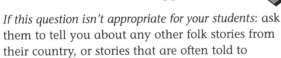

**Exercise 6: alternative suggestion**

*If this question isn't appropriate for your students*: ask them to tell you about any other folk stories from their country, or stories that are often told to children.

**Vocabulary: additional suggestion**

If you want to introduce some more common irregular verbs in future lessons, use the *Vocabulary booster: Irregular verbs* on page 144 of the Resource bank (instructions on page 98).

**Past tenses: additional suggestions**

Here are some ways to revise all the irregular past tenses from this module.

a   *If you have a small class*: write the verbs on separate cards. You need one set of cards for the whole class. Distribute the cards so that each student has an equal number. Students move around the room and ask their classmates to tell them the past tenses of the verbs on their cards. If a student doesn't know one of the past tenses, he/she must take the card and add it to his/her deck. The aim of the activity is to get rid of all your cards. The student who has the fewest cards when you call an end to the activity is the winner. It is advisable to demonstrate this activity before handing out the cards. (This activity works equally well to revise other vocabulary, too.)

b   *If your students cannot move around the room*: write all the verbs on the board. Students work in pairs. Students take it in turns to say a verb, and their partner must say the past tense. If a student doesn't know the past tense, his/her partner scores a point. The person with the most points at the end is the winner.

c   Write all the verbs on cards. Give a set of cards (shuffled) to each group of three or four students. Students place the pack face down in between them. Student A turns over a card and says the verb. The student on his/her right must say the past tense. If he/she is correct, he/she keeps the card. If he/she is not correct, the turn passes to the next student. Students take it in turns to turn over the cards and ask the person on their right for the past tense. The student with the most cards at the end is the winner.

## ADDITIONAL PRACTICE

[RB] **Resource bank:** *Vocabulary booster: Irregular verbs*, page 144 (instructions on page 98)

## Real life (PAGES 88–89)

Months and dates

**1 a)** board 🔲 [10.7] Teach students the word *month* /mʌnθ/ and drill this with the class. Students work individually or in pairs and put the months in the box in the correct place on the line. Play the recording for students to check their answers. Write the months on the board. Highlight the use capital letters for months in English.

**b)** Play the recording again for students to mark the stress in their books. Check the answers on the board. Play the recording a third time (or model the months yourself), pausing after each word for students to repeat. Pay particular attention to the pronunciation of *February* /ˈfebruəri/; *April* /ˈeɪprəl/; *August* /ˈɔːɡəst/, and the /dʒ/ sound in *January* /ˈdʒænjuəri/, *June* /dʒuːn/ and *July* /dʒuˈlaɪ/.

**ANSWERS**

January  February  March  April  May
June  July  August  September  October
November  December

### Exercise 1: additional suggestions

a  Students work in pairs and say the months alternately. They can then do the same backwards starting with *December*. Alternatively, students can say the months in turn around the class.

b  You may also wish to teach the words for the seasons at this point: *spring, summer, autumn* /ˈɔːtəm/ (or *fall* in the USA) and *winter*.

**2 a)** Students do the exercise individually or in pairs.

**b)** board 🔲 [10.8] Play the recording for students to check their answers. Write these on the board. Highlight the use of 'st', 'nd' and 'th' in dates, and explain what they are short for. Drill the dates on the board chorally and individually. You will probably need to focus particularly on the /θ/ sound in words like *fourth, thirteenth, thirtieth*, etc., which most students find difficult to pronounce. Write some more dates on the board and see if students can pronounce them correctly.

### Exercise 2: additional suggestion

Students work in pairs and count alternately up from *first, second*, etc. Students can also do this backwards from *31st*. Circulate and correct any pronunciation mistakes you hear. Alternatively, students can count up from *first* around the class.

**3** 🔲 [10.9] Play the recording and allow students to circle the date that they hear. Check the answers with the whole class, referring back to the recording if there are any disagreements.

**ANSWERS**
**a** 21st **b** April 15th **c** October 9th
**d** December 30th **e** January 16th **f** March 12th

## Grammar

board Write *March 17th* and *July 24th* on the board and ask students how to say the dates. Write *March the seventeenth* and *July the twenty-fourth* next to the dates in speech bubbles. Highlight the use of *the* in the spoken form but not the written form, and the hyphen in *twenty-fourth*.

Write the following on the board using the date for your birthday, for example: *I was born ... (December 30th)* and *I was born ... (December)*. and ask the students for the correct prepositions in each sentence. Highlight that we use *on* with dates (you can compare this to using *on* with days of the week) and *in* with months (which you can compare with using *in* with years).

LANGUAGE NOTES:
a) We realise this is not the only way to say dates. For example, May 30th can also be said as *the thirtieth of May* in British English, and in American English it would be said as *May thirtieth*. If you have a strong class, or your students are exposed to a lot of American English, you may wish to teach them the alternative versions. You may also want to point out that dates are also commonly written the other way round, for example, *30th May*.
b) Numbered dates are written differently in British and American English. For example, 3/9/01 is September 3rd in the UK, but March 9th in the USA. You may wish to point this out if you feel this is relevant to your students.

**4** Introduce the question *When's your birthday?* and drill this with your class. (*birthday* is pronounced /ˈbɜːθdeɪ/). Use the speech balloons to remind students that we use *on* with birthdays. Students move around the room and try to find someone who has a birthday close to theirs. If your students cannot move around the room they should ask as many people as they can from their seats. At the end of the activity students can tell the class who has a birthday close to them.

### Exercise 4: additional suggestions

a  Ask students to line up in order of birthdays at the front of the class.

b  Students write down the names of six people they know very well, for example family members, partners and close friends. Students work in pairs and ask questions about the people on their partner's paper. They should first ask questions to establish who each person is, then ask about his/her birthday. You may also wish to use this exercise to revise Present Simple questions with *he/she,* such as: *What's his/her job? Where does he/she live? Is he/she married? Does he/she have any children? What does he/she study?,* etc.

c  Use activity 10D *The date game* in the Resource bank on page 145 (instructions on page 98). Note that this activity practises how to say years as well as dates.

**5** Focus students on the photographs at the top of pages 88 and 89 and discuss them with your students (see notes below). Students then do the exercise individually. If you have a monolingual class, discuss their dates with the whole class and ask individual students to explain why they are important. If you have a multilingual class, put students in different nationality groups and allow them to explain their dates to their classmates. Circulate and help with vocabulary as necessary. Students can then tell the whole class about one date that is significant in their country.

**The Venice Carnival**: This colourful festival takes place in February each year. Originally the festival was to mark the period before people gave up eating meat for Lent, which is the forty-day period of fasting that precedes Easter. (The Italian word *carnevale* actually comes from the Latin meaning 'farewell to meat'.) Nowadays, festival-goers often wear costumes and masks, and there are many balls and concerts around the city.

**Independence Day**: This holiday is on July 4th, and celebrates the day the Declaration of Independence from Britain was formally adopted by Congress in 1776. Today, it is one of the most important holidays in the USA, and families celebrate July 4th with parties, family gatherings and barbecues. There are also large parades with fireworks in cities all over the country.

**Seville Spring Fair**: This festival in Andalucia, southern Spain, dates back over 150 years, and is usually held at the end of April. During the festival the local people dress up in their finest traditional clothes to enjoy street processions, parades and parties at the many fairgrounds that spring up around the city. There are also over a hundred 'casetas' – large canvas pavilions with dancing and Flamenco music all through the night.

**The Day of the Dead**: This important Mexican festival takes place in November, and dates back to Aztec times. It is a time when people remember their dead friends and relatives, and reflect on the cycle of life and death. Children who have died are honoured on November 1st, and adults on the 2nd. However, it is not a sombre occasion. People give presents of sugar skeletons or skulls, have large feasts and parades, and decorate their houses with flowers.

## ADDITIONAL PRACTICE

**Workbook:** Spelling: months, page 51

RB **Resource bank:** 10D *The date game*, page 145 (instructions on page 98)

## Do you remember? (PAGE 89)

**ANSWERS**

**1**

| O | S | T | U | D | Y | M | S |
|---|---|---|---|---|---|---|---|
| F | B | O | N | G | I | A | L |
| I | A | D | W | O | R | K | H |
| N | Z | G | S | E | E | E | A |
| I | M | E | E | T | J | J | V |
| S | U | T | M | E | U | L | E |
| H | S | E | L | L | R | I | L |
| I | K | N | A | W | N | V | X |
| V | W | A | T | C | H | E | P |

**2  Regular verbs:** studied; worked; watched; finished; returned; lived
**Irregular verbs:** met; sold; got; went; made; had; saw

**3**  a  met      d  changed
   b  got      e  wrote
   c  moved    f  had

**4a** January 1st; February 14th; March 1st; April 16th; May 1st; June 4th; July 22nd; August 3rd; September 30th; October 2nd; November 21st; December 25th.

# module 11

## Focus 1  (PAGES 90–91)

### Vocabulary: holidays

**1** Focus students on the pictures on page 90, and use them to teach the expression *in the country*. Students work in pairs and discuss which they think is the best place to go on holiday. Compare ideas with the whole class.

**2** **board** Focus students on the box and the speech balloon, highlighting the use of *can* in the example. Students do the exercise in pairs, referring to the *Vocabulary book* on page 52 as necessary. Compare ideas with the whole class. Write *go, go to, go for* and *stay* on the board and add the expressions as below.

**go**      shopping / skiing / swimming

**go to**   the beach / museums / restaurants

**go for**  a walk

**stay**    in a hotel

Highlight the prepositions *to* and *for*, and the use of *the* in *go to the beach*. Drill the expressions chorally and individually, paying particular attention to the pronunciation of *skiing* /ˈskiːɪŋ/; *museums* /mjuˈziːəmz/, and the weak forms of *to* /tə/ and *for* /fə/. Also point out that *go* is often followed by an *-ing* word (a gerund).

> **Exercise 2: additional suggestions**
>
> a Students work in pairs. One student says a noun (e.g. *restaurants*) and the other student says the whole expression (e.g. *go to restaurants*). Alternatively, these can be put onto cards for students to match in pairs.
>
> b **board** *If you have a strong class*: ask students to work in groups and think of some more expressions with *go, go to, go for* and *stay*. Add these to the expressions already on the board and allow students time to copy. Some suggestions are: ***go** sailing / waterskiing / camping*; ***go to** art galleries / street markets / cafés*; ***go for** a run / a drive / a swim*; ***stay** with friends / at a campsite / at home*.

**3** **a)** Students do the exercise individually. You may need to check the meaning of *mountains, lake* and *river* before they begin.

> **Exercise 3a: alternative suggestion**
>
> *If you have a monolingual class*: you may like to ask your students to write down the names of places in another country they know well, for example somewhere they have been on holiday. This might prevent them from all writing down the same places!

**b)** Draw students' attention to the speech balloons. Students work in pairs or small groups and tell each other what people do in the places they have written down in Exercise 3a. Students should use the vocabulary in Exercise 2, or their own ideas. If you have a multilingual class, put students from different countries together. Discuss a few of their ideas with the whole class.

### Listening

**4** **a)** Focus students on the pictures of New York on page 91. Students work in small groups and think of three places people can visit there. Discuss their ideas with the class and (if appropriate) ask your class if anyone has been to New York. If they have, ask them to share their experiences with the group.

**b)** 🖭 [11.1] Play the recording and ask students to listen and decide if Matt enjoyed his holiday (he did!).

**5** Go through the list of activities in New York with the class. You may wish to check the pronunciation of *Metropolitan* /metrəˈpɒlɪtən/ and *Statue* /ˈstætʃuː/. Play the recording again, and ask students to put a tick or a cross in the boxes. Students compare answers in pairs before checking with the whole class.

> **ANSWERS**
> a (✓)   b (✓)   c (✗)   d (✓)   e (✗)
> f (✗)   g (✓)   h (✓) i (✗)

> **Exercise 5: additional suggestion**
>
> You may use activity 11A *Collocation pelmanism* on page 146 of the Resource bank (instructions on page 98) at any time after this activity.

### Past Simple negative

## Grammar

**board** Write *We … … to expensive restaurants.* and *They … … a lot of money.* on the board and ask students to complete the sentences in the negative. Ask students to give you one or two more sentences about themselves (**not** about Matt and Claire). Drill the sentences with the class chorally and individually, focusing on natural rhythm and stress:

**We didn't go to expensive restaurants.**

**They didn't have a lot of money.**

Highlight:

- we use *didn't* to make the Past Simple negative.

- the word order: **subject + *didn't* + verb.**

- *didn't* /ˈdɪdənt/ is a contraction of *did not*, and is always stressed.

- the negative form is the same for all subjects
(*I/you/he/she/we/they*).

Refer students to *Language summary* 11A on page 118 of
the *Students' Book*.

**6 a)** Go through the example before asking students to
do the exercise individually. They should refer to the
answers for Exercise 5 if necessary to see if the sentences
should be positive or negative.

**b)** [recording icon] [11.2] Play the recording for students to check their
answers. You may wish to write the negative sentences on
the board. Play the recording again, pausing after each
sentence for students to repeat chorally and individually.

**ANSWERS**
**a** They went for a walk in Manhattan
**b** They went shopping.
**c** They didn't go the Metropolitan Museum.
**d** They went to the Statue of Liberty.
**e** They didn't go to the Empire State Building.
**f** They didn't stay in a hotel.
**g** They stayed with friends.
**h** They went for a walk in Central Park.

**7 a)** Students do the exercise individually. Tell students
to tick the sentences that are correct for them, and to
write both a negative and a positive sentence for the
sentences that need correcting, as in the example. Circulate
and help students with problems and any new vocabulary
they need.

**b)** Use the speech balloons to remind students of the
question: *What about you?*. Put students into pairs to
compare sentences. As they are talking, circulate and
correct students as necessary.

### ADDITIONAL PRACTICE

**Workbook:** Vocabulary: holiday expressions, page 54; Past
Simple negative, page 54

[RB] **Resource bank:** 11A *Collocation pelmanism,* page 146
(instructions on page 98)

## Focus 2 (PAGES 92–93)

### Vocabulary and speaking: holidays

**1** [board] Do one or two examples before asking the
students to do the exercise individually. The following
vocabulary may be new to your students: *boat, plane, relax*
/rɪˈlæks/; *do nothing*. Ask students to compare answers in
pairs or small groups. Check the answers with the whole
class. Highlight the use of the preposition *by* in expressions
of travelling, e.g. *go by train*. You may also wish to drill the
phrases with the class.

LANGUAGE NOTE:
You may wish to extend the vocabulary of ways to travel by
teaching: *go by bicycle / taxi / motorbike / tube
(underground)*. You can also teach the exception *on foot*
and highlight that *by walk* is not English!

**2** Students discuss the questions in small groups.
Encourage students to give reasons for their answers
where possible.

**3** Ask students to think of a holiday they remember well.
Allow students a few moments to read the
questionnaire, but tell them **not** to fill in the answers. Deal
with any questions about vocabulary students may have.
Put students into pairs. Student A asks Student B the
questions, and writes the answers in his/her *Students' Book*.
When they have finished, students swap roles so that
Student B is asking the questions and writing down Student
A's answers. Encourage students to give more information
in their answers if possible. At the end of the activity, ask a
few students to tell the class about their partner's holiday.

### Past Simple questions

## Grammar

[board] Write *Where ... you go?* and *What ... you do there?* on
the board, and ask students to help you complete the
questions. You may wish to add one or two other *Wh-*
questions, such as *Where did you stay?* It is useful to write
the questions so that similar words are above each other, as
this helps students see the underlying pattern.

Write *... have a good time?* on the board and ask students
to help you complete the question. Put a tick and a cross
next to this question and elicit, *Yes, I did.* and *No, I didn't.*
from the class. You may wish to add one or two other
*yes/no* questions from the questionnaire, such as *Did you
travel by car?* Leave the examples on the board if possible
to help students in the next activity.

Highlight:
- we use *did* in Past Simple questions.
- the word order: **(Question word) + *did* + subject + verb.**
- we do not use the past tense (e.g. *went*) in questions.
- the use of *did* and *didn't* in short answers.
- the question form is the same for all subjects
(*I/you/he/she/we/they*).

Refer students to *Language summary* 11B on page 118 of
the *Students' Book*.

LANGUAGE NOTE:
It may be useful to show the similarity in grammar between Present Simple questions and Past Simple questions, particularly the fact that *do/does* simply changes to *did* to make a question in the past. This is covered in *Language summary* 11A, and you may wish to write some of these examples on the board to highlight this in front of the class.

**4** **a)** Students do the exercise individually before checking in pairs. Refer students to the examples of Past Simple questions on the board (or in the *Grammar* box) if they are having problems with the word order.

**b)** 🖥 [11.3] Play the recording for students to check their answers. Play the recording again (or model the sentences yourself), pausing after each sentence for students to repeat chorally and individually. When drilling, focus on natural rhythm and stress, and highlight that *did* is not usually stressed.

**c)** Students work in pairs and ask each other at least three questions from Exercise 4b. Remind students of the short answers *Yes, I did.* and *No, I didn't.* before they begin. Students should also try to give some additional information in their answer, e.g. *Yes, I did. I went to the cinema.* or *No, I didn't. I stayed in.* for question 3.

**Exercise 4c: alternative suggestions**

a If you feel one or two of the questions are inappropriate for your students to ask each other during the lesson (e.g. questions 1 and 4), write alternative questions on the board for the students to put in order for Exercise 4a. Some suggestions are:

- did / yesterday / have lunch / Where / you?
- do / did / this morning / What / you?
- How / come / today / did / to school / you?

b *If your students are able to move around the room:* ask your students to circulate and ask at least four other people the questions.

**5** **a)** Students do the exercise individually or in pairs.

**b)** board 🖥 [11.4] Play the recording for students to check their answers. Write the expressions on the board and check students understand the meaning of *last* by asking them the dates of last weekend. Highlight the stress in the words and phrases (see below), and that *last* is usually pronounced without the 't' /lɑːs/. Drill the new language chorally and individually.

**ANSWERS**
last year > last month > last weekend >
yesterday > last night > this morning

**Exercise 5: additional suggestions**

a *For extra practice of* yes/no *questions*: Use activity 11B *Did you or didn't you?* on page 147 of the Resource bank (instructions on page 98).

b *For extra practice of* Wh- *questions*: Use activity 11C *Madonna's life story* on pages 148 and 149 of the Resource bank (instructions on page 99).

**6** Focus students on the game board on page 93 and go through the example with the class, on the board if necessary. Students then work individually or in pairs and make questions for the other prompts on the game board (for some squares students must make two questions). Depending on your class, you may want your students to say the questions to each other, or to write them down. With a weak class, you may wish to check the questions for all the squares before continuing.

**Speaking task**

Put the students into groups of three or four. Give each group dice and counters (or they may use something of their own, like a pen top, as a counter). Tell each group to turn to page 112 of the *Students' Book* and read the rules of the game. Check that students have understood these before continuing and demonstrate how to play the game in front of the whole class. Teach the language in the *Don't forget!* box on page 93, and check they understand the language on the non-question squares on the board. Students then play the game in their groups. As they are playing, circulate and note down any common errors for later correction. These can be written on the board for the class to correct as a group or in pairs. If a group finishes early, they can play the game again. At the end of the activity, don't forget to ask each group who won their game!

**Workbook:** Past Simple, *yes/no* questions, page 54; Short answers, page 55; *Wh-* questions, page 55; Vocabulary: time phrases, page 56

RB **Resource bank:** 11B *Did you or didn't you?*, page 147 (instructions on page 98); 11C *Madonna's life story*, pages 148 and 149 (instructions on page 99)

## Focus 3 (PAGES 94–95)
Reading: Around the World

**1** Students discuss the questions in pairs or small groups. Ask students to share any interesting experiences with the whole class.

**2** **a)** Focus students on the pictures on pages 94 and 95, and the title of the article. Check that they understand the expression *sail around the world*. Students do the exercise individually, but do not tell them the answer at this stage.

**b)** 📼 [11.5] Students read and listen to the text to check their answer to Exercise 2a. When they have finished, check that they have the correct answer to Exercise 2a (the answer is c). Alternatively, you may prefer your students to simply read the text at this stage, and to play recording [11.5] after Exercise 3 as consolidation. If so, it is useful to set students a time limit of three or four minutes to encourage them to read for gist. Check students understand the following words before they read the article again: *a dream*; *a journey* /ə ˈdʒɜːni/; *a whale* /ə weɪəl/; *took*; *argue*.

**3** Students read the text again and correct sentences (a–i) on their own. Circulate and help students with vocabulary as necessary while they are reading. Students compare answers in pairs. Check the answers with the whole class, and refer them to the *Vocabulary book* on page 54.

> **ANSWERS**
> a  Alison is a **teacher** and Jeff is an **engineer**.
> b  They met at a **sailing** club.
> c  Their dream was to sail **around the world**.
> d  They took their **three** children with them.
> e  Their boat, the *Charlotte Rose*, was **eight** metres long.
> f  They went to **South Africa** first, then Australia, then **South America**.
> g  Alison **enjoyed** the journey.
> h  One day the children saw **three** whales near their boat.
> i  Jeff says that their family argued **sometimes**.

**4** **a)**  Begin by checking that students understand the meaning of all the verbs in the box. Tell students that the past tenses are in the same order in the article, and that they can refer to the Verb tables on pages 62 and 63 of the *Vocabulary book* as necessary. Students then do the exercise individually or in pairs.

> **ANSWERS**
> meet    **met** (irregular)
> decide    **decided** (regular)
> buy    **bought** (irregular)
> want    **wanted** (regular)
> take    **took** (irregular)
> arrive    **arrived** (regular)
> see    **saw** (irregular)
> argue    **argued** (regular)

**b)** 🔲board 📼 [11.6] Play the recording for students to check their answers, and write the past tenses on the board.  Ask the students which verbs are regular and which are irregular. Play the recording again (or model the words yourself) and ask students to repeat the verbs and past tenses. Pay particular attention to the pronunciation of *bought* /bɔːt/; *took* /tʊk/; *saw* /sɔː/, and the extra syllable in *wanted* /wɒntɪd/.

**5** Students do the exercise individually before checking the answers with the whole group. The following words may be new to your students: *boring* /ˈbɔːrɪŋ/; *exciting* /ɪkˈsaɪtɪŋ/ and *stupid* /ˈstjuːpɪd/.

**6** Students do the exercise in groups. Encourage students to give reasons for their answers where possible. Conclude the activity by discussing their ideas with the whole class.

## Grammar

Draw students' attention to the sentences in the *Grammar* box, or write them on the board. Check that students understand the difference between *and* and *but*, and ask them to give you some more examples if necessary. Highlight that we usually use *and* and *but* in the middle of sentences.

LANGUAGE NOTE:
The rules on whether to use a comma before *and* and *but* are complex, if indeed they exist at all! At this level we suggest that you simply teach students to use *and* and *but* without commas, and that they should use these words in the middle of the sentence rather than at the beginning. They can break these rules later in their language development!

**7** Students look back at the article on page 94 and underline all the *and*s and *but*s they can find. Check the answers with the whole group.

**8** Students do the exercise individually. Check the answers with the whole class.

> **ANSWERS**
> a  Tom's married **and** he has two children.
> b  They went to Rome **but** they didn't go to Venice.
> c  Marta went to Thailand on holiday **and** she had a great time.
> d  I like English **but** I don't understand everything.
> e  This is a good hotel **and** the rooms are very quiet.
> f  Sue had a ticket for a concert **but** she didn't go.
> g  I can play the guitar **but** I can't sing.

**9** Students do the exercise individually, using their own ideas. While they are working, circulate and help students with vocabulary as necessary. Students compare sentences in pairs or small groups.

> **Grammar/Vocabulary: additional suggestions**
>
> a  For extra practice of all aspects of the Past Simple, use activity 11D *Past Simple snakes and ladders* on pages 150 and 152 of the Resource bank (instructions on page 99).
>
> b  *Vocabulary booster: The weather* on page 153 of the Resource bank (instructions on page 99) may be used at any time during the module.

## ADDITIONAL PRACTICE

**Workbook:** *did*, *was* and *were*, page 56; Past Simple verbs, page 56; *and* and *but*, page 56

[RB]  **Resource bank:** 11D *Past Simple snakes and ladders*, pages 150 and 152 (instructions on page 99); *Vocabulary booster: The weather*, page 153 (instructions on page 99)

## Real life  (PAGES 96–97)

Buying a train ticket

**1** Focus students on the pictures on page 96. Students work individually or in pairs and try to match the words with the pictures. Check the answers with the whole group. Drill the words with the class and check the pronunciation of *ticket* /ˈtɪkɪt/. Also explain that people usually just say *a single* or *a return* when buying tickets.

**2** **a)**  [11.7] Focus students on the photograph of Veronica and the ticket seller on page 97. Play the recording and ask students to circle the correct answers. Students can compare answers in pairs before checking with the whole class. Play the recording again if there are any disagreements in the class.

> **ANSWERS**
> return; £23.50; next; 10.54; platform; sixteen

**b)** Play the recording again, pausing after each sentence for students to repeat. When drilling these sentences, encourage students to say them with natural rhythm and stress. Students then practise the conversation in pairs. After they have repeated the conversation two or three times, ask them to close their books and try to repeat the conversation from memory. You may wish to conclude by asking one or two pairs to perform the conversation in front of the class (students do not need to leave their seats).

**3** Put students in different pairs, Student A and Student B. In order to do the first roleplay, Student A should read the information on page 96, and Student B should turn to page 110 of the *Students' Book* and read the information on the timetable. Students then do the roleplay in pairs. When they have finished, Student B reads the information on page 96 and Student A reads the timetable on page 112 of the *Students' Book*. Remind students to base their

conversation on the dialogue in Exercise 2a, and check they know the question *How much is that?* before they begin. You may also wish to check that students can say the times correctly (i.e. 10.48 = *ten forty-eight*; 11.45 = *eleven forty-five*, etc.). As they are working, circulate and help as necessary.

> **Exercise 3: alternative suggestion**
>
> If it is possible to get hold of a set of railway timetables, you can make a similar version of Exercise 3 based on train travel in the country you are teaching in. This use of authentic (i.e. real) material is often very motivating for students, particularly if they are studying in an English-speaking country.

(W) Use the suggested links to buy tickets online with your students.

## Do you remember?  (PAGE 97)

> **ANSWERS**
> **1**  various answers
>
> **2**  a  When **did** he go to bed last night?
>  b  Did **he** come to school by train?
>  c  What did they **do** last night?
>  d  What **time** did you get up this morning?
>  e  **Did** your sister go shopping last week?
>  f  Where did you **meet** your husband?
>
> **3**  1 d    4 b
>  2 e    5 a
>  3 f    6 c
>
> **4**  **go to** a restaurant; the beach; a museum
>  **go** shopping; swimming; skiing
>  **have** a good time; breakfast; a lot of money
>  **stay** with a family; in a hotel; with friends

# module 12

## Focus 1 (PAGES 98–99)

### Vocabulary: things you buy

**1 a)** Focus students on the adverts on pages 98 and 99 and use these to teach *advert* /'ædvɜːt/. Students do the exercise individually or in pairs. Alternatively, you can teach the new vocabulary in front of the class (e.g. by using pictures from magazines) before they begin the exercise. Words that may be new to students are: *clothes, make-up, shampoo, jeans, a jacket, boots, a carpet*. Check the answers with the whole group. Students may use page 57 of the *Vocabulary book* as consolidation of these new words.

> **ANSWERS**
> **Advert 1:** a carpet, a book, coffee
> **Advert 2:** jeans, a jacket, boots
> **Advert 3:** clothes, make-up, a mobile phone

LANGUAGE NOTE:
*Advert* is a shortened form of *advertisement*, and is commonly used in British English. In American English, *ad* is more common. Note also that *advertisement* is pronounced /əd'vɜːtɪsmənt/ in British English, and /'ædvətaɪzmənt/ in American English.

**b)** [12.1] Play the recording (or model the words yourself), pausing after each word for students to repeat chorally and individually. Words that are often difficult for students to pronounce are *jeans* /dʒiːnz/; *jacket* /'dʒækɪt/ and *clothes* /kləʊðz/ (which actually sounds the same as *close* /kləʊz/ in normal spoken English). Also check the word stress on *make-up* /'meɪkʌp/ and *shampoo* /ʃæm'puː/, and any other words students have problems with. Also point out that *jeans* is always plural in English (e.g. *These jeans are nice*.)

**2** Draw students' attention to the speech balloons before asking them to do the exercise in pairs. Students should choose between the items in Excercise 1. Ask each pair what they think the answers are before allowing them to turn to page 109 of the *Students' Book* to check their answers.

> **ANSWERS**
> **1** carpets **2** boots **3** a mobil phone

**3** **board** Check that students understand the categories, and teach the new verbs *carry* and *wear* /weə/, using examples from Exercise 1 if necessary. Students do the exercise in pairs. Check the answers with the whole class by writing them on the board in the correct category. Note that some words can go in more than one category.

> **ANSWERS**
> **a** a mobile phone; make-up; a book
> **b** jeans; a jacket; boots; a watch; make-up
> **c** shampoo; coffee; a carpet

**4** **board** [12.2] Students do the exercise in the same pairs. Play the recording to check their answers and add them to the categories on the board. Play the recording again (or model the words yourself) and drill the words with your students. Pay particular attention to the pronunciation of *chair* /tʃeə/ and *handbag* /'hænbæg/. Also check the word stress in *T-shirt* /'tiːʃɜːt/.

> **ANSWERS**
> **a** a handbag; a briefcase
> **b** a jumper; a T-shirt; shoes
> **c** a chair; a table; a lamp

LANGUAGE NOTE:
*T-shirt* can also be spelt *tee-shirt*. Other words for *jumper* are *sweater* /'swetə/ and *pullover* /'pʊləʊvə/. You may also wish to check your students understand the difference between *a lamp* (which you can move around) and *a light* (which is fixed in a wall or ceiling). It is also useful to teach the expression of *a pair of (shoes/jeans)*.

> ............................................................
> **Exercise 4: additional suggestions**
>
> a Put students into pairs. One student draws one of the items in the *Students' Book*, and the other person must guess what it is.
>
> b For revision of this vocabulary, as well as other common nouns covered in the *Students' Book*, use activity 12A *Shopping crossword* on page 154 of the Resource bank (instructions on page 99).
>
> c If you want to teach your students more clothes vocabulary, use the *Vocabulary booster: Clothes* on page 155 of the Resource bank (instructions on page 100).
> ............................................................

### want to

**5** [12.3] Play the recording and ask students to write down what the four people want to buy. Students compare answers in pairs. Play the recording again if necessary, and check the answers with the whole class (note that *Bon Jovi* are an American rock band). You may wish to pre-teach *leather* /'leðə/ before you play the tape.

> **ANSWERS**
> **a** Yuko: a (Bon Jovi) CD; some shoes
> **b** Antonia: nothing
> **c** Ali: a (leather) jacket
> **d** Lucas: a lamp

## Grammar

**board** Draw two columns on the board headed *nouns* and *verbs*. Write *I want a CD.* on the board in the *nouns* column. Ask students what the other people on recording [12.3] wanted and write *I want a new leather jacket.* and *I want a lamp.* in the same column. Ask students how they would say these sentences with the verb *buy*. Write *I want to buy a CD.* on the board in the *verbs* column. Ask the class how they would make this sentence negative, and write *I don't want to buy a CD.* in the same column. Add more examples if necessary.

Highlight:

- the use of *to* in **want + to + verb**.
- *want* is in the Present Simple, so we would say *he/she wants*.
- the use of *don't* (or *doesn't*) in negatives.

Refer students to *Language summary* 12A on page 118 of the *Students' Book*. You may also wish to draw students' attention to the question forms.

**6** Check that students understand the headings (including the new word *furniture* /ˈfɜːnɪtʃə/), and draw their attention to the speech balloons (note that Radiohead are a British rock band). Students do the activity in pairs. Encourage students to use both *want* + noun and *want* + to + verb in their answers. At the end of the exercise students can share some of their ideas with the whole class.

**7** **a)** Focus students on the circles A, B and C, and check they understand all the vocabulary. The following words or phrases may be new to your students: *to see a film, to go for a coffee, tonight, tomorrow, next* (as in *next weekend* and *next week*). Students do the exercise individually. You may wish students to use only the language in the book, or add their own ideas as well.

**b)** Students do the exercise in pairs or groups. At the end of the activity each student can tell the whole class one of his/her sentences.

**Exercise 7b: additional suggestion**

*If you want to practise questions with 'want'*: Students work on their own and write down six things they want to do or buy, or places they want to go to. Students then move around the room asking other people if they want to do the same things, using questions such as *Do you want to buy a car?*. When students find someone who wants to do the same thing as them, they write the person's name next to their sentence. The aim of the activity is to find a different person for each of their six sentences. At the end of the activity students can compare answers in pairs or with the whole class.

## ADDITIONAL PRACTICE

**Workbook:** Vocabulary: things you buy, page 59; *want to*, page 59

**RB** **Resource bank:** 12A *Shopping crossword*, page 154 (instructions on page 99); *Vocabulary booster: Clothes*, page 155 (instructions on page 100)

## Focus 2 (PAGES 100–101)

Vocabulary: colours and sizes

**1** Students do the exercise individually before checking the answers in pairs or with the whole class. Drill the words for the colours with the whole class.

> **ANSWERS**
> **a** brown **b** yellow **c** black **d** white **e** green **f** blue **g** red

**Exercise 1: additional suggestion**

*If this is easy for your students*: use items in the room or pictures from magazines to teach other colours. You may also wish to teach *dark* and *light*, as in *dark/light blue*.

**2** **a) and b)** [12.4] Students do the exercise individually. Play the recording for students to check their answers. Play the recording again, pausing after each question for students to repeat chorally and individually. Also check the pronunciation of the new words *medium* /ˈmiːdiəm/ and *large* /lɑːdʒ/.

> **ANSWERS**
> **1** c **2** b **3** a

Reading

**3** Focus students on the two Internet shopping sites on page 100. Students work in pairs and try to name the things they can see in the pictures. Check the answers with the whole group.

> **ANSWERS**
> **1** a jacket, a briefcase, a wallet, two bags
> **2** a jumper, a coffee table, a carpet, a lamp

LANGUAGE NOTE:
You may wish to point out that *.com* at the end of website addresses is pronounced *dot com*.

**Exercise 3: additional suggestion**

*If you have a strong class*: begin by having a class discussion about shopping on the Internet with your class, if you feel this is appropriate for your students.

Write the following questions on the board and ask students to discuss them in groups:

- Do you shop on the Internet? Why/Why not?
- Do you like shopping on the Internet?
- What do people usually buy?
- What was the last thing you bought?

Students can then compare their answers with their classmates in a class discussion.

**4** Direct students to the 'Extra information' boxes on page 101. Students read the information and match the descriptions to the pictures on the websites. Check the answers with the whole group. The following words may be new to students: *short*; *extra large/small*; *wool*; *handmade*; *high*. You may wish to check that students understand these words before moving on to the next exercise.

**5** Teach the meaning of *cheaper* (question 7), for example by drawing two TVs on the board with different prices and asking students which one is cheaper. Ask the class to close their books and put the students into pairs. Start the clock and tell students to open their books and answer as many questions as they can in three minutes. Stop them after three minutes are up and see which pair has answered the most questions, or completed all the questions in the shortest time. Check the answers with the whole class.

**ANSWERS**
1 medium, large, extra large
2 no
3 $58
4 Brazil
5 no
6 $105
7 the women's jacket
8 black or brown
9 both men and women
10 30 centimetres

## Speaking task

1 Teach students *present* /ˈprezənt/, meaning *a gift*. Students do the exercise individually, choosing the presents from the pictures on the websites. Encourage them to think of a reason why they have chosen each present. Allow students a few minutes for this.
2 Draw students' attention to the speech balloons and the language in the *Don't forget!* box, particularly the use of the preposition *for* in *For my sister*. Students do the exercise in small groups, giving reasons for their choices where possible. As they are working, circulate and help as necessary, noting down common errors for later correction on the board. If a group finishes early, ask them to decide what they want to buy for

each other! Conclude the activity by asking a few students to tell the whole class about one thing they want to buy.

**Speaking task: alternative suggestion**

If you feel the items on the websites are not appropriate gifts for your students, bring into the class some photographs of other possible presents, taken from magazines or downloaded from the Internet. Stick these on the board or on a worksheet, and check that students know all the relevant vocabulary. Students can then do Exercises 1 and 2 of the Speaking task as above.

## ADDITIONAL PRACTICE

**Workbook:** Vocabulary: colours, page 59; Sizes, page 60

 Go shopping online with your students and use the related activities in the Resources section of the website.

## Focus 3 (PAGES 102–103)

*going to*

TEACHER'S NOTE:
We have chosen to introduce *going to* as the future tense in this book rather than *will + verb*, as we feel it is more relevant to low-level students' immediate communicative needs, for example talking about their plans for the evening or next weekend.

**1** Introduce the topic by asking students where they like to shop and what they like (and don't like) buying. Focus students on the picture of the shopping mall on page 102. Students work in pairs and write down all the places they see. Check any new vocabulary with the class.

**ANSWERS**
a café, a flower shop, a newsagents, clothes shops, a computer shop (or electric shop)

**2** Students do the exercise in pairs before comparing answers with a partner. Check the answers with the whole group. You may wish to pre-teach the following words: *flowers*; *a football match*; *a girlfriend*, or refer students to page 59 of the *Vocabulary book*. You may also wish to teach *boyfriend* at this point if it is appropriate for your students.

**ANSWERS**
**a** 6 **b** 7 **c** 4 **d** 5 **e** 2 **f** 3 **g** 1

TEACHER'S NOTE:
Students at this point may ask you what *going to* means. We suggest you simply tell them that it's a future tense – which should be obvious from the context – but leave the detailed explanation of the grammar until later in the lesson.

**3** **a)** ▭ [12.5] Tell students they are going to listen to four of the people in the picture talking. Play the recording, and ask the students to write down which people they think they are. Check the answers with the whole class.

> **ANSWERS**
> **a** 6  **b** 7  **c** 2  **d** 1

**b)** ▭ [12.6] Students work in pairs and try to complete the sentences. Play the recording for students to check their answers, and write them on the board if necessary. Check also that students have included '*re* where appropriate.

> **ANSWERS**
> **1** going to  **2** going to; re going to  **3** not
> **4** going to; 're going to

**Exercise 3b: alternative suggestion**
*You may wish to play recording [12.6] and ask the students to fill in the correct answers as they listen to the tape.*

# Grammar

**board** Write *I ... ... ... visit my mother in hospital.* on the board. Ask students to tell you which words are missing and write them in the gaps. Write *... buy a computer.* on the board and ask students to complete the sentence, based on the information from the recording. Finally, write *What ... you ... ... do tomorrow?* on the board and again ask students to help you complete the question.

Highlight:

● *going to* refers to the future.

● the word order: **subject + be + going to + verb.**

● the position of *not* in negative sentences.

● the change of word order in questions: *you are > are you?*

● the *he/she/we/they* forms in the *Grammar* box.

Drill the sentences chorally and individually, focusing on natural sentence stress.

Refer students to *Language summary* 12B and 12C on page 118 of the *Students' Book*.

LANGUAGE NOTE:
Point out that *going to* is often used with a word or phrase that indicates future time, such as *tomorrow, next weekend / week / month / Tuesday, on Sunday, this evening, tonight,* etc. You may wish to write these on the board for students to copy.

**4** Go through the language in the speech balloons, and drill the questions: *What's he/she going to do?* with the whole class. Students do the activity in pairs.

**5** ▭ [12.7] Students match the questions to the answers individually before comparing answers in pairs. You may need to pre-teach *aunt* /ɑːnt/ and *uncle* /ˈʌŋkəl/ in answer c). Play the recording for students to check their answers.

> **ANSWERS**
> **1** d  **2** f  **3** a  **4** b  **5** c  **6** e

LANGUAGE NOTE:
When the main verb in the sentence is *go* we sometimes leave out this verb to avoid repeating it. For example, we might say: *Are you going out tonight?* and *Are you going to the shops this morning?* for questions 3 and 4. We have included the full version here as we feel that it is important for students at this level to learn the general rule and the word order. You may wish to point out the shorter versions to your class.

# Pronunciation

**1** ▭ [12.8] Play the recording for students to listen and read. Highlight the weak pronunciation of *to* /tə/ in the sentences. Play the recording again (or model the sentences yourself), pausing after each sentence for students to repeat chorally and individually. One useful drilling technique is to build up the sentences 'block by block', with the whole class repeating each phrase after you: *going to > going to phone > going to phone Linda today? > Are you going to phone Linda today?*

**2** Students practise the dialogues in Exercise 5 with a partner. As they are working, circulate and help students with pronunciation as necessary.

# Speaking task

**1** Focus students on the prompts 1–8 and allow students a few moments to read them and check any vocabulary with you. Tell the class that they are going to ask each other about next weekend, and go through the example question with the class. Students work individually and write down the questions for the other seven prompts. Check these with the whole class, and also remind students of the short answers: *Yes, I am.* and *No, I'm not.*

2 Demonstrate the activity with the whole class, showing students that they should write the name of one person for each of the prompts in the boxes provided. Students move around the room and ask each other the questions they have prepared. They should try to find a different person for each prompt if possible. If your students are not able to move around the room, they should ask as many people as possible from where they are sitting.

3 Students tell the class some of their answers, as in the speech balloon. Alternatively, students can compare answers in pairs before sharing one or two of their answers with the whole class.

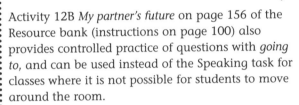

**Speaking task: additional suggestion**

Activity 12B *My partner's future* on page 156 of the Resource bank (instructions on page 100) also provides controlled practice of questions with *going to*, and can be used instead of the Speaking task for classes where it is not possible for students to move around the room.

## ADDITIONAL PRACTICE

**Workbook:** *Going to*, page 60; Positive and negative sentences, page 61; Questions, page 61

RB **Resource bank:** 12B *My partner's future*, page 156 (instructions on page 100)

## Real life (PAGES 104–105)

Best wishes for the future

1 Focus students on the pictures on page 104, and allow students time to read the captions underneath them. Students can then do the exercise on their own.

2 a) 🔲 [12.9] Play the recording for students to check their answers. Drill the phrases with the class by playing the recording again (or modelling them yourself), and encourage students to sound interested and cheerful! Also check that students know the following responses from the recording: *You too.*; *Thanks, and you.*; *See you.*

**ANSWERS**
a Good luck with your new job!
b Have a nice weekend!
c Good luck with your new school!
d Have a nice holiday!
e See you in September!

b) Students practise the phrases and appropriate responses in pairs.

3 a) Students work in pairs and make similar phrases from the prompts. Check that students understand and can pronounce the new vocabulary *meal*, *test* and *interview* before they begin. You may also wish to teach *Good luck with your exam!* if your students are facing end-of-course examinations!

b) 🔲 [12.10] Play the recording once for students to listen to the phrases. Play the recording again, pausing after each phrase for students to repeat chorally and individually.

4 Students work individually and write down one phrase for each situation. Early finishers can compare answers in pairs. Check the answers with the whole group. Students can then practise the phrases in pairs. Student A says, for example, *It's my birthday tomorrow!*, and Student B responds with *Have a nice birthday!*.

**ANSWERS**
1 Have a nice birthday! *or* Happy birthday!
2 Have a nice meal!
3 Good luck with your new flat! *or* Good luck with the move!
4 Have a nice holiday! *or* Have a nice time!
5 See you at three (o'clock).

5 Students write down at least three things they are going to do soon. If they are having problems thinking of ideas, then allow them to make up a few things! Students move around the room and tell other students what they are going to do. Students must respond to their classmates' plans with the appropriate phrase. Encourage students to talk to as many people as possible. If your students cannot move around the room, do the activity in groups of four or six.

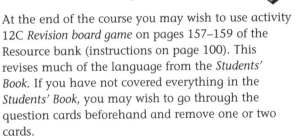

**Revision: additional practice**

At the end of the course you may wish to use activity 12C *Revision board game* on pages 157–159 of the Resource bank (instructions on page 100). This revises much of the language from the *Students' Book*. If you have not covered everything in the *Students' Book*, you may wish to go through the question cards beforehand and remove one or two cards.

## ADDITIONAL PRACTICE

RB **Resource bank:** 12C *Revision board game*, pages 157–159 (instructions on page 100)

## Do you remember? (PAGE 105)

**ANSWERS**
**1**

| O | K | J | S | H | O | E | S | K | R |
|---|---|---|---|---|---|---|---|---|---|
| J | N | U | K | M | S | I | J | B | P |
| E | U | M | C | T | S | H | I | R | T |
| A | P | P | I | I | H | D | E | I | O |
| N | S | E | D | M | A | R | G | E | G |
| S | G | R | E | E | N | E | N | F | B |
| A | B | O | N | U | D | K | I | C | L |
| T | A | B | L | E | B | N | M | A | U |
| M | P | R | A | E | A | A | F | S | E |
| X | O | G | M | W | G | W | R | E | D |
| C | A | R | P | E | T | E | S | R | A |

| clothes: | jeans T-shirt jumper |
|---|---|
| colours: | blue green red |
| things in the house: | carpet table lamp |
| made of leather: | shoes handbag briefcase |

**2** various answers

**3** a I'm not going to play football tomorrow.
  b My sister's going to buy a new car.
  c They're going to visit their friend in hospital.
  d I'm not going to go to university next year.
  e Marta's going to meet me at the airport.
  f We're going to stay with my parents next weekend.

## Consolidation modules 9–12

**A**
**1** a was
  b had
  c listened
  d didn't have
  e went
  f didn't study
  g left
  h weren't
  i met
  j played
  k sold
  l moved

**B**
  a were; On
  b start; was
  c do you want; to go
  d did you go; by
  e are you going; I'm
  f Were; weren't

**D**
  a Where were you born?
  b He wasn't very old.
  c I went to a museum at the weekend.
  d She didn't come to school.
  e What are you going to do?
  f I'm going to meet my friends.

**E**
**1** a 4 (wealthy man)
  b 2 (rich man)
  c 3 (win a fortune)
  d 1 (pay a bill)

**2**
**Chorus**
Money, money, money,
Must be **funny**,
In the **rich** man's world.
Money, money, money,
**Always** sunny,
In the rich **man's** world.
Aha-ahaaa
All the **things** I could do
if I **had** a little money.
It's a rich man's **world.**

**3**

| Verse 1 | | Verse 2 | |
|---|---|---|---|
| 1 | e | 8 | i |
| 2 | f | 9 | m |
| 3 | a | 10 | k |
| 4 | g | 11 | n |
| 5 | b | 12 | h |
| 6 | d | 13 | l |
| 7 | c | 14 | j |

# Resource bank
## Index of activities

**Instructions for activities** pages 89–100    **Resource bank key** pages 188–191

# Instructions

## Classroom language

### Questions in the classroom

*You will need: one copy of the worksheet per student*

This worksheet is designed to be used at any time in the course. If you have a strong class or mainly false beginners, you might like to introduce these questions sometime during Modules 1 or 2. If all your class are real beginners, you might choose to teach this language a little later in the course.

- Distribute copies of the worksheet to the class. Students work individually or in pairs and match the questions to the pictures (Exercise 1). Check the answers with the whole class (see **Key**). Students can then write the questions in the correct speech bubbles. We suggest that you teach these questions as lexical 'chunks', rather than focusing on the grammatical form of each question.
- Practise the pronunciation of all the questions with the class, drilling each question chorally and individually and focusing on natural rhythm and stress. Students can then do Exercise 2 in pairs.
- Allow students the opportunity to ask you questions using the language from the worksheet. Also encourage students to keep the worksheet handy and refer to it during future lessons. You might also like to write the questions on cards and display them around the room, along with other useful expressions such as *I'm sorry, I don't understand.* and *I'm sorry I'm late.*

## 1A What's your job?

### Names and jobs with *I* and *you*

*You will need: one role card per student*

This activity can be used as an alternative to Focus 2, Exercise 4 in the Students' Book for classes where the students don't have jobs.

- Pre-teach the words *actress*, *waitress* and *singer*.
- Give one role card to each student. If you have more than twelve students, use duplicate role cards. If possible, give cards with male characters to the male students, and female characters to the female students. (The names on the first six cards can be both male and female names in English.) If you have already done the *Vocabulary Booster* on page 103, or taught other job vocabulary in class, consider making extra role cards.
- Students move around the room introducing themselves, using the new names on the cards, and asking about each other's jobs. Encourage students to use the following language during the activity: *Hello/Hi, my name's (Sally). What's your name? Nice to meet you. What's your job? I'm a (doctor).*
- If it is not possible for your students to move around the room, they can ask the students sitting near them.
- **Optional stage:** If this activity is used after Exercise 2 on

p8 of the Students' Book, students can work in pairs and test each other on the other students' jobs. For example, Student A points to another student in the class and asks: *What's her job?*, and Student B must try to answer correctly.

## Vocabulary Booster – Jobs

*You will need: one copy of the worksheet per student*

- Give a copy of the worksheet to each student. Students do Exercise 1 in pairs or small groups. Check the answers with the whole class (see **Key**). Check that students can pronounce the new vocabulary items before continuing. Note that secretary can be pronounced with three or four syllables: /sekrətri/ or /sekrəteri/.
- Tell students to cover the list of jobs at the top of the worksheet. Students then do Exercise 2 in pairs.
- Students do Exercise 3 individually or in pairs. Check the answers with the whole class (see **Key**). This final stage can also be done as a race, with the first person/pair to finish being the winner.

## 1B What's his surname?

### Names and jobs with *he* and *she;* spelling

*You will need: one copy of the* Time for a break! *picture per pair of students; one copy of Worksheet A or Worksheet B per student*

- Put the students into pairs. Give each pair a copy of the *Time for a break!* picture and allow them a few moments to study it.
- Give one student from each pair *Worksheet A* and the other student *Worksheet B*. **Students are not allowed to look at each other's worksheets.**
- Students take it in turns to point to a person on the *Time for a break!* picture (*not* the picture on their worksheets) and ask a question which will help them fill in the spaces on their worksheet. For example, Student A should point to Fiona and ask: *What's her surname?*.
- When Student B gives the answer, Student A must write it on his/her worksheet. If Student A does not know how to spell the name, he/she must ask Student B to spell it.
- Encourage students to use the following questions during the activity: *What's his/her first name? What's his/her surname? What's his/her (full) name? What's his/her job? How do you spell it?*
- When students have finished the activity, they can look at each other's worksheets and check their spelling.

## 2A  Where are you from?

Countries; *to be* with *I* and *you*

***You will need:*** *one role card per student*

- Pre-teach the following countries: *Australia*, *Egypt*, *Thailand* and *Germany*. Alternatively, discard the bottom four cards.
- Give one role card to each student. There are seven cards for male students and seven for female students. If you have more than fourteen students, use duplicate role cards.
- Students move around the room introducing themselves and asking each other's names, countries and jobs. If it is not possible for your students to move around the room, they can ask the students sitting near them.
- Encourage students to use the following language during the activity: *Hello/Hi, my name's (Francisco). What's your name? Nice to meet you. Where are you from? I'm from (Brazil). What's your job? I'm a (doctor).*
- If this activity is used after Exercise 8 on p17 of the *Students' Book*, students can work in pairs and try to remember where all the people in the class are from. Encourage students to use the following language: *What's his/her name? His/Her name's ...; Where's he/she from? He/She's from ...; What's his/her job? He/She's a ... .* If you are planning to do this stage of the activity, tell the class beforehand that they must remember the names, jobs and countries of the people they talk to.

## Vocabulary Booster – Nationalities

***You will need:*** *one worksheet per student*

- Give a copy of the worksheet to each student. Allow students to work in pairs and complete the table in Exercise 1. All the countries are taken from Module 2 of the *Students' Book*. Encourage the class to look back at page 14 or page 17 of the *Students' Book* if necessary. Check the answers with the whole class (see **Key**).
- Students work individually or in pairs and put the nationalities from Exercise 1 in the correct place according to their endings in the table in Exercise 2. Check the answers with the whole class (see **Key**).
- Ensure that students can pronounce all the nationality words before allowing them to do Exercise 3 in pairs. One student should say a country, and his/her partner should say the corresponding nationality.
- Students work in new pairs or small groups and do Exercise 4. It may be advisable to demonstrate this activity with the whole class beforehand by pretending to be a different nationality yourself.
- Refer students to the map. Ask them to do Exercise 5 on a separate sheet. If you have a monolingual class, allow students to do the exercise in pairs or small groups. If you have a multilingual class, allow students from the same country to work together if possible. While the students are working, the teacher moves around the room helping students with the words for the countries

and nationalities. It may be useful to have an atlas or some bilingual dictionaries available for the students to refer to.

- At the end of the activity students can compare maps, or they can be displayed around the classroom.

## 2B  Bingo!

Numbers 1–100

***You will need:*** *at least one Bingo Card per student*

- Give one Bingo Card to each student, and allow them a few moments to check the numbers on their cards.
- Sit or stand in front of the class with a copy of the Master Bingo Card. Call out the numbers on the card in any order, and cross them off the card at the same time.
- If a student has the number on his/her card, he/she should put a line through it. The first student who completes either a **horizontal** or a **vertical** line is the winner. The card can be checked against the Master Bingo Card if necessary.
- To repeat the activity, distribute new cards to the students and play again.

## 2C  The numbers game

Numbers 1–100

***You will need:*** *one copy of both sets of cards per three students*

- Before class cut out the two sets of cards, ensuring that you keep the cards for GAME 1 and GAME 2 **separate**.
- Divide the class into groups of three and distribute the cards for GAME 1. Give the first student Card A, the second student Card B, and the third student Card C. If you have extra students, put two students together so that they are working with one card.
- Students must listen to the numbers their partners say and find them in the **HEAR** column on their card. They must then say the corresponding number in the **SAY** column for the other students to recognise.
- The student with START on his/her card begins by saying the number indicated. The turn then passes from student to student until they reach the FINISH square. Students can tick off the numbers on their cards if they wish.
- If necessary, demonstrate the activity to the whole class before allowing the students to work in groups.
- When the students have finished, distribute the cards for GAME 2 and allow the groups to repeat the activity with the new cards. Alternatively, this second set of cards can be used for revision later in the course.

## 2D What's your address?

Personal information questions with *you* (and *he/she*)

***You will need:*** *one role card per student; one blank form per student (for Procedure B)*

**Procedure A**

This procedure uses the role cards to complete the Real Life Speaking Task on page 21 of the *Students' Book*, providing practice of questions with *you*.

- Put the students in pairs and give a role card to each student. There are three 'women' role cards and three 'men' role cards. **Students are not allowed to look at each other's role cards.**
- Student A asks Student B questions in order to fill in the form on page 21 in the *Students' Book*. Student B answers the questions using the new identity on the role cards. Encourage students to check spelling by asking *How do you spell it?* where appropriate.
- When Student A has completed his/her form, the students change roles so that Student B interviews Student A and fills in the form in his/her copy of the *Students' Book*. Student A responds to the questions using the new identity on his/her role card.
- When both students have finished, they should compare their forms and check their answers (and spelling) are correct.

**Procedure B**

This procedure provides practice of questions with *he* and *she*.

- Give each student a copy of the blank form at the bottom of the photocopiable page. Students work in pairs and write down questions with *he/she* for each of the blank spaces on the form. (For example: *What's his/her first name?*). Check these questions with the whole class before continuing.
- Put the students in pairs, and give each student a role card. Student A asks questions about the person on Student B's role card and completes his/her form.
- When Student A has completed his/her form, Student B then asks questions about the person on Student A's role card and completes his/her own form.
- When both students have finished, they should compare their forms and check their answers (and spelling) are correct.

## 3A What are their names?

*be* with plural forms

***You will need:*** *one copy of Worksheet A and one copy of Worksheet B per pair of students*

- Before you begin, check the students understand the meaning of *their* and *our*, and know how to pronounce these words.
- Divide the class into pairs and give one student a copy of Worksheet A and the other a copy of Worksheet B. Allow students time to read the information about the four people (Exercise 1). **Students are not allowed to look at each other's worksheets.**

- Students work individually and complete the questions in Exercise 2. Check that all the students have the correct answers before continuing (see **Key**).
- Students work in their pairs. Student A asks the questions he/she has prepared, and writes the answers in the correct spaces in the second text on Worksheet A. Remind the students of the question: *How do you spell it?* before they begin.
- When Student A has completed his/her worksheet, Student B asks the same questions in order to complete the second text on Worksheet B.
- When both students have completed their texts, they can look at each other's worksheets to check their answers and spelling.

## Vocabulary Booster – Food and drink

***You will need:*** *one worksheet per student*

- Give a copy of the worksheet to each student. Put the students into pairs and allow them time to do as much of Exercise 1 as they can. Check the answers with the whole class (see **Key**). Check the students can pronounce all the words correctly before continuing. Pay particular attention to *sausages* /ˈsɒsɪdʒɪz/; *orange juice* /ˈɒrɪndʒ dʒuːs/ and *chocolate* /ˈtʃɒklət/.
- Students work in pairs and do Exercise 2. Check the answers with the whole class (see **Key**). Check also that students know the spelling of the singular nouns (particularly *tomato* and *potato*). With a strong class you may choose to teach some other items of food and drink vocabulary which are particularly useful for your students, and ask them to put them in the right category on their worksheet.
- Tell the class to cover all the words on the worksheet with a piece of paper. Students then do Exercise 3 in pairs, taking it in turns to ask their partner what the items are.
- Finally, students do Exercise 4 in small groups.

## 3B What's this?

Vocabulary revision: *this, that, these, those*

*You will need:* one set of cards per group of three or four students

- Check that you have covered all the items of vocabulary on the cards (all of which come from Modules 1 to 3 of the *Students' Book*). If there are any items you haven't taught, either pre-teach them before beginning the activity or remove the cards.
- Divide the students into groups of three or four. Give each group a set of picture cards **face down in a pile**. Shuffle the cards beforehand.
- Student A turns over the first card. He/She asks the student on his/her right (Student B) what the word is in English by asking: *What's this?* or *What are these?*. Student B must then give the word in English, using the plural form if appropriate.
- If Student B is correct, Student A gives him/her the card. If Student B doesn't know the word, the turn passes to the next student in the group. If none of the students can guess the word, the card goes back to the bottom of the pile.
- The students continue taking it in turns to hold up a card and ask the person on their right what the word is in English. The student who collects the most cards by the end of the game is the winner.
- **Optional stage:** When the students have finished, they spread the cards out on the floor in front of them and take turns in pointing to each of the cards, this time asking *What's that?* or *What are those?* for each item. Alternatively, the teacher can stick one set of cards around the room and students point to them from their seats.

**Note:** it would be advisable to demonstrate this activity to the whole class before they begin working in groups.

## 4A Where's the cinema?

Places in a town; prepositions

*You will need:* one copy of Worksheet A and Worksheet B per pair of students

- Put students into pairs. Give a copy of Worksheet A to one student, and a copy of Worksheet B to the other. **Students are not allowed to look at each other's worksheets.**
- Check that students can pronounce all the street names on the map; this is a good opportunity to teach the English words for the points of the compass (i.e. *north, south, east* and *west*). Also check that they can find *the square* and *the park*.
- Tell the class that the places that are shaded (i.e. *the post office, the station, Pizza Land* and *McDonald's*) are on **both** maps, so they may refer to them when doing the activity.
- Students take it in turns to ask each other for the location of the places listed at the bottom of the

worksheet. Students should use the language in the *Don't forget!* box to help them. For example, Student B might ask: *Where's the Hilton Hotel?*, and Student A could reply: *It's in Station Road, on the left of the station*.

- When a student has identified the correct location, he/she writes the place in one of the boxes on his/her map. If students are unsure, they should check that they have written the name in the correct place by asking questions. For example: *'Is it near North Street, or near the park?'*. **Students are not allowed to look at each other's pictures at any time.**
- When a pair of students have located all the places, they compare their maps and see if they have written them in the correct spaces.
- As a follow-up activity, students can test each other on where places are on the map.

## 4B Vocabulary pelmanism

### Vocabulary: places and people

*You will need:* one set of cards per pair of students

- Put students into pairs (or groups of three). Give each pair (or group) a set of cards and tell them to spread them out in front of them **face down**, with the bigger cards on one side and the smaller cards on the other. Shuffle the cards before the class.
- Students take it in turns to turn over one big card and one small card. If the word matches the picture, the student keeps the cards as a 'trick' and has another turn. If the cards do not match, the student must put them back **in exactly the same place**.
- The activity continues until all the cards are matched up. The student with the most tricks is the winner.
- If one group finishes early, they can test each other by holding up the picture cards and asking their partner for the correct word.

## Vocabulary Booster – Places in a town

*You will need:* one copy of the worksheet per student

- Give a copy of the worksheet to each student. Allow students to do Exercise 1 in pairs or small groups. Students can use bilingual dictionaries if available. Check the answers with the whole group (see **Key**). Ensure that students can pronounce all the words with correct stress before continuing.
- Put the students into pairs. Tell students to cover the vocabulary box at the top of the worksheet before allowing them to do Exercise 2.
- Students work individually and do Exercise 3 before comparing answers in pairs or small groups. Students can share their best sentences with the whole class.
- Students do Exercise 4 in small groups, taking it in turns to mime being in one of the places in Exercise 1. It would be helpful for the teacher to demonstrate this activity before they begin.

## 4C  Spot the difference

Questions with *there is/there are*

*You will need: one copy of Picture A and one copy of Picture B per pair of students*

- Divide students into pairs. Give a copy of Picture A to one student, and a copy of Picture B to the other. **Students are not allowed to look at each other's pictures.**
- Tell the students that there are **ten** differences between the pictures. Students must find the differences by asking their partner questions using *there is/there are*. Encourage them to use the language in the *Don't forget!* box during the activity. Set a time limit of ten minutes.
- When students find a difference, they should mark it on their pictures. The activity continues until each pair has found all the differences, or the time limit has expired. The pair who finishes first, or finds the most differences in the time allowed, are the winners.
- At the end of the activity students can compare their pictures with each other or in small groups to check that they have found all the differences.

## 5A  Bob's family

Relationship vocabulary; possessive *'s*

*You will need: one copy of Worksheet A and one copy of Worksheet B per pair of students*

- Pre-teach the following items of vocabulary: *to be retired; a housewife.*
- Divide the students into pairs. Give a copy of Worksheet A to one student and a copy of Worksheet B to the other. If you have an odd number of students, pair two students together with one worksheet. **Students are not allowed to look at each other's worksheets until the end of the activity.**
- Check that students understand the information given is each person's name, age and job. Also check they understand the questions in the *Don't forget!* box.
- Students must ask their partner questions in order to complete their version of Bob's family tree. Students should ask questions about Bob initially. For example, Student A will need to ask *Who is Bob's father?* while Student B will need to ask *Who is Bob's mother?*. When students have more names on both worksheets they should refer to those where necessary. For example: *Who is Olivia's daughter?*
- Where possible, students should check that they have the information in the correct place by referring to other people on the worksheet. For example: *Is Bob his brother?; Are Lisa and Paul his parents?*
- When a pair have finished, they can look at each other's worksheets and check their answers and spelling.
- As a follow-up activity, students can test each other on the family relationships, or write some sentences about Bob's family.

## 5B  Present Simple dominoes

Present Simple with *I* and *you*; verb/noun combinations

*You will need: one set of dominoes per pair of students*

- Students work in pairs. Give one set of dominoes to each pair, and ask them to share them out equally. If you have an odd student, have one group of three.
- One student places a domino in front of them, and the other student has to make a complete sentence by placing one of his/her dominoes at either end of the first domino. Encourage students to look at the articles, prepositions and punctuation to ensure the sentence is accurate. Students then take it in turns to put down their dominoes at either end of the domino chain.
- If a student thinks his/her partner's sentence is not grammatically correct or doesn't make sense, he/she can challenge the other student. If the students cannot agree, the teacher adjudicates. If the sentence is incorrect, the student must take back the domino and miss a turn.
- If a student cannot make a sentence, the turn passes to his/her partner.
- The game continues until one student has used all his/her dominoes, or until neither student can make a correct sentence. The student who finishes first, or has the fewest dominoes remaining, is the winner.

## Vocabulary Booster – Rooms in a house

*You will need: one copy of the worksheet per student*

- Give a copy of the worksheet to each student. Students do Exercise 1 individually or in pairs. Check the answers with the whole class (see **Key**). Check that the students can pronounce all the words correctly before continuing.
- Students do Exercise 2 in pairs or small groups. Check the answers with the whole class (see **Key**). Again check that students can pronounce all the words correctly before allowing them to do Exercise 3 in pairs. Students can then change roles, so that Student B has his/her book closed, and Student A is asking the questions.
- Allow students about five minutes to draw a plan of their house or flat (Exercise 4a). Tell them to draw the items in each room (tables, chairs, TV, etc.) but **not** to write the English words. It might be useful for the teacher to prepare a plan of his/her own flat as a lead-in for this activity.
- Students work with a partner and describe where they live, using the vocabulary from the worksheet (Exercise 4b). At this stage the teacher can move around the room and help students with any new vocabulary they may need.
- Alternatively, Exercise 4 can be done without asking the students to draw their plan first. They can simply describe where they live to their partner from memory.
- As a follow-up activity, students can write a paragraph about their home, which can be put up round the classroom for other students to read.

## 6A  Like, love and hate

Present Simple with *you*; likes and dislikes; object pronouns

*You will need: one copy of the worksheet per student*

* Distribute one worksheet to each student. Students work individually and write their answers to the prompts in the second column. They should only write one or two words (e.g. *cartoons, football, Tom Hanks,* etc.), not complete sentences. Set a time limit of five minutes. As they are working, the teacher can move around the class and help students with vocabulary.
* **The aim of the activity is for each student to find a person who has the same opinion as him / her for each of the items on his / her worksheet.** Students move around the room and ask their classmates questions about the items they have written in the second column, beginning with *Do you like ...?* Encourage students to refer to the *Don't forget!* box while they are working, and to choose the correct pronoun in their response.
* If Student B has the same opinion as Student A, Student A should write Student B's name in the third column of the worksheet. If it is not possible for your students to move around the room, they can ask the people sitting close to them instead.
* Finally, students tell the whole class some things they both like or don't like. For example: *Mario and I both hate shopping.*

## 6B  Pronoun snap

Subject and object pronouns with *like, love* and *hate*

*You will need: one set of Question cards and one set of Answer cards for each pair of students.*

* Check that students know all the famous people in the activity before you begin. (If they don't know them, make sure they realise which people are women and which are men.)
* Students work in pairs. Give a set of *Question cards* to Student A and a set of *Answer cards* to Student B. Tell students to shuffle the cards and put them face down in a pile in front of them. Students will also need a pen and paper to keep score.
* Both students turn over a card from their pile at the same time and place them down next to each other. If the answer matches the question grammatically, the first student to say *'Snap!'* gets a point. Students then pick up **their own cards only**, shuffle their pack, and play again. Students do **not** pick up their partner's cards.
* If the answer doesn't match the question, the students continue turning over cards from their piles until someone says *'Snap!'*. If they reach the end of their cards without a match occurring, students pick up their own cards, shuffle them and play again.
* If a student says *'Snap!'* when the answer *doesn't* match the question, his/her partner gets a point and the students continue with the activity. If there is

disagreement whether the cards match, the teacher adjudicates. The first student to get 10 points is the winner.

* As a follow-up activity, students can ask each other the questions on the cards and give their own answers.
* It would be advisable to demonstrate this activity with the whole class before allowing the students to work in pairs.

## Vocabulary Booster – Sports

*You will need: one copy of the worksheet per student*

* Distribute a copy of the worksheet to each student, and allow them to do Exercise 1 alone or in pairs. Check the answers with the whole group (see **Key**).
* Ensure that students can pronounce the new vocabulary items before allowing the students to do Exercise 2 in pairs.
* Students work in pairs or small groups and do Exercise 3. This stage could also be done as a mingle activity if it is possible for students to move around the room.
* Students work individually and do Exercise 4. Put the class into pairs or small groups and allow them to compare their answers. If you are working with a monolingual group, you may want to teach the English words for other popular sports in their country before they begin this exercise.

## 6C  Does he or doesn't he?

Present Simple with *does* and *doesn't*

*You will need: one copy of the worksheet per student*

* Distribute copies of the worksheet to each student. Students work individually and choose the correct verb in each of the questions. Allow students to compare their answers in pairs before checking with the whole class (see **Key**).
* Tell students to write the name of someone they know well and their relationship to them in the box at the top of their worksheet (e.g. *Her name is Claudia. She is my sister*).
* Put students into pairs and tell them to **swap worksheets**. Students ask their partner questions about the person at the top of the worksheet, using the prompts in the first column. Encourage students to use the language in the *Don't forget!* box during the activity.
* When Student A has finished asking all his/her questions, Student B completes his/her worksheet in the same way. Encourage students to include more details in their answers if possible (e.g. *Yes, he does. He speaks English and French.*).
* **Optional stage:** Students write sentences using the information they have on the worksheet. For example: *Claudia is Paolo's sister. She doesn't watch sport on TV but she uses the Internet every day.*
* Finally, students can share the most interesting things they have found out about the person with the whole class.

## 7A  A footballer's day

Present Simple with *he*; daily routine vocabulary

***You will need:*** *one copy of Worksheet A and one copy of Worksheet B per pair of students*

- Pre-teach the following vocabulary items: *toast; pasta; a football match; a stadium.*
- Divide the class into two groups, A and B. Give a copy of Worksheet A to each student in group A, and a copy of Worksheet B to each student in group B.
- Students work in pairs or small groups with people **with the same worksheet**, and write down the questions they need to ask to complete the gaps on their worksheet (see **Key**). For example, students with Worksheet A will need to write: *What time does he get up?* for question 1, and students with Worksheet B should write: *What time does he have breakfast?* for question a.
- Pair one student with Worksheet A with another student with Worksheet B. **Students are not allowed to look at each other's worksheets.** They must ask their new partners the questions they have prepared and fill in the gaps on their worksheets. Remind students of the question: *How do you spell it?* before they begin.
- When the students have asked all their questions, they can look at each other's worksheets and compare answers and spelling.

## 7B  Adverb partners

Adverbs of frequency

***You will need:*** *one copy of Worksheet A or Worksheet B per student*

- Divide the class into pairs. If possible put students with someone they don't usually work with or don't know very well.
- Give one student in each pair a copy of Worksheet A and the other student a copy of Worksheet B. Each student should write their partner's name in the space at the top of the worksheet. **Students are not allowed to look at their partner's worksheets.**
- Students work individually and choose the word or phrase in italics that they think is true for their partner. Students are not allowed to ask their partners any questions at this stage of the activity.
- Students then take it in turns to tell their partner what they have written. For example, Student A might say: *'You always get up before ten o'clock.'* Student B then tells Student A if this statement is true or not. If the statement is not true, Student B should try to explain why. For example: *'No, that's false. I usually get up at eleven.'*
- For each statement students get right they put a tick in the second column on the worksheet, and for each one they get wrong they put a cross. The student who gets the most statements correct is the winner.

- As a follow-up activity, students can swap partners and tell each other what they found out about their original partners. For example: *Pablo usually watches TV in the evening, and he never reads magazines.*

## 7C  A classroom survey

Time expressions

***You will need:*** *one card per student*

- Give one card to each student. If you have more than twelve students in the class, use duplicate cards. Tell students that they must find out the number of students who do the activity on their card by talking to every member of the class.
- Allow students time to write down the questions with *'you'* they will need to ask the other students. For example, a student with Card A will need to ask: *Do you usually get up before nine o'clock on Saturday?*. (This question is formed by substituting *'Do you'* for *'____ people in the class'*, and can be highlighted on the board if necessary). Go round the class and check that all the students have appropriate questions before continuing.
- Students move around the room and ask the questions they have prepared. They must talk to every student in the class, and should keep a record of the answers on the back of their cards or in a notebook.
- Students write the correct number on their card, then report back to the class. For example, a student with Card A might say: *Five people in the class get up before nine o'clock on Saturday.*

If it is not possible for your students to move around the room, the activity can be adapted as follows:

- Put the students into groups of three or four, and give each group a set of cards. Tell the class to share the cards out equally between them, and allow them time to prepare the questions with *'you'* they need to ask, as above.
- Students take it in turns to ask the rest of the group their questions, and make a note of the answers on the card or in a notebook.
- Each group shares some of their answers with the whole class.

## Vocabulary Booster – Verbs and nouns

***You will need:*** *one copy of the worksheet per student*

- Distribute a copy of the worksheet to each student. Students work in pairs or small groups and do Exercise 1. Students can use monolingual dictionaries if available. Allow time for the class to ask you the meanings of any words before continuing. Also ensure that students can pronounce all the new vocabulary items correctly.
- Students do Exercise 2 individually or in pairs. Check the answers with the whole class (see **Key**).
- Put students into pairs, and tell them to test each other on the collocations in Exercise 2. One student says a noun from the box (e.g. *shopping*), and his/her partner

says the complete expression (e.g. *go shopping*).

- Students work individually and complete the gaps in Exercise 3. Check the answers with the whole class (see **Key**) before allowing students to ask and answer the questions in pairs.
- Students work individually and write six sentences about themselves using adverbs of frequency and time phrases (Exercise 4). Students can then work in pairs and compare their sentences.
- Finally, students can tell the whole class some of the things they have found out about their partners.

## 8A What can you do?

*can* and *can't*

***You will need:*** *one* Find someone who ... *worksheet per student; one role card per student*

- Pre-teach the following items of vocabulary: *to type; to play the piano/guitar; to ski; a vet; a musician.*
- Give each student a copy of the *Find someone who ...* worksheet and allow students time to read the sentences.
- Give each student a role card in random order, and allow them time to read the information on the card. **They must not look at one another's cards.** (If you have more than ten students, the cards can be duplicated without affecting the outcome of the activity.)
- Tell students that they must find one person in the room who can do the things on the *Find someone who ...* worksheet. If necessary, check that students know the questions with 'you' they need to ask for each sentence before they begin (e.g. *Can you cook very well? Can you speak four languages?*).
- Students move around the room and have conversations with one another. When they find someone who can do one of the things on the worksheet, they write their name in the second column.
- Encourage students to introduce themselves and use 'getting to know you' questions to start the conversation (e.g. *My name's ...; What's your name? Where are you from? What's your job?*), rather than just asking the questions required to complete the worksheet.
- Students check their answers in pairs or with the whole class.

## Vocabulary Booster – Parts of the body

***You will need:*** *one copy of the worksheet per student*

- Distribute a copy of the worksheet to each student. Put students into pairs or small groups and allow them to do Exercise 1. Check the answers with the whole group, pointing out the irregular plurals (*foot, tooth*). Ensure that students can pronounce the new vocabulary before continuing. Words that often cause problems are *mouth* /maʊθ/, *teeth* /tiːθ/, *hair* /heə‖her/ and *stomach* /stʌmək/.
- Put students in pairs and allow them to do Exercise 2.
- Students work alone and do Exercise 3a, using a clean

sheet of paper to draw the monster. If necessary, check that students know the meaning of *short*, *long* and *round* before they begin. Set a time limit of five minutes.
- When students have finished their pictures, put them in small groups or allow them to move around the class and compare drawings (Exercise 3b).
- **Optional stage – Picture Dictation:** Each student draws another monster of their own. Students then take it in turns to describe their monster to a partner, who must draw the monster from the description given (but without looking at the original drawing). Finally, students compare pictures to see if their drawings are correct.
- Students do Exercise 4 on their own or in pairs. Set a time limit of three minutes, and check the answers with the whole class (see **Key**).

## 8B Question word quiz

Question words

***You will need:*** *one copy of the worksheet per student*

- Pre-teach the following items of vocabulary: *volleyball, a team, a tiger, Asia, Africa, Europe.*
- Divide the class into teams of three or four, and give a copy of the worksheet to each student. Allow them time to read the instructions, and use the example to check they have understood what to do. Tell students that they will need to use some of the question words more than once.
- Students do the quiz in their teams. Set a time limit of ten minutes.
- Check the answers with the whole class (see **Key**). Students get one point for each correct question word, and two points for each correct answer. The team with the most points are the winners.

## 9A Adjective dominoes

Adjectives and nouns

***You will need:*** *one set of dominoes per group of three students*

- Students work in groups of three. Give one set of dominoes to each group, and ask them to share them out equally.
- One student places a domino in front of them, and the other student must place one of his/her dominoes at either end of the first domino so that the adjective and noun match. Students then take it in turns to put down their dominoes at either end of the domino chain.
- If another student thinks the adjective and noun do not match, he/she can challenge the other student. If the students cannot agree, the teacher adjudicates. If the adjective and noun do not match, the student must take back the domino and miss a turn.
- If a student cannot make a matching adjective–noun combination, the turn passes to the next student.
- The game continues until one student has used all his/her dominoes, or until no student can make a correct

match. The student who finishes first, or has the fewest dominoes remaining, is the winner.

## 9B  Where were you?

*was* and *were*

*You will need: one copy of the worksheet per student*

- Pre-teach the following vocabulary items: *yesterday, last (Sunday), your first (teacher)*.
- Distribute a copy of the worksheet to each student. Students work individually and write their answers in the boxes (Exercise 1). Make sure they write their answers in **random order**, and encourage them to answer all the questions if possible. They should write names, single words or short phrases, **not** complete sentences. Demonstrate this on the board if necessary.
- Put students into pairs and tell them to swap worksheets. Students work individually and write *yes/no* questions for each of the words or phrases in the boxes on their partner's worksheet (Exercise 2). Check that students have understood the instructions and examples, and refer them to the *Don't forget!* box while they are working. **Students must not speak to their partners at this stage of the activity.**
- Students work in pairs with the same partner and ask each other the questions they have prepared. Encourage students to use the short answers in the *Don't forget!* box when answering questions.
- When a student gets a positive answer to a question, he/she should put a cross through the relevant box. Students must continue asking *yes/no* questions until all the words or phrases in the boxes have been crossed out.
- At the end of the activity, students report back to the class on the most interesting things they found out about their partner.

## Vocabulary Booster – Describing people

*You will need: one copy of the worksheet per student*

- Give each student a copy of the worksheet. Students work in pairs or small groups and do Exercise 1. Check the answers with the whole class (see **Key**). Ensure that students can pronounce all the new vocabulary before continuing. It is also useful to point out to students that we use *be* with adjectives (e.g. *tall*), and **have** with nouns (e.g. *a beard*) and adjective + noun (e.g. *short hair*).
- Students do Exercise 2 individually. Check the answers with the whole class (see **Key**). Use this opportunity to teach: *She has brown/blue/green eyes.*
- Students do Exercise 3 individually before reading out their description to the whole class. If you have a large class, consider dividing the students into smaller groups for the second stage of this exercise.
- Tell students to write the names of three people they know well (either family members or friends) in the boxes (Exercise 4). Allow students a few minutes to think how to describe these people using the language in the *Don't*

*forget!* box and from the worksheet.
- Students work in pairs and take it in turns to describe the people whose names they have written in the boxes.
- **Follow-up activity:** Students find a photograph of a person (either someone they know or a person from a newspaper or a magazine). The students stick the picture on a piece of paper and write a description. These can be displayed around the classroom in the next lesson.

## 10A  Past Simple quiz

Past Simple (statements)

*You will need: one copy of the worksheet per student*

- Pre-teach the following vocabulary items: *to die; a war; a GameBoy; wives; a king; the moon.* (A GameBoy is a handheld computer games console.)
- Divide the class into teams of three or four, and give a copy of the worksheet to each student. Allow them time to read the instructions, and use the example to check they have understood what to do.
- Allow students to do the quiz in their teams. Set a time limit of ten minutes.
- Check the answers with the whole class (see **Key**). Students get one point for each correct past tense and two points for each correct answer. The team with the most points are the winners. The maximum score is 34 points.

## 10B  Ten things about me

Past Simple (statements)

*You will need: one copy of the worksheet per student*

- Give a copy of the worksheet to each student. Students work individually and write their answers in the circles. Make sure they write their answers in **random order**, and encourage them to answer all the questions if possible. They should write names, single words or short phrases, **not** complete sentences. Demonstrate this on the board if necessary.
- Students work in pairs and swap worksheets with their partner. Students must try to work out why their partner has written the items on their worksheet, and the partner should say if they are right or wrong. For example: Student A has written *1994*. Student B: *I think you started school in 1994.* Student A: *No, that's wrong.* Student A: *You met your best friend in 1994.* Student B. *Yes, that's right.* If necessary, write the responses on the board before they begin.
- At the end of the activity, students report back to the class on the most interesting things they found out about their partner.

## 10C  Past Simple bingo

Irregular and regular past tenses

*You will need: at least one* Bingo Card *per student*

- Give one *Bingo Card* to each student, and allow them a

few moments to check the past tenses on their cards. If you have more than eight students, distribute duplicate cards.

- Sit or stand in front of the class with a copy of the *Master Bingo Card*. Call out the **infinitives** on the card in any order, and cross them off the card at the same time.
- If a student has the corresponding past tense on his/her card, he/she should cross it out. The first student who crosses out *all* the verbs on his/her card should shout 'Bingo', and is the winner. (Alternatively, students can shout 'Bingo' if they get one horizontal line on their card.) The student's card can be checked against the Master Bingo Card if necessary.
- To repeat the activity, distribute new cards to the students and play again.

## Vocabulary Booster – Irregular verbs

***You will need:*** *one copy of the worksheet per student*

- Give a copy of the worksheet to each student. Put the students in pairs and allow them time to do Exercise 1a. Check any words they don't understand with the whole class before students do Exercise 1b with their partner.
- Students work individually and do Exercise 2. Check the answers with the whole class (see **Key**). Ensure that students can pronounce all the Past Simple forms correctly before continuing. Words that students often have difficulty with are *saw* /sɔː/, *read* /red/ and *bought* /bɔːt/.
- Students do Exercise 3 individually before comparing answers in pairs. Check the answers with the whole class (see **Key**).
- Put students into new pairs and allow them to do Exercise 4. You can also write the other irregular past tenses from Module 10 on the board and tell the class to include them in the activity.

## 10D The date game

Dates, months and years

***You will need:*** *one copy of both sets of cards per three students*

- Before class cut out the two sets of cards, ensuring that you keep the cards for Game 1 and Game 2 **separate**.
- Divide the class into groups of three and distribute the cards for **Game 1**. Give the first student Card A, the second student Card B, and the third student Card C. If you have extra students, put two students together so that they are working with one card. Check students understand that there are both dates and years on the cards.
- Students must listen to the dates/years their partners say, and find the *same* date/year in the HEAR column on their card. They must then say the corresponding date/year in the SAY column for the other students to recognise.
- The student with 'start' on his/her card begins by saying

the date indicated. The turn then passes from student to student until they reach the 'finish' square. Students can tick off the numbers on their cards if they wish.

- If necessary, demonstrate the activity to the whole class before students begin working in their groups.
- When the students have finished, distribute the cards for **Game 2** and allow the groups to repeat the activity with the new cards. Alternatively, this second set of cards can be used for revision later in the course.

## 11A Collocation pelmanism

Verb/noun collocations

***You will need:*** *one set of cards per group of three students*

- Put students into groups of three. Give each group a set of cards and tell them to spread them out in front of them **face down**. Students should put the small cards on the left and the big cards on the right. Shuffle the cards before the class. (All the collocations are taken from Focus 1, Module 11 in the *Students' Book*, or from earlier modules).
- Students take it in turns to turn over one small card and one big card. If the words on both cards go together, the student keeps the cards as a 'trick' and has another turn. If the cards do not match, the student must put them back **in exactly the same place**, and the turn passes to the next student. If students cannot agree whether cards match or not, the teacher adjudicates.
- The activity continues until all the cards are matched up. The student with the most tricks is the winner.
- If one group finishes early, they can test each other on the collocations on the cards.

## 11B Did you or didn't you?

Past Simple (*yes/no* questions)

***You will need:*** *one copy of the worksheet per student*

- Give a copy of the worksheet to each student. Tell the class that they must find one student who did each activity on the worksheet and write his/her name at the beginning of the sentence.
- Students work alone or in pairs and write down the questions they must ask, using '*you*' as the subject for each question, as in the example. Check that all the students have the correct questions before continuing.
- Students move around the room asking each other the questions they have prepared. Remind students to use *Yes, I did./No, I didn't.* when answering.
- When a student gets a positive answer, he/she should write the other student's name along the line at the beginning of the sentence. He/She should then move on and talk to another student. **Students only need to collect one name for each activity**, but they should try to collect as many different names as possible.
- If you have a strong class, encourage students to ask a follow-up question for each activity before moving on to someone else. For example, students could ask: *What*

*did you see?/Where did you go?* as follow-up questions for 1.

- If it is not possible for your students to move around the room, students should ask as many people as possible sitting close to them.
- Students work in pairs or small groups and tell each other what they have found out about their classmates. Finally, students can share the most interesting things they have found out with the whole class.

# 11C Madonna's life story

Past Simple (*Wh-* questions)

***You will need:*** *one copy of Worksheet A or Worksheet B per student.*

- Ask the class what they know about Madonna, and write their ideas on the board.
- Pre-teach the following vocabulary items: *to die; a hit (record); a model; to get divorced; a party.*
- Divide the class into two groups, A and B. Give a copy of Worksheet A to each student in group A and a copy of Worksheet B to each student in group B. Allow students time to read their worksheets and ask any questions about the vocabulary.
- Students work in pairs or groups with people who have **the same worksheet** and write down the questions in the Past Simple they will need to ask to complete their version of the text.
- Rearrange the class so that each student with Worksheet A is working with a student with Worksheet B. **Students are not allowed to look at each other's worksheets.** Students take it in turns to ask the questions they have prepared. Student A must ask the first question (i.e. Question 1 on his/her worksheet.) They should write the answers in the spaces on their worksheet.
- When they have finished they can look at each other's worksheets and check their answers and spelling.
- As a follow-up activity, students can see how much their partner remembers about the person by turning over the worksheets and asking their questions again.

# 11D Past Simple snakes and ladders

Past Simple review

***You will need:*** *one* Snakes and Ladders *board per group of three students; one set of Question cards per group; dice and counters*

- Put students into groups of three, and give each group a *Snakes and Ladders* board, a set of Question cards (shuffled, **face down**), counters and dice.
- Students take it in turns to throw the dice. When they land on a square with a question mark on it, they must take a Question Card from the top of the pile. The student places it down next to the board so all the students can see it, then must answer the question. If the student answers the whole question correctly, he/she stays on the square and the next student takes his/her turn.

- If another player thinks the student's answer is wrong, he/she can challenge him/her. If they cannot agree, the teacher adjudicates (see **Key**).
- If a student lands at the foot of a ladder, he/she must answer the question correctly *before* he/she is allowed to go up it. If a student lands on the head of a snake, he/she must always slide down the snake to its tail.
- The game continues until one student reaches the *Finish* square (or until the group runs out of Question cards).
- At the end of the game students can discuss the cards they got wrong, or go through the question cards they didn't answer.

## Vocabulary Booster – The Weather

***You will need:*** *one copy of the worksheet per student*

- Give a copy of the worksheet to each student, and ask them to do Exercise 1 in pairs or small groups. Check the answers with the whole class. Point out that we use *be* with weather adjectives, and check they can pronounce all the new vocabulary items before continuing.
- Check that students understand and can pronounce the question: *What's the weather like?* before allowing them to do Exercise 2 in pairs. Also point out that *like* is used in the question, but not the answer.
- Students work individually and complete the sentences in Exercise 3 for the weather in their countries. If your class are all from the **same country**, allow the students to check their answers together in pairs or small groups. If your students are from **different countries**, put students into pairs or small groups. They should ask their partner(s) about the weather in different months of the year. For example: *What's the weather like in July? In Portugal it's usually hot and dry.*
- Check that students can pronounce the Past Simple question: *What was the weather like?* before allowing them to do Exercise 4 in pairs or small groups.

# 12A Shopping crossword

Things you buy

***You will need:*** *a copy of Crossword A and Crossword B per pair of students*

- Pre-teach the following vocabulary items: *socks, film, CD player, motorbike, bicycle.* All the other words in the crossword are taken from Module 12 or earlier modules of the *Students' Book.*
- Divide the class into two groups, A and B. Give a copy of Crossword A to each student in group A, and a copy of Crossword B to each student in group B. Check that students understand how to refer to words in a crossword, i.e. *3 across* and *7 down.*
- Firstly students should work together in their separate groups to check they know all the meanings of the words on their worksheet.
- Put students into pairs so that one student with Crossword A and one student with Crossword B are working together. **They are not allowed to look at each**

other's crossword.

- Students take it in turns to give clues for the words that appear on their half of the crossword. These clues can be either verbal, visual or through mime, but students are not allowed to translate any words, give letters as clues, or use their own language during the activity.
- The other student must guess the words and write them on his/her own crossword. Remind students of the question: *How do you spell it?* before they begin.
- The activity continues until both students have a completed version of the crossword.

## Vocabulary Booster – Clothes

*You will need: one copy of the worksheet per student*

- Give a copy of the worksheet to each student, and allow them to do Exercise 1 in pairs or small groups. Check the answers with the whole class (see **Key**), and check that students know the words for the other clothes in the picture.
- Ensure that students can pronounce all the new words before continuing. Also point out that *trousers* and *jeans* are always plural, and *boots*, *shoes* and *trainers* are usually plural. Note also that *a suit* can be used for women as well as men.
- Students do Exercise 2 individually before checking their sentences in pairs or with the whole class. Check that students understand the meaning of *He's wearing* ... in the example before they begin. (We suggest not teaching this as the Present Continuous, but as a lexical phrase.)
- Put students into pairs or small groups and allow them to do Exercise 3. Teach *bought* via the examples and remind students of the English words for colours before they begin.
- Allow students a minute or two 'thinking time' before doing Exercise 4 in groups of three or four. When they have finished students can report back to the whole class on interesting clothes they talked about.
- Put students into different pairs for Exercise 5. Student A should describe the clothes that somebody in the class is wearing, but without mentioning the person's name. Student B must guess which person his/her partner is describing. Students then continue taking it in turns to describe their classmates. (It is often helpful to ask Student B to close his/her eyes while Student A is talking, so that he/she can't see who Student A is looking at!)

## 12B My partner's future

*going to*

*You will need: one copy of Worksheet A or Worksheet B per student*

- Divide the class into pairs. If possible, put students with someone they don't usually work with or don't know very well.
- Give one student in each pair Worksheet A and the other student Worksheet B. Each student should write their partner's name in the space at the top of the worksheet.

**Students are not allowed to look at their partner's worksheets.**

- Students work individually and decide if their partner is going to do the activities listed on their worksheet by circling *is* or *isn't* in each sentence. Students are not allowed to ask their partners any questions at this stage of the activity.
- Check that students can make questions with 'you' for each of the sentences on the worksheets. For example, students with Worksheet A should ask: *Are you going to get up early tomorrow morning?* for No 1. If necessary write some examples on the board before continuing.
- Students then take it in turns to ask their partner if he/she is going to do the activities on their worksheet. For each statement students have guessed right they put a tick in the second column on the worksheet, and for each one they get wrong they put a cross. The student in the pair who gets the most answers correct is the winner.
- As a follow-up activity students can work with a new partner and tell him/her about the person they have just been talking to. For example: *I talked to Yoko. She's going to meet friends this evening, and she isn't going to get up early tomorrow.*

## 12C Revision board game

All the language in the *Students' Book*

*You will need: one copy of the board and one set of Question Cards per group of three or four students; dice and counters*

- Put students into groups of three or four. Give each group a copy of the board, a set of *Question Cards* (shuffled), dice and counters. Tell students to put the *Question Cards* face down in a pile on the appropriate space on the board, and their counters on the *Start* square.
- Students take it in turns to throw a number. If Student A lands on a square with a question mark on it, he/she must pick up a *Question Card*. He/She should place the card down so that all the students can read it, then try to answer the question.
- If the other students think that the answer is correct, Student A stays on the square. If the answer is not correct, or Student A cannot answer the question, he/she should move back to his/her original square. If the students cannot agree, the teacher adjudicates (see **Key**).
- If a student lands on a square with a speech bubble on it, he/she must talk about that topic for fifteen seconds without stopping. (If one of the students in each group has a watch with a second hand, make him/her the timekeeper). If the student cannot think of anything to say, or stops talking before the fifteen seconds are up, he/she must return to his/her original square.
- The first student to reach the *Finish* square is the winner. Groups who finish first can go through the *Question Cards* and check their answers.

# Classroom language

## Questions in the classroom

**1** Match these questions with the pictures.

a  Can you write it on the board, please?

b  How do you pronounce this word?

c  How do you say *Merhaba* in English?

d  Can you say that again, please?

e  How do you spell *today*?

f  What does *bag* mean?

**2** Practise the dialogues in pairs.

**3** Ask your teacher a question!

## 1A What's your job?

Names and jobs with *I* and *you*

| Pat | Sam | Jo |
|---|---|---|
| 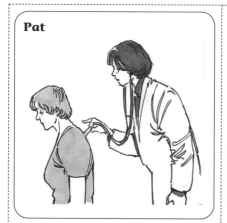 |  |  |
| **Chris** | **Frankie** | **Alex** |
|  |  |  |
| **Tim** | **Sally** | **Brad** |
|  |  |  |
| **Karen** | **Mark** | **Rebecca** |
|  |  |  |

PHOTOCOPIABLE

## Vocabulary Booster – Jobs

**1** Match the jobs with the pictures.

| | | | |
|---|---|---|---|
| a secretary | a nurse | a taxi driver | a journalist |
| a travel agent | a lawyer | a musician | a salesperson |

**2** Point at the pictures. Ask your partner.

What's his job?

He's a lawyer.

What's her job?

She's a musician.

**3** Put the jobs in Exercise 1 in the crossword.

## 1B  What's his surname?

Names and jobs with *he* and *she*; spelling

**Time for a break!**

 **PHOTOCOPIABLE**

## Worksheet A

**Name:** Erika Schmitt
**Job:** ..............................

**Name:** Fiona .......................
**Job:** teacher

**Name:** Julius Soyinka
**Job:** ..............................

**Name:** .............. ..............
**Job:** businessman

**Name:** ..................... Zampa
**Job:** actress

**Name:** Abdul Razzaq
**Job:** ..............................

## Worksheet B

**Name:** .............. ..............
**Job:** doctor

**Name:** Fiona Matthews
**Job:** ..............................

**Name:** Julius .......................
**Job:** engineer

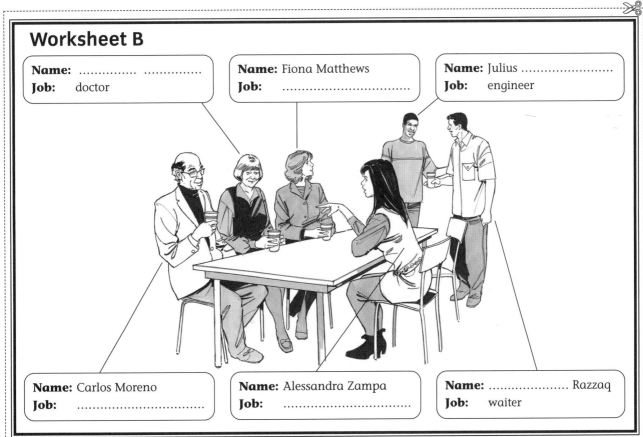

**Name:** Carlos Moreno
**Job:** ..............................

**Name:** Alessandra Zampa
**Job:** ..............................

**Name:** ..................... Razzaq
**Job:** waiter

© Pearson Education Limited 2002

## 2A Where are you from?

Countries; *to be* with *I* and *you*

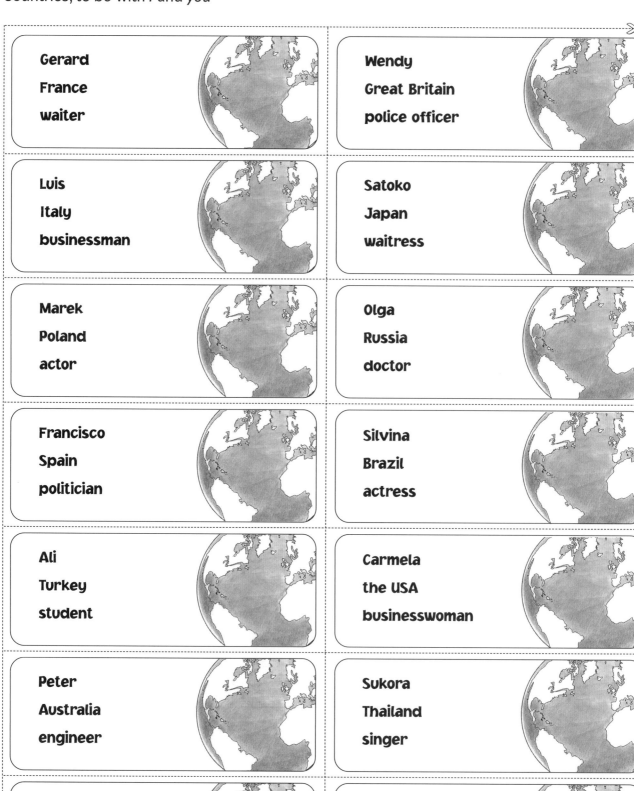

| | |
|---|---|
| **Gerard** <br> **France** <br> **waiter** | **Wendy** <br> **Great Britain** <br> **police officer** |
| **Luis** <br> **Italy** <br> **businessman** | **Satoko** <br> **Japan** <br> **waitress** |
| **Marek** <br> **Poland** <br> **actor** | **Olga** <br> **Russia** <br> **doctor** |
| **Francisco** <br> **Spain** <br> **politician** | **Silvina** <br> **Brazil** <br> **actress** |
| **Ali** <br> **Turkey** <br> **student** | **Carmela** <br> **the USA** <br> **businesswoman** |
| **Peter** <br> **Australia** <br> **engineer** | **Sukora** <br> **Thailand** <br> **singer** |
| **Karl** <br> **Germany** <br> **footballer** | **Mufana** <br> **Egypt** <br> **teacher** |

# Vocabulary Booster – Nationalities

**1** Write the country for the nationality.

| Country | Nationality | Country | Nationality |
|---|---|---|---|
| 1 *the USA* | American | 9 ................ | Polish |
| 2 ................ | British | 10 ................ | Turkish |
| 3 ................ | Japanese | 11 ................ | German |
| 4 ................ | French | 12 ................ | Australian |
| 5 ................ | Russian | 13 ................ | Egyptian |
| 6 ................ | Italian | 14 ................ | Thai |
| 7 ................ | Spanish | 15 ................ | Chinese |
| 8 ................ | Brazilian | 16 ................ | English |

**2** Put the **nationalities** in the correct box below.

| -n, -an, -ian | -ish | -ese | other |
|---|---|---|---|
| American | British | Japanese | French |
| | | | |

**3** Test your partner, like this:

Turkey

Turkish.

**4** Work with a partner. Imagine you're from a **different** country. Ask questions, like this:

Are you Turkish?

No, I'm not.

Are you German?

Yes, I am!

**5** Look at this example. Draw **your** country. What are the countries around it? How do you say the nationalities?

## 2B Bingo!

Numbers 1–100

### Bingo Card A

| 1 | 6 | 9 | 14 | 16 |
|----|----|----|----|----|
| 24 | 25 | 29 | 30 | 37 |
| 43 | 47 | 51 | 54 | 58 |
| 68 | 69 | 70 | 74 | 80 |
| 81 | 85 | 88 | 91 | 98 |

### Bingo Card B

| 3 | 4 | 9 | 12 | 19 |
|----|----|----|----|----|
| 23 | 28 | 29 | 33 | 40 |
| 41 | 45 | 52 | 57 | 59 |
| 61 | 64 | 67 | 70 | 75 |
| 83 | 87 | 91 | 99 | 100 |

### Bingo Card C

| 5 | 8 | 10 | 15 | 20 |
|----|----|----|----|----|
| 24 | 27 | 31 | 34 | 39 |
| 41 | 47 | 52 | 54 | 60 |
| 62 | 67 | 68 | 71 | 74 |
| 82 | 86 | 92 | 94 | 99 |

### Bingo Card D

| 1 | 7 | 13 | 16 | 18 |
|----|----|----|----|----|
| 22 | 25 | 32 | 36 | 40 |
| 42 | 46 | 48 | 55 | 57 |
| 65 | 69 | 71 | 75 | 77 |
| 84 | 88 | 90 | 92 | 95 |

### Bingo Card E

| 8 | 5 | 11 | 12 | 15 |
|----|----|----|----|----|
| 23 | 27 | 32 | 38 | 39 |
| 44 | 48 | 53 | 56 | 59 |
| 61 | 65 | 72 | 79 | 80 |
| 84 | 87 | 93 | 95 | 98 |

### Bingo Card F

| 2 | 4 | 10 | 17 | 18 |
|----|----|----|----|----|
| 22 | 28 | 31 | 35 | 37 |
| 45 | 42 | 50 | 56 | 60 |
| 63 | 64 | 72 | 76 | 78 |
| 81 | 85 | 89 | 93 | 96 |

### Bingo Card G

| 2 | 3 | 11 | 14 | 20 |
|----|----|----|----|----|
| 21 | 26 | 33 | 35 | 38 |
| 44 | 46 | 49 | 50 | 53 |
| 62 | 66 | 73 | 76 | 78 |
| 83 | 86 | 90 | 94 | 97 |

### Bingo Card H

| 6 | 7 | 13 | 17 | 19 |
|----|----|----|----|----|
| 21 | 26 | 30 | 34 | 36 |
| 43 | 49 | 51 | 55 | 58 |
| 63 | 66 | 73 | 77 | 79 |
| 82 | 89 | 96 | 97 | 100 |

### MASTER BINGO CARD

| 1 | 2 | 3 | 4 | 5 | 6 | 7 | 8 | 9 | 10 |
|----|----|----|----|----|----|----|----|----|----|
| 11 | 12 | 13 | 14 | 15 | 16 | 17 | 18 | 19 | 20 |
| 21 | 22 | 23 | 24 | 25 | 26 | 27 | 28 | 29 | 30 |
| 31 | 32 | 33 | 34 | 35 | 36 | 37 | 38 | 39 | 40 |
| 41 | 42 | 43 | 44 | 45 | 46 | 47 | 48 | 49 | 50 |
| 51 | 52 | 53 | 54 | 55 | 56 | 57 | 58 | 59 | 60 |
| 61 | 62 | 63 | 64 | 65 | 66 | 67 | 68 | 69 | 70 |
| 71 | 72 | 73 | 74 | 75 | 76 | 77 | 78 | 79 | 80 |
| 81 | 82 | 83 | 84 | 85 | 86 | 87 | 88 | 89 | 90 |
| 91 | 92 | 93 | 94 | 95 | 96 | 97 | 98 | 99 | 100 |

**PHOTOCOPIABLE**

## 2C The numbers game

Numbers 1–100

| GAME 1 CARD A | |
|---|---|
| **HEAR** | **SAY** |
| 41 | 22 |
| 20 | 81 |
| 38 | 14 |
| **START ➡** | 3 |
| 100 | 45 |
| 69 | 33 |
| 54 | 75 |
| 1 | 26 |

| GAME 1 CARD B | |
|---|---|
| **HEAR** | **SAY** |
| 22 | 54 |
| 62 | 87 |
| 93 | 70 |
| 56 | 9 |
| 3 | 29 |
| 81 | **FINISH!** |
| 26 | 38 |
| 17 | 69 |

| GAME 1 CARD C | |
|---|---|
| **HEAR** | **SAY** |
| 45 | 62 |
| 70 | 41 |
| 33 | 56 |
| 29 | 100 |
| 14 | 93 |
| 9 | 20 |
| 87 | 1 |
| 75 | 17 |

| GAME 2 CARD A | |
|---|---|
| **HEAR** | **SAY** |
| 59 | 30 |
| 32 | 64 |
| 16 | 47 |
| 67 | 8 |
| 28 | 35 |
| 72 | 6 |
| 95 | 11 |
| 19 | 24 |

| GAME 2 CARD B | |
|---|---|
| **HEAR** | **SAY** |
| 64 | 46 |
| 78 | 32 |
| 30 | 91 |
| **START ➡** | 53 |
| 35 | 67 |
| 13 | 72 |
| 47 | 60 |
| 90 | 19 |

| GAME 2 CARD C | |
|---|---|
| **HEAR** | **SAY** |
| 24 | 59 |
| 8 | **FINISH!** |
| 60 | 95 |
| 6 | 28 |
| 11 | 78 |
| 53 | 16 |
| 91 | 13 |
| 46 | 90 |

## 2D    What's your address?

Personal information questions with *you* (and *he/she*)

---

| | |
|---|---|
| **Name:** | Janet Simmons |
| **Age:** | 26 |
| **Single / married:** | single |
| **Address:** | 94 Collins Street |
| | Melbourne |
| | Victoria 3001 |
| | Australia |
| **Home phone number:** | 03 9617 4485 |
| **Work phone number:** | 03 4556 2097 |
| **Job:** | teacher |

| | |
|---|---|
| **Name:** | Greg Alexander |
| **Age:** | 19 |
| **Single / married:** | married |
| **Address:** | 23 Bush Street |
| | San Francisco |
| | California 94108 |
| | USA |
| **Home phone number:** | 415 786 4320 |
| **Work phone number:** | 415 894 7703 |
| **Job:** | waiter |

| | |
|---|---|
| **Name:** | Carol Bailey |
| **Age:** | 22 |
| **Single / married:** | single |
| **Address:** | 22, Deacon Road |
| | Liverpool |
| | L4 7TQ |
| | England |
| **Home phone number:** | 0151 268 9743 |
| **Work phone number:** | 0151 343 7769 |
| **Job:** | student |

| | |
|---|---|
| **Name:** | Andrew Robertson |
| **Age:** | 33 |
| **Single / married:** | married |
| **Address:** | 56 Phillip Street |
| | Sydney |
| | NSW 1223 |
| | Australia |
| **Home phone number:** | 02 9252 6670 |
| **Work phone number:** | 02 5319 6778 |
| **Job:** | actor |

| | |
|---|---|
| **Name:** | Suzannah Atkins |
| **Age:** | 43 |
| **Single / married:** | married |
| **Address:** | 11, Franks Street |
| | Austin |
| | Texas 45701 |
| | USA |
| **Home phone number:** | 614 542 45701 |
| **Work phone number:** | 614 322 98602 |
| **Job:** | businesswoman |

| | |
|---|---|
| **Name:** | Tom Arnold |
| **Age:** | 26 |
| **Single / married:** | single |
| **Address:** | 69, Mallett Road |
| | Maidstone |
| | ME6 2JP |
| | England |
| **Home phone number:** | 01622 649382 |
| **Work phone number:** | 020 7491 3346 |
| **Job:** | engineer |

| | |
|---|---|
| First Name: | ............................... |
| Surname: | ............................... |
| Age: | ............................... |
| Single/married: | ............................... |
| Address: | ............................... |
| | ............................... |
| Home phone number: | ............................... |
| Work phone number: | ............................... |
| Job: | ............................... |

| | |
|---|---|
| First Name: | ............................... |
| Surname: | ............................... |
| Age: | ............................... |
| Single/married: | ............................... |
| Address: | ............................... |
| | ............................... |
| Home phone number: | ............................... |
| Work phone number: | ............................... |
| Job: | ............................... |

## 3A  What are their names?

*be* with plural forms

---

### Worksheet A

**1** Read about the four people.

**A**

Hello. Our names are Miguel and Carola, and we're from Granada, in Spain. It's a beautiful city, and it's very hot. I'm a businessman, and Carola's an English teacher. We're 25 years old, and we're married. Our address is 34, Camino de Ronda and our phone number is 958 65 43 27. See you!

**B**

Hi! Our names are a) ........................ and ........................ . We're from b) ........................ , in ........................ . It's a big city, and it's very expensive. I'm c) ........................ , and George is ............ . He's d) ............ years old and I'm ............ , and e) *we're /we aren't* married. Our address is f) .............. ............... .............., and our phone number is g) ........................ . Have a nice day!

**2** Complete the questions using *'s*, *are*, *they* and *their*.

a  What .............. .............. names?
b  Where .............. .............. from?
c  What .............. .............. jobs?
d  How old .............. .............. ?
e  .............. .............. married?
f  What .............. .............. address?
g  What .............. .............. phone number?

**3** Ask your partner the questions and complete text B.

---

## Worksheet B

**1** Read about the four people.

A

Hi! Our names are Hilary and George. We're from San Francisco, in the USA. It's a big city, and it's very expensive. I'm a doctor, and George is an engineer. He's 54 years old and I'm 50, and we're married. Our address is 1627, Sea Drive, San Francisco, and our phone number is 0044 456 7612. Have a nice day!

B

Hello. Our names are a) ........................ and ........................ , and we're from b) ........................ , in ........................ . It's a beautiful city, and it's very hot. I'm c) ........................ , and Carola's ............ . We're d) ............ years old, and e) *we're / we aren't* married. Our address is f) .............. .............. .............. and our phone number is g) ........................ . See you!

**2** Complete the questions using *'s*, *are*, *they* and *their*.

a   What .............. .............. names?
b   Where .............. .............. from?
c   What .............. .............. jobs?
d   How old .............. .............. ?
e   .............. .............. married?
f   What .............. .............. address?
g   What .............. .............. phone number?

**3** Ask your partner the questions and complete text B.

© Pearson Education Limited 2002

# Vocabulary Booster – Food and drink

**1** Match the words with the pictures.

| | | | | |
|---|---|---|---|---|
| sausages ......... | tomatoes ......... | chicken ......... | potatoes ......... | orange juice ......... |
| chocolate ........ | wine ........ | bananas ......... | beer ......... | apples ......... | tea ........ |

**2** Write the words in the correct boxes.

| meat | vegetables | fruit | drinks | other words |
|---|---|---|---|---|
| *sausages* | | | | |

**3** Look at the picture and test your partner, like this:

What's this?          Orange juice.

What are these?          Potatoes.

**4** Choose four things you like and four things you don't like from the picture. Tell the other students.

I like bananas.          I don't like beer.

## 3B   What's this?

Vocabulary revision: *this, that, these, those*

© Pearson Education Limited 2002     **PHOTOCOPIABLE**

## 4A  Where's the cinema?

Places in a town; prepositions

### Worksheet A

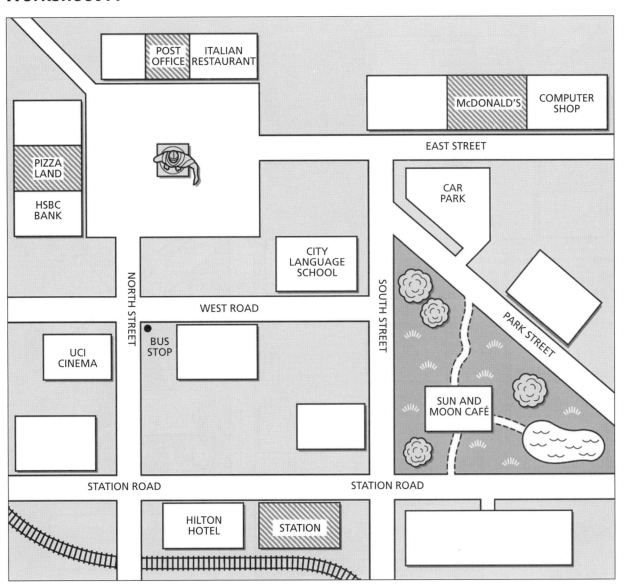

Ask your partner where these places are. Write them on your map.

a   the Pasta Café
b   the ABC Cinema
c   the school
d   the Japanese restaurant
e   the supermarket
f   the Citibank
g   the Ritz Hotel
h   the bookshop

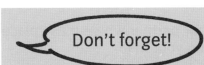

### Don't forget!

Where's (the Pasta Café)?

It's **in** Station Road/East Street.

It's **in** the square/the park.

It's **on the left of** (the post office).

It's **on the right of** (the station).

It's **near** (the bus stop).

# Worksheet B

| | | |
|---|---|---|
| PASTA CAFÉ | POST OFFICE | |

| | | |
|---|---|---|
| CITIBANK | McDONALD'S | |

JAPANESE RESTAURANT

PIZZA LAND

EAST STREET

NORTH STREET

SOUTH STREET

PARK STREET

RITZ HOTEL

WEST ROAD

BUS STOP

ABC CINEMA

BOOKSHOP

SUPERMARKET

STATION ROAD

STATION ROAD

STATION

SCHOOL

Ask your partner where these places are. Write them on your map.

a   the Hilton Hotel
b   the HSBC Bank
c   the Sun and Moon Café
d   the car park
e   the Italian restaurant
f   the UCI Cinema
g   the City Language School
h   the computer shop

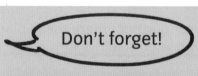

Don't forget!

Where's (the Hilton Hotel)?

It's **in** Station Road/East Street.

It's **in** the square/the park.

It's **on the left of** (the post office).

It's **on the right of** (the station).

It's **near** (the bus stop).

© Pearson Education Limited 2002

## 4B  Vocabulary pelmanism

Vocabulary: places and people

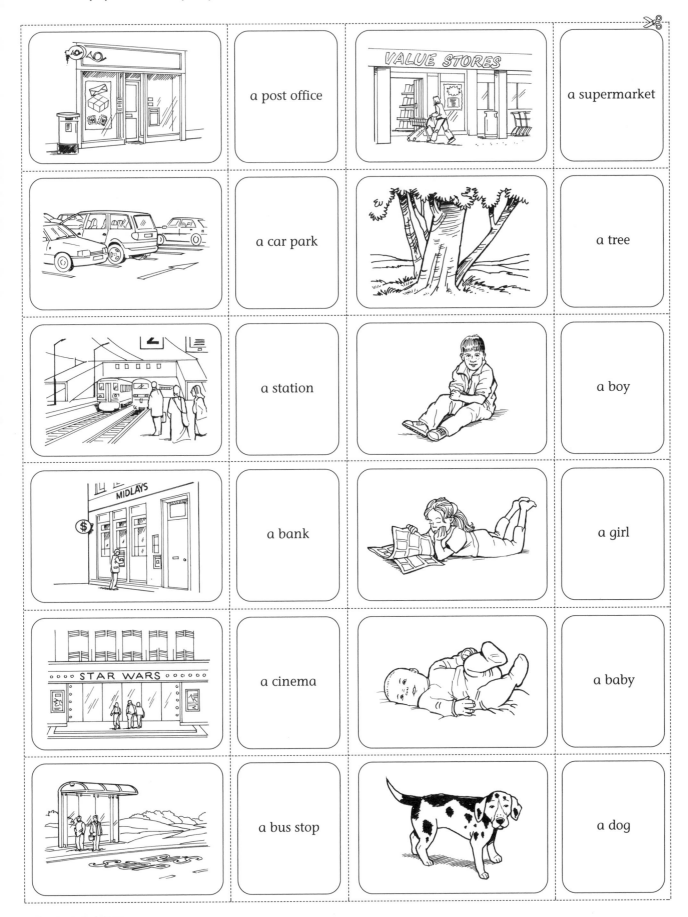

| | | | |
|---|---|---|---|
| | a post office | | a supermarket |
| | a car park | | a tree |
| | a station | | a boy |
| | a bank | | a girl |
| | a cinema | | a baby |
| | a bus stop | | a dog |

## Vocabulary Booster – Places in a town

**1** Match these words with the pictures.

> an airport .........   a bus station .........   a theatre .........   a museum .........
>
> a library .........   a market .........   a football stadium .........   a bookshop .........
>
> a clothes shop .........   a pharmacy .........

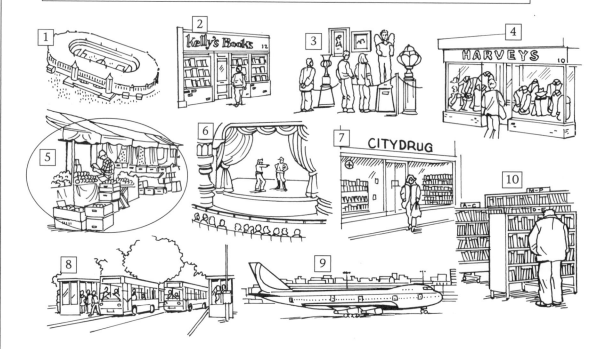

**2** Test your partner, like this:

> What's number 6?    It's a theatre.
>
> What's number 8?    I don't know!

**3** Complete these sentences using words from Exercise 1. Then write two more sentences.

1 There's a/an ..................... near my house.
2 There isn't a/an ..................... in my town/city.
3 There are some good ..................... in my town/city.
4 There aren't any ..................... near my house.
5 There ............................................................. .
6 There ............................................................. .

Compare your sentences with another student.

**4** Imagine you are at one of the places in Exercise 1. Don't say anything! The other students must say where you are.

**4C** **Spot the difference**

Questions with *there is/there are*

## Picture A

**Don't forget!**

Is there a (hotel) in your picture?
Yes, there is. No, there isn't.

Are there any (people in the restaurant)?
Yes, there are.   No, there aren't.

There are some cars in my picture.
There are five people. There's a bus stop.

© Pearson Education Limited 2002

## Picture B

**Don't forget!**

Is there a (hotel) in your picture?
Yes, there is. No, there isn't.

Are there any (people in the restaurant)?
Yes, there are.    No, there aren't.

There are some cars in my picture.
There are five people. There's a bus stop.

## 5A  Bob's family

Relationship vocabulary; possessive 's

**Worksheet A**

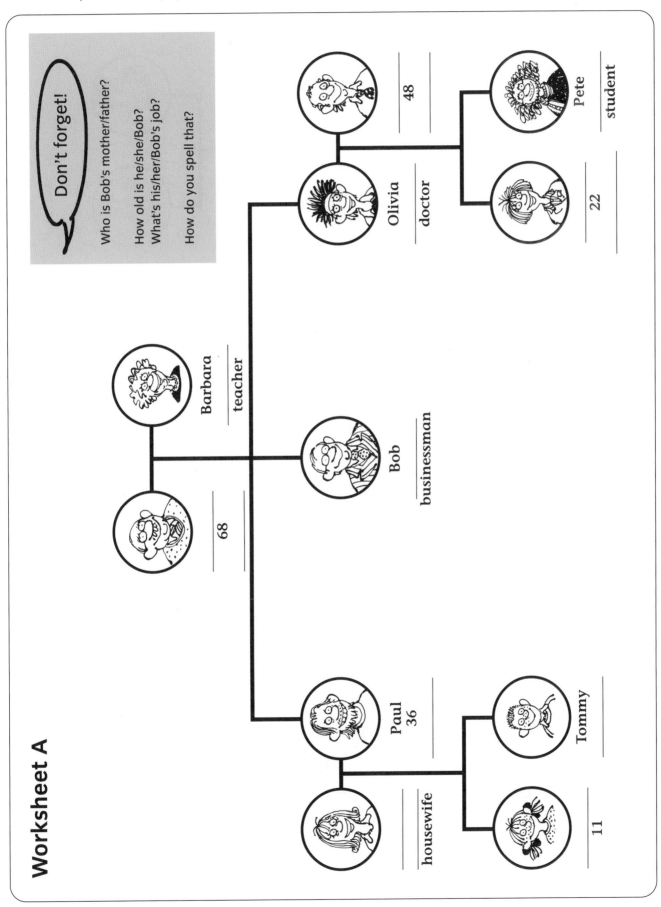

**Don't forget!**

Who is Bob's mother/father?

How old is he/she/Bob?

What's his/her/Bob's job?

How do you spell that?

© Pearson Education Limited 2002  **121**

# Worksheet B

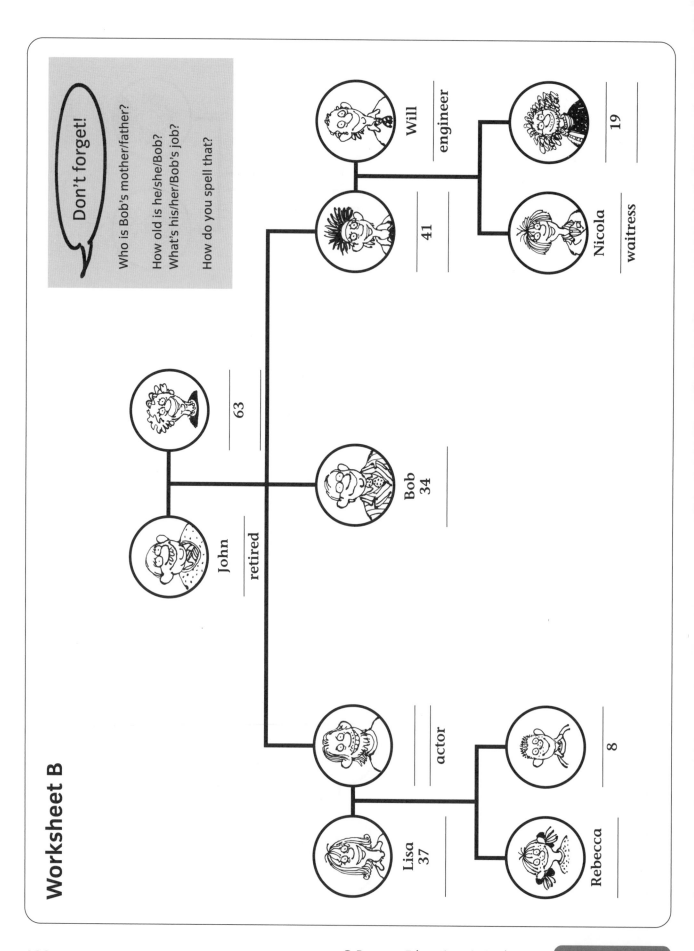

Don't forget!

Who is Bob's mother/father?

How old is he/she/Bob?
What's his/her/Bob's job?

How do you spell that?

Will
engineer

41

19

Nicola
waitress

63

John
retired

Bob
34

actor

8

Lisa
37

Rebecca

## 5B   Present Simple dominoes

Present Simple with *I* and *you*; verb/noun combinations

| | | | |
|---|---|---|---|
| *... computers.* | **Where do ...** | **... you live?** | **I work for ...** |
| **... an American company.** | **Do you have any ...** | ... brothers and sisters? | I study German and Italian in .. |
| *... a language school.* | **I don't live in ...** | ... the centre of the city. | Do you study other ... |
| **... languages?** | **Who do you live ...** | ... with? | Do you live with ... |
| *... your parents?* | **I don't live with my ...** | ... family, I live alone. | **What do you ...** |
| **... study?** | **I live near ...** | ... Cordoba, in Spain. | I don't have a car ... |
| *... or a bicycle.* | **Do you work for ...** | ... a big company? | Do you have a ... |
| **... job?** | **Where do you ...** | ... work? | I have a dog ... |
| *... and two cats.* | **Do you live in a ...** | ... house or a flat? | I don't study ... |
| **... French, I study English.** | **I don't have any sons ...** | ... but I have two daughters. | I work with ... |

© Pearson Education Limited 2002          **123**

# Vocabulary Booster – Rooms in a house

**1** Match these words with the letters on the picture.

| kitchen | bathroom | toilet | living room | hall | balcony | bedroom |

**2** Find these things in the picture. What other things are in the house?

a table ...*4*.....   a chair .........   a shower .........   a sofa .........   a picture .........
a bed .........   a bath .........   a cooker .........   a fridge .........

**3** Look at the picture for one minute.

Student A: close your book.
Student B: ask your partner what is in each room.

What's in the bedroom?      There's a bed, two chairs ...

**4** a  Draw a plan of your house or flat. Draw the items from Exercise 2 on your plan, and any other things you have (a CD player, a computer, a TV, a video ...).

   b  Tell your partner about your house or flat.

In my flat there are three bedrooms.      There's a TV in the kitchen.

We don't have a garden.      We have two bathrooms.

     **PHOTOCOPIABLE**

## 6A Like, love and hate

Present Simple with *you*; likes and dislikes; object pronouns

| | Write your answers here | Name |
|---|---|---|
| A type of food you love. | | |
| A type of food you hate. | | |
| The name of an actor/actress that you like. | | |
| The name of an actor/actress that you don't like. | | |
| A drink you really like. | | |
| A drink you hate. | | |
| An activity (e.g. reading, shopping, dancing) that you like. | | |
| An activity that you don't like. | | |
| The name of a singer/band you really like. | | |
| The name of a singer/band you don't like. | | |

## 6B Pronoun snap

Subject and object pronouns with *like*, *love* and *hate*

**Question cards**

| | | |
|---|---|---|
| Do you like Bruce Willis? | Do you like Michael Jackson? | Do you like George Michael? |
| Do you like Jennifer Lopez? | Do you like Madonna? | Do you like Celine Dion? |
| Do you like meat? | Do you like shopping? | Do you like coffee? |
| Do you like burgers? | Do you like cartoons? | Do you like cats? |
| Do you like cooking? | Do you like Ricky Martin? | Do you like your English lessons? |

**Answer cards**

| | | |
|---|---|---|
| Yes, I like him a lot. | He's okay. | No, I hate him! |
| Yes, she's great. | She's okay. | Yes, I really like her. |
| Yes, I love it. | It's okay. | No, I hate it. |
| Yes, I love them. | They're okay. | No, I hate them. |
| Yes, I like it a lot. | Yes, I really like him. | Yes, they're great! |

# Vocabulary Booster – Sports

**1** Match the words with the pictures.

basketball ...c.....    swimming .........    volleyball .........    cycling .........

jogging .........    tennis .........    golf .........    skiing .........    motor racing .........    boxing .........

**2** Test your partner.

> What's picture c?

> Basketball.

**3** Ask other students about the sports in the pictures, like this:

> Do you like basketball?

> Yes, it's great.

> Do you like swimming?

> No, I don't.

**4** Complete the sentences with words from the box, or your own ideas. Compare your sentences with another student.

a ................. is popular in my country.

b I like watching ................. on TV.

c ................. isn't popular in my country.

d I don't like watching ................. on TV.

e My favourite sport is ................. .

f I also like ................. .

g I really hate .................!

## 6C    Does he or doesn't he?

Present Simple with *does* and *doesn't*

> ### Don't forget!
>
> | | |
> |---|---|
> | **Does (Alex) like …?** | Yes, he/she does. |
> | **Does he/she watch …?** | No, he/she doesn't. |
> | **Does he/she play …?** | I don't know. |

| His/Her name is _____<br>He/She is _____ | ✓, ✗ or ? |
|---|---|
| a (**speak**) / **eat** / **talk** any foreign languages? | |
| b **use** / **watch** / **read** sport on TV? | |
| c **speak** / **like** / **work** shopping? | |
| d **play** / **read** / **use** the Internet? | |
| e **do** / **study** / **read** a lot of books? | |
| f **like** / **go** / **play** cooking? | |
| g **play** / **watch** / **do** computer games? | |
| h **do** / **work** / **read** a newspaper every day? | |
| i **watch** / **play** / **study** TV a lot? | |
| j **study** / **watch** / **eat** meat every day? | |
| k **eat** / **like** / **speak** jazz or opera? | |

© Pearson Education Limited 2002

## 7A  A footballer's day

Present Simple with *he*; daily routine vocabulary

### Worksheet A

My name is Franco Bonelli, and I'm from Italy. I'm a footballer, and I play for Chelsea in the English Premiership. In England, football matches are usually on Saturday. I get up at 1) ............ and I have breakfast at nine. I usually have 2) ..................................... . In the morning I 3) ........................ .............. and read the newspaper. I go to the stadium at about half past eleven, and have lunch at 4) ............ with the other players. We usually have pasta and salad. The match starts at 5) ............ and finishes at about quarter to five. After the match I 6) ..................................... with the other players, and in the evening I usually go to a restaurant with my wife and some friends. When I get home I 7) ..................................... and then I go to bed at about half past eleven. I'm usually very tired, and sleep for ten or eleven hours!

Write questions about Franco's day.

1  What time ............... he ............... ............... ?

2  What ............... he ............... for breakfast?

3  What ............... ............... do ............... ............... morning?

4  What time ............... ............... ............... lunch?

5  What time ............... the match ............... ?

6  What ............... ............... do after the match?

7  What ............... ............... do when he ............... home?

## Worksheet B

My name is Franco Bonelli, and I'm from Italy. I'm a footballer, and I play for Chelsea in the English Premiership. In England, football matches are usually on Saturday. I get up at half past eight, and I have breakfast at a) ............ . I usually have eggs, toast and coffee. In the morning I b) ..................................... and watch TV with my children. I go to the stadium at about c) ............ and have lunch at quarter past twelve with the other players. We usually have d) ..................................... . The match starts at three o'clock, and finishes at e) ............ . After the match I have a drink with the other players, and in the evening I usually f) ..................................... with my wife and some friends. When I get home I watch football on TV and then I go to bed at about g) ............ . I'm usually very tired, and sleep for ten or eleven hours!

Write questions about Franco's day.

a  What time ............... he ............... breakfast?

b  What ............... ............... do ............... ............... morning?

c  What time ............... ............... ............... to the stadium?

d  What ............... ............... have for lunch?

e  What time .............. the match ............... ?

f  What ............... ............... do ............... ............... evening?

g  What time ............... ............... ............... to bed?

## 7B  Adverb partners

Adverbs of frequency

### Worksheet A

Choose the answer in *italics* that you think is correct for your partner. Choose **one** answer for each sentence.

| Partner's name ................................................................ | True or false? |
|---|---|
| 1  He/She *always / usually / sometimes / never* gets up before ten o'clock. | |
| 2  He/She *sometimes listens / doesn't usually listen / never listens* to rock music. | |
| 3  He/She *always / sometimes / never* drinks coffee with his/her breakfast. | |
| 4  He/She *sometimes watches / doesn't usually watch / never watches* cartoons. | |
| 5  He/She *always / usually / sometimes / never* goes to the theatre at the weekend. | |
| 6  He/She *always / usually / sometimes / never* reads a newspaper in the morning. | |
| 7  He/She *sometimes plays / doesn't usually play / never plays* computer games in the evening. | |
| 8  He/She *always / usually / sometimes / never* studies English in the evening. | |

### Worksheet B

Choose the answer in *italics* that you think is correct for your partner. Choose **one** answer for each sentence.

| Partner's name................................................................ | True or false? |
|---|---|
| 1  He/She *always / usually / sometimes / never* goes to bed before half past eleven. | |
| 2  He/She *sometimes listens / doesn't usually listen / never listens* to dance music. | |
| 3  He/She *always / sometimes / never* drinks tea in the afternoon. | |
| 4  He/She *always / usually / sometimes / never* watches TV in the evening. | |
| 5  He/She *always / usually / sometimes / never* goes to a restaurant at the weekend. | |
| 6  He/She *sometimes reads / doesn't usually read / never reads* magazines. | |
| 7  He/She *sometimes watches / doesn't usually watch / never watches* videos at the weekend. | |
| 8  He/She *always / usually / sometimes / never* studies English at the weekend. | |

## 7C  A classroom survey

Time expressions

**Card A**

......... people in the class usually get up before nine o'clock on Saturday.

**Card B**

......... people in the class usually go to the cinema at the weekend.

**Card C**

......... people in the class watch sport at the weekend.

**Card D**

......... people in the class have a big breakfast every morning.

**Card E**

......... people in the class read a newspaper every day.

**Card F**

......... people in the class have dinner at about nine o'clock in the evening.

**Card G**

......... people in the class usually go to bed at about eleven o'clock.

**Card H**

......... people in the class usually get home at five o'clock in the afternoon.

**Card I**

......... people in the class sleep in the afternoon.

**Card J**

......... people in the class watch television every day.

**Card K**

......... people in the class use the Internet every week.

**Card L**

......... people in the class start work/school/ university at nine o'clock.

**PHOTOCOPIABLE**

# Vocabulary Booster – Verbs and nouns

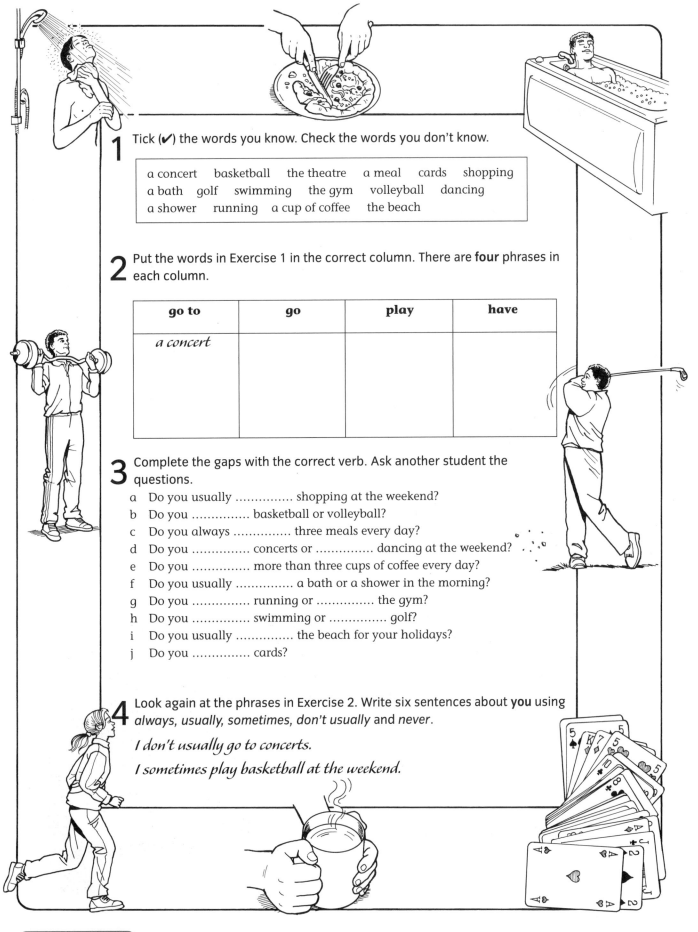

**1** Tick (✔) the words you know. Check the words you don't know.

> a concert   basketball   the theatre   a meal   cards   shopping
> a bath   golf   swimming   the gym   volleyball   dancing
> a shower   running   a cup of coffee   the beach

**2** Put the words in Exercise 1 in the correct column. There are **four** phrases in each column.

| go to | go | play | have |
|-------|-----|------|------|
| a concert | | | |
| | | | |
| | | | |
| | | | |

**3** Complete the gaps with the correct verb. Ask another student the questions.

a   Do you usually ............... shopping at the weekend?
b   Do you ............... basketball or volleyball?
c   Do you always ............... three meals every day?
d   Do you ............... concerts or ............... dancing at the weekend?
e   Do you ............... more than three cups of coffee every day?
f   Do you usually ............... a bath or a shower in the morning?
g   Do you ............... running or ............... the gym?
h   Do you ............... swimming or ............... golf?
i   Do you usually ............... the beach for your holidays?
j   Do you ............... cards?

**4** Look again at the phrases in Exercise 2. Write six sentences about **you** using *always, usually, sometimes, don't usually* and *never*.

*I don't usually go to concerts.*
*I sometimes play basketball at the weekend.*

## 8A  What can you do?

*can* and *can't*

| Find someone who ... | Name(s) |
|---|---|
| 1   ... can cook very well. | |
| 2   ... can speak four languages. | |
| 3   ... can talk to animals. | |
| 4   ... can type very fast. | |
| 5   ... can swim 30 kilometres. | |
| 6   ... can ski very well. | |
| 7   ... can run 100 metres in ten seconds. | |
| 8   ... can eat seven burgers in two minutes. | |
| 9   ... can play the piano and the guitar. | |
| 10 ... can dance and sing very well. | |

© Pearson Education Limited 2002

**Role card A**

Your name is Carola (woman)/Marcos (man), and you're a teacher. You live in Buenos Aires, in Argentina. You can speak four languages – French, Japanese, Spanish and English.

**Role card B**

Your name is Olga (woman)/Stefan (man), and you're from Bonn, in Germany. You're a famous musician and you can play the piano and the guitar brilliantly.

**Role card C**

Your name is Rita (woman)/Rolf (man), and you're a student. You live in Switzerland, and you study French at university. You can also ski very well.

**Role card D**

Your name is Samantha (woman)/Steve (man) and you're a student. You live in Texas, in the USA, and you really love food. You can eat seven burgers in two minutes!

**Role card E**

Your are a waitress/waiter from France, and your name is Veronica (woman)/ Pierre (man). You work in a restaurant in Paris, and you can also cook very well.

**Role card F**

Your name is Motoko (woman)/Toshi (man), and you're from Osaka, in Japan. You're a famous actor/actress, and you can dance and sing very well.

**Role card G**

You are Michelle (woman)/Mike (man). You live in Cape Town, in South Africa, and you're a police officer. You live near the beach, and you can swim 30 kilometres!

**Role card H**

Your name is Barbara (woman)/Luca (man), and you live in Napoli, in Italy. You are a very famous vet in your country, because you can talk to animals!

**Role card I**

Your name is Ada (woman)/Adam (man), and you're from Poland. You're a secretary for an American company, and you can type very fast – 100 words a minute!

**Role card J**

You are from Spain, and your name is Silvia (woman)/Roberto (man). You are a famous footballer in your country, and you can also run 100 metres in ten seconds.

## Vocabulary Booster – Parts of the body

**1** Put these words in the correct place on the picture.

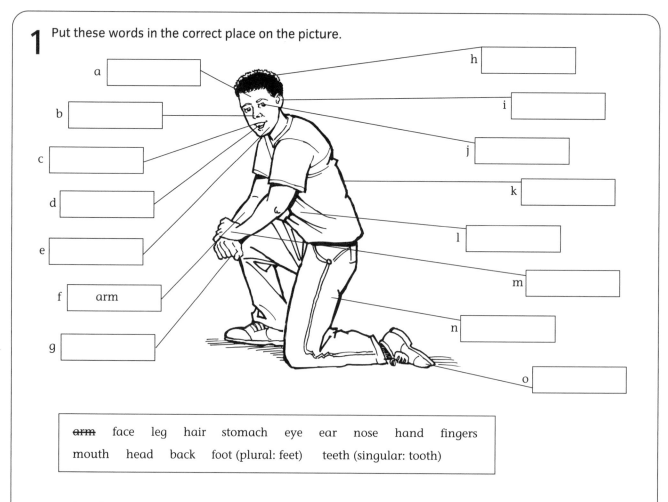

a
b
c
d
e
f    arm
g
h
i
j
k
l
m
n
o

~~arm~~   face   leg   hair   stomach   eye   ear   nose   hand   fingers

mouth   head   back   foot (plural: feet)   teeth (singular: tooth)

**2** Work with a partner. Point to a part of your body. Your partner says what it is.

**3** a   Draw the monster!

A Boogle has a big head, a round face, six eyes and a very big nose. His mouth is also very big, and he has lots of teeth. His hair is very long, and he has four small ears. He has four arms, but there are only three fingers on each hand. He has a big stomach, two short legs, and very big feet!

b   Show your drawing to some other students. Which drawing is the best?

**4** Find the words from Exercise 1 in the box. You have three minutes!

| E | Y | E | S | L | E | G | H |
|---|---|---|---|---|---|---|---|
| F | O | O | T | D | R | F | E |
| T | F | N | O | S | E | I | A |
| E | A | R | M | H | A | N | D |
| E | C | R | A | T | R | G | B |
| T | E | N | C | E | W | E | A |
| H | A | Q | H | A | I | R | C |
| M | O | U | T | H | O | S | K |

© Pearson Education Limited 2002   **PHOTOCOPIABLE**

## 8B  Question word quiz

Question words

| When | Where | Why | Who | What | How many |
|------|-------|-----|-----|------|----------|

**Instructions**

* Complete the gaps in the questions with one of the words in the box above. Your team scores **1** point for each correct word.
* Answer the questions. Your team scores **2** points for each correct answer.

*Where.* is Buckingham Palace?  ✔ *1 point*

a) in England  b) in Germany  c) in the USA  ✔ *2 points*

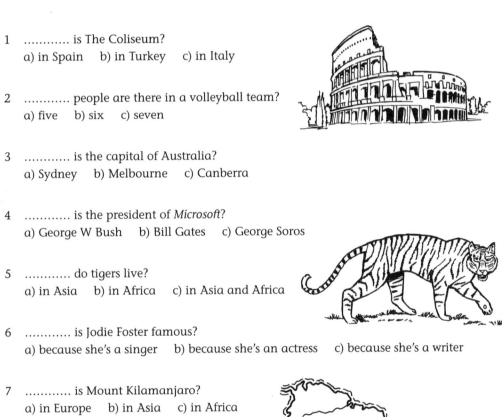

1  ............ is The Coliseum?
a) in Spain    b) in Turkey    c) in Italy

2  ............ people are there in a volleyball team?
a) five    b) six    c) seven

3  ............ is the capital of Australia?
a) Sydney    b) Melbourne    c) Canberra

4  ............ is the president of *Microsoft*?
a) George W Bush    b) Bill Gates    c) George Soros

5  ............ do tigers live?
a) in Asia    b) in Africa    c) in Asia and Africa

6  ............ is Jodie Foster famous?
a) because she's a singer    b) because she's an actress    c) because she's a writer

7  ............ is Mount Kilamanjaro?
a) in Europe    b) in Asia    c) in Africa

8  ............ countries are there in South America?
a) eight    b) thirteen    c) eighteen

9  ............ is the next Olympic Games?
a) 2004    b) 2006    c) 2008

10  ............ is this person's job?
a) an engineer    b) a vet    c) a doctor

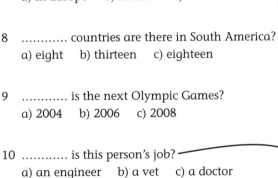

© Pearson Education Limited 2002    **137**

## 9A Adjective dominoes

Adjectives and nouns

| town | **YOUNG** | boy | **SLOW** |
| car | **OLD** | man | **FAST** |
| train | **HAPPY** | children | **SAFE** |
| city | **UNHAPPY** | girl | **DANGEROUS** |
| country | **RICH** | woman | **EXPENSIVE** |
| shop | **POOR** | family | **CHEAP** |
| school | **NEW** | house | **HOT** |
| day | **OLD** | hotel | **COLD** |
| drink | **BUSY** | road | **BEAUTIFUL** |
| park | **QUIET** | place | **EXPENSIVE** |
| bicycle | **BEAUTIFUL** | beach | **POOR** |
| people | **UGLY** | building | **BUSY** |

© Pearson Education Limited 2002     **PHOTOCOPIABLE**

## 9B Where were you?

*was* and *were*

**1** Write short answers to these questions in the boxes below.
Write the answers in a **different order** to the questions.

- Where were you at half past six yesterday afternoon?
- Who was your first friend?
- Who were you with last Sunday?
- Who was your favourite teacher at your first school?
- Where were you at nine o'clock last Saturday?
- What was your favourite sport when you were twelve?
- Where were you at eleven o'clock yesterday morning?
- What was the name of your first English teacher?
- What was your grandfather's first name?

**Don't forget!**

Were you (with Ana) ...?
Were you (at home) ...?
Was (Marco/Rita) ...?
Was (football) ...?
Was your grandfather's name ...?

Yes, I was.
No, I wasn't.

Yes he/she/it was.
No, he/she/it wasn't.

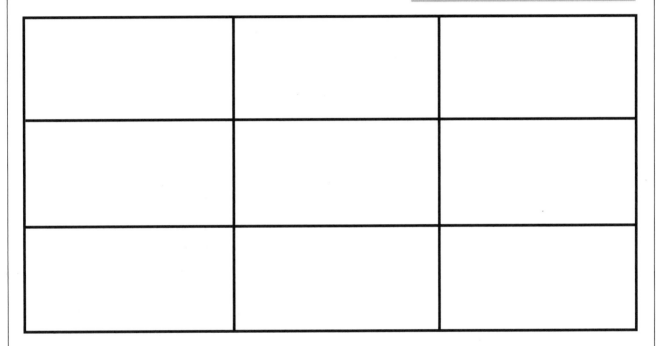

**2** Look at the words in your partner's boxes above, and write questions about them.

Franco     *Was Franco your first friend?*

a ................................................................................................................

b ................................................................................................................

c ................................................................................................................

d ................................................................................................................

e ................................................................................................................

f ................................................................................................................

g ................................................................................................................

h ................................................................................................................

i ................................................................................................................

© Pearson Education Limited 2002

## Vocabulary Booster – Describing people

**1** Match the sentences to the people. Sometimes there is more than one answer.

| Chris | Mark | Alan |

a   He's tall.          *Chris*
b   He's short.
c   He's slim.
d   He's fat.
e   He's good-looking.
f   He has long hair.
g   He has short hair.
h   He has fair hair.
i   He has dark hair.
j   He has a moustache.
k   He has a beard.

> **Don't forget!**
>
> He's my brother/father/son.
> She's my sister/mother/daughter.
> He's/She's my friend.
> He's from (Poland).
> She's (about) forty.
> He's a (doctor).
> He/She lives in (Istanbul).

**2** Put *'s* or *has* in the gaps.

a   Tom ..*has*.. long hair and brown eyes.
b   She ......... short hair and she ......... very slim.
c   Marco ......... a very big moustache.
d   My father ......... quite tall, and he ......... fair hair.
e   He ......... dark hair, big blue eyes, and he ......... very good-looking.
f   Ana ......... very beautiful, and she ......... also very tall.

**3** Write four sentences about a person in the classroom. Say the sentences to the class. Can they guess who it is?

**4** Write the names of three friends or people in your family in the boxes below. Describe these people to another student.

| 1 | 2 | 3 |

**PHOTOCOPIABLE**

## 10A  Past Simple quiz

Past Simple (statements)

**Instructions**
- Put each verb in brackets in the Past Simple. Your team scores **1** point for each correct past tense.
- Answer the questions. Your team scores **2** points for each correct answer.

Example
John Lennon ...*died*... (die) in:          ✔ *1 point*
a) 1970   b) (1980)   c) 1990          ✔ *2 points*

1   The artist Pablo Picasso ......... (be) born in:
    a) Spain   b) France   c) Italy.

2   David Beckham ......... (get) married to Victoria Adams in:
    a) 1993   b) 1996   c) 1999.

3   The Second World War ......... (start) in:
    a) 1935   b) 1939   c) 1945.

4   Mother Teresa ......... (live) most of her life in:
    a) Rome   b) Calcutta   c) Delhi.

5   John F Kennedy ......... (become) President of the USA when he ......... (be):
    a) 33   b) 43   c) 53.

6   Nintendo ......... (sell):
    a) 10 million   b) 50 million   c) 100 million   GameBoys in the 1990s.

7   The English king Henry the Eighth ......... (have):
    a) two wives   b) four wives   c) six wives.

8   The Russian Fyodor Dostoyevsky:
    a) ......... (write) books   b) ......... (paint) pictures   c) ......... (make) films.

9   Bjørn Borg ......... (be) famous because he ......... (play):
    a) tennis   b) golf   c) football.

10  Man ......... (go) to the moon for the first time in:
    a) 1959   b) 1969   c) 1979.

## 10B Ten things about me

Past Simple (statements)

Write short answers to these questions in the circles below. Write the answers in a **different order** to the questions.

- a place you went to last year
- a person you met last week
- the year you started school
- the name of a film (or a TV programme) you watched last month
- a person you know who got married last year
- the town or city you lived in when you were a child
- a person you wrote a letter or an email to last month
- the year you met your best friend
- a person you know who went to university
- a restaurant, café or shop you went to last week

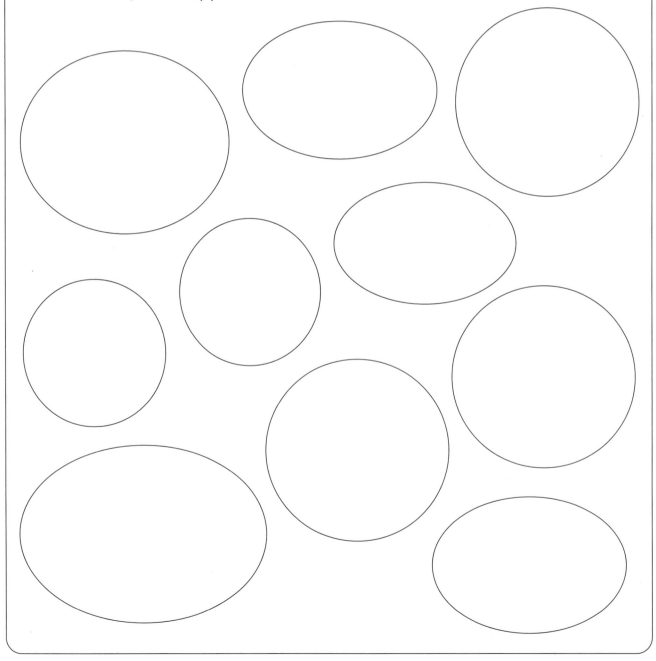

**PHOTOCOPIABLE**

## 10C  Past Simple bingo

Irregular and regular past tenses

---

### BINGO CARD A

| left | hated | was/were | played |
| got | worked | started | loved |
| had | watched | met | liked |

### BINGO CARD B

| moved | went | returned | became |
| made | studied | wrote | lived |
| finished | wanted | talked | sold |

### BINGO CARD C

| studied | sold | played | wrote |
| hated | got | started | made |
| met | finished | moved | returned |

### BINGO CARD D

| worked | left | was/were | talked |
| wanted | lived | loved | went |
| watched | had | liked | became |

### BINGO CARD E

| moved | sold | studied | returned |
| worked | had | wrote | watched |
| was/were | met | finished | liked |

### BINGO CARD F

| went | got | started | talked |
| made | lived | left | hated |
| wanted | became | played | loved |

### BINGO CARD G

| loved | wanted | met | made |
| started | got | lived | became |
| watched | sold | liked | moved |

### BINGO CARD H

| hated | had | finished | was/were |
| wrote | studied | worked | went |
| returned | talked | left | played |

---

### MASTER BINGO CARD

| leave | sell | go | meet | write | become |
| make | have | get | be | study | work |
| start | return | live | finish | want | love |
| talk | watch | hate | like | play | move |

---

© Pearson Education Limited 2002     **143**

## Vocabulary Booster – Irregular verbs

**1 a** Work with a partner. Do you know these verbs?

| see | know | drink | give | understand |
|---|---|---|---|---|
| eat | do | buy | read | come |

**b** Say one noun you can use with each verb.

( see a film )    ( say a sentence )

**2** Write the correct verb from Exercise 1. Practise the pronunciation of the Past Simple forms with your teacher.

| Verb | Past Simple | Verb | Past Simple |
|---|---|---|---|
| a *know* ............... | knew | f ................... | saw |
| b ................... | understood | g ................... | came |
| c ................... | drank | h ................... | read /red/ |
| d ................... | ate | i ................... | gave |
| e ................... | did | j ................... | bought |

**3** Put the past tenses from Exercise 2 in the gaps.

a I ...*understood*... all the words in the text.

b They .................... a lot of water because it was very hot.

c She .................... me her address and telephone number.

d We .................... a new TV last weekend. It was very expensive!

e The children .................... all the pizza.

f All the students .................... their homework last week.

g We .................... a good programme on TV yesterday.

h I .................... the first Harry Potter book when I was 14.

i Lots of friends .................... to my house for dinner last weekend.

j I .................... four of these past tenses before the class!

**4** Test your partner on the Past Simple forms.

( see )  ( saw )

( do )  ( did )

**PHOTOCOPIABLE**

# 10D The date game

Dates, months and years

| GAME 1 CARD A | |
|---|---|
| HEAR | SAY |
| 1969 | June 4th |
| June 20th | 1983 |
| START ➡ | April 1st |
| April 25th | August 4th |
| December 30th | 2010 |
| 1914 | October 13th |
| October 31st | February 6th |
| February 16th | December 13th |

| GAME 1 CARD B | |
|---|---|
| HEAR | SAY |
| 1983 | April 25th |
| June 4th | 1996 |
| February 12th | FINISH! |
| April 11th | February 16th |
| 2001 | October 31st |
| October 3rd | 1914 |
| August 14th | December 30th |
| December 25th | 1940 |

| GAME 1 CARD C | |
|---|---|
| HEAR | SAY |
| 1996 | August 14th |
| August 4th | February 12th |
| October 13th | December 25th |
| 2010 | April 11th |
| April 1st | 2001 |
| 1940 | June 20th |
| December 13th | October 3rd |
| February 6th | 1969 |

| GAME 2 CARD A | |
|---|---|
| HEAR | SAY |
| March 25th | January 23rd |
| May 19th | 2003 |
| 1974 | July 4th |
| January 1st | March 2nd |
| 2006 | November 15th |
| July 14th | 1947 |
| 1918 | September 23rd |
| November 15th | 1949 |

| GAME 2 CARD B | |
|---|---|
| HEAR | SAY |
| September 23rd | 1980 |
| 1949 | March 25th |
| July 4th | May 17th |
| START ➡ | January 1st |
| 1947 | September 20th |
| September 18th | 2006 |
| 2003 | November 5th |
| January 11th | 1994 |

| GAME 2 CARD C | |
|---|---|
| HEAR | SAY |
| January 23rd | September 18th |
| March 2nd | 1918 |
| 1994 | November 15th |
| May 17th | July 14th |
| November 5th | 1974 |
| 1980 | May 19th |
| November 15th | FINISH! |
| September 20th | January 11th |

## 11A Collocation pelmanism

Verb/noun collocations

| | | | |
|---|---|---|---|
| go | shopping | go for | a walk |
| go | skiing | get up | late |
| go to | the beach | get | married |
| go to | a restaurant | become | famous |
| have | lunch | move | house |
| have | dinner | watch | television |
| stay | in a hotel | listen to | rock music |
| go on | holiday | study | languages |

## 11B  Did you or didn't you?

Past Simple (*yes*/*no* questions)

---

**Find one student in the class who did each of these things. Write their names at the beginning of the sentence.**

1 ............................. went to the cinema last week.

**Question:** *Did you go to the cinema last week?* ..............................................

2 ............................. had a big breakfast this morning.

**Question:** *Did you* ..............................................................................

3 ............................. used a computer yesterday.

**Question:** *Did* ..................................................................................

4 ............................. went for a walk last weekend.

**Question:** ..........................................................................................

5 ............................. had lunch or dinner in a restaurant last week.

**Question:** ..........................................................................................

6 ............................. stayed at home on Friday evening.

**Question:** ..........................................................................................

7 ............................. went shopping last Saturday.

**Question:** ..........................................................................................

8 ............................. met some friends last weekend.

**Question:** ..........................................................................................

9 ............................. got up before seven o'clock this morning.

**Question:** ..........................................................................................

10 ............................. went to bed after twelve o'clock last night.

**Question:** ..........................................................................................

 © Pearson Education Limited 2002

## 11C  Madonna's life story

Past Simple (*Wh-* questions)

### Worksheet A

# Madonna – *Her Life Story*

Madonna Louise Ciccone was born on (1) ............... in Michigan, USA, and her mother died (2) .............. ............... . Madonna studied acting at college and then she went to live in (3) ............... in 1977. When she arrived there she only had $35! Before she became a singer she worked as a dancer and a model.

She made her first record in (4)............... and in 1983 she had her first hit with *Holiday*. She met (5) .............................. at a party in Los Angeles, and they got married in 1985. The marriage wasn't a happy one, and they got divorced in (6) ............... . Madonna also wanted to be a movie star, and she made *Evita* (the story of Eva Peron) in 1996.

In 1998 she met (7) .............................. , a British film director, at her friend Sting's house. On (8) .............................. they got married in Scotland. Madonna has two children, Lourdes and Rocco, and she now lives in London.

Write questions in the Past Simple for the gaps in the text above.

1  When ..................... she born?

2  When ..................... her mother ..................... ?

3  Where ................... ................... ................... to live in 1977?

4  When ................... ................... ................... her first record?

5  Who ................... ................... ................... in Los Angeles?

6  When ................... ................... ................... divorced?

7  Who ................... ................... ................... in 1998?

8  When ................... ................... ................... married?

**Worksheet B**

# Madonna – *Her Life Story*

Madonna Louise Ciccone was born on 16th August 1958 in (a) ......................... , and her mother died when she was six. Madonna studied (b) .............. at college and then she went to live in New York in 1977. When she arrived there she only had (c) $.............. ! Before she became a singer she worked as a dancer and a model.
She made her first record in 1982, and in (d) .............. she had her first hit with *Holiday*. She met actor Sean Penn at a party in Los Angeles, and they got married in (e) .............. . The marriage wasn't a happy one, and they got divorced in 1989. Madonna also wanted to be a movie star, and she made *Evita* (the story of Eva Peron) in (f) .............. . In 1998 she met Guy Richie, a British film director, at (g) .............. . On 22nd December 2000 they got married in (h) .............. . Madonna has two children, Lourdes and Rocco, and she now lives in London.

Write questions in the Past Simple for the gaps in the text above.

a Where .............. she born?

b What .............. she .............. at college?

c How much money .............. .............. .............. when she arrived?

d When .............. .............. .............. her first hit?

e When .............. .............. .............. married?

f When .............. .............. .............. *Evita*?

g Where .............. .............. .............. Guy Richie?

h Where .............. .............. .............. married?

## 11D  Past Simple snakes and ladders

Past Simple review

© Pearson Education Limited 2002    **PHOTOCOPIABLE**

# Questions

✂

---

1 What is the Past Simple of these verbs?

- leave
- make
- walk

---

2 Put these words in order to make a question.

weekend did do last you What ?

---

3 Is this sentence right or wrong? (If it's wrong, correct it.)

Where did you went last month?

---

4 Put *was* or *were* in the gaps.

'......... you at home last night?'
'Yes, I ......... .'

---

5 Put *did* or *didn't* in the gaps.

'......... you go to the cinema last night?'
'No, I ......... .'

---

6 Answer this question.

What did you do last month?
(Say at least <u>three</u> things.)

---

7 Which is correct?

Sam *did/was* a teacher, but he *didn't/wasn't* like his job.

---

8 Make this sentence negative.

I went for a walk last Monday.

---

9 How do you spell the Past Simple of these verbs?

- study
- sell
- hate

---

10 Put *did* or *didn't* in the gaps.

'......... you study English at school?'
'Yes, I ......... .'

---

11 Make this sentence positive.

Frank didn't study French at school.

---

12 Put these words in order to make a question.

did on Where go holiday you year last ?

---

13 Is this sentence right or wrong? (If it's wrong, correct it.)

We didn't stay in an expensive hotel when we were on holiday.

---

14 What is the Past Simple of these verbs?

- watch
- meet
- have

---

15 Make this sentence negative.

He started work at nine o'clock in the morning.

---

 © Pearson Education Limited 2002

# Questions

---

16 Make this sentence positive.

We didn't live in a big house, and we weren't rich.

---

17 Put *was* or *were* in the gaps.

Peter ......... born in 1974, and his parents ......... very happy.

---

18 Answer this question.

What did you do last weekend?
(Say at least <u>three</u> things.)

---

19 Which is correct?

They *didn't/wasn't* like the food because it *was/did* cold.

---

20 How do you spell the Past Simple of these verbs?

• finish
• become
• write

---

21 Put these words in order to make a question.

school in many were people How there your ?

---

22 Put *did* or *didn't* in the gaps.

'What ......... we do in the last class?'
'I don't know. I ......... come to the last class.'

---

23 Is this sentence right or wrong? (If it's wrong, correct it.)

Tom and Susan didn't studied English at school.

---

24 Make this sentence negative.

I did my homework last night.

---

25 What is the Past Simple of these verbs?

• want
• go
• get

---

26 Which is correct?

'Where *did/was* Tom go last night?'
'He *was/did* at a friend's house.'

---

27 Answer this question.

What did you do yesterday? (Say at least <u>three</u> things.)

---

28 Put *was* or *were* in the gaps.

We ......... in a restaurant last night, and my husband ......... very ill.

---

29 Is this sentence right or wrong? (If it's wrong, correct it.)

When I was young I lived in France, but we moved to Germany when I was six.

---

30 Put these words in order to make a question.

get this time did you What up morning ?

---

## Vocabulary Booster – The weather

**1** Match the sentences with the places.

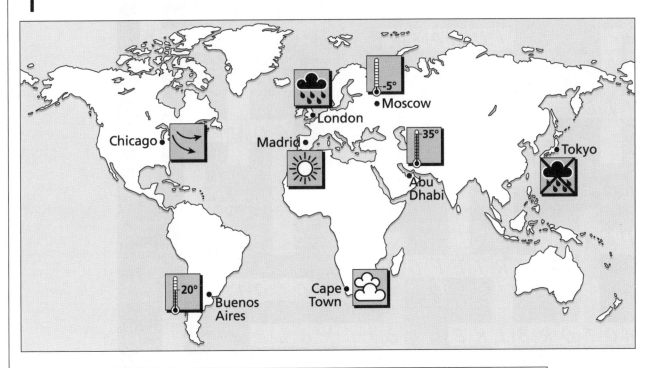

It's dry. *Tokyo* ...... It's hot. ............ It's cloudy. ............ It's cold. ............

It's sunny. ............ It's wet. ............ It's warm. ............ It's windy. ............

**2** Ask and answer with your partner.

What's the weather like in Moscow?

It's cold.

**3** What's the weather like in your country? Complete these sentences.

a   In December and January it's usually ............................... .

b   In March and April it's ............................... and ............................... .

c   In May and June it's usually ............................... and ............................... .

d   In July and August it's usually ............................... .

e   In September and October it's ............................... and ............................... .

f   In November and December it's ............................... .

**4** Ask and answer with a partner.

What was the weather like ... ?

- yesterday
- last weekend
- last month
- six months ago
- on your last holiday
- on your last birthday

 © Pearson Education Limited 2002    **153**

## 12A Shopping crossword

Things you buy

**Worksheet A**

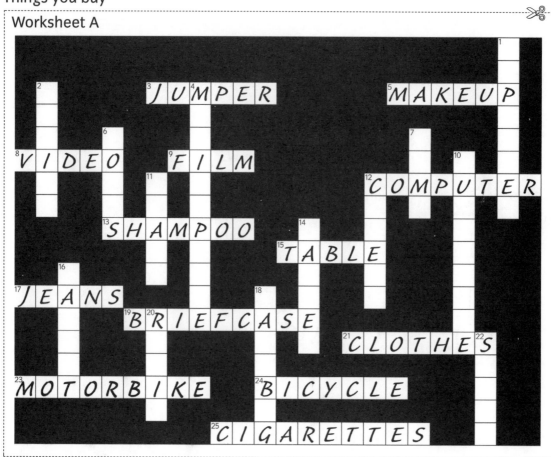

**Worksheet B**

**PHOTOCOPIABLE**

# Vocabulary Booster – Clothes

**1** Match the words with the clothes. What other clothes can you see?

a hat .........    a dress .........    a tie .........    a coat .........    boots .........

trousers .........    trainers .........    a shirt .........    a skirt .........    a suit .........

**2** Write sentences about the people in the picture.

*He's wearing a suit, a tie and a shirt.*

**3** Work with a partner. Did you buy any clothes last week/last month/last year? When did you buy the clothes you're wearing now?

> I bought some new shoes last weekend.

> I bought this skirt last month.

**4** What are your favourite clothes? Tell other students about them.

> I have a long red coat. It's beautiful.

> These are my favourite trainers.

**5** Work with a partner. Describe another student's clothes, but don't say who it is. Your partner must guess his/her name.

  

## 12B  My partner's future

*going to*

### Worksheet A

| Partner's name ................................................................................ | Right or wrong? |
|---|---|
| 1   My partner *is/isn't* going to get up early tomorrow morning. | |
| 2   My partner *is/isn't* going to watch sport on TV next weekend. | |
| 3   My partner *is/isn't* going to go on holiday next month. | |
| 4   My partner *is/isn't* going to have dinner in a restaurant this weekend. | |
| 5   My partner *is/isn't* going to stay in tomorrow evening. | |
| 6   My partner *is/isn't* going to be in a different country on his/her next birthday. | |
| 7   My partner *is/isn't* going to go to the supermarket today. | |
| 8   My partner *is/isn't* going to meet friends this evening. | |

### Worksheet B

| Partner's name ................................................................................ | Right or wrong? |
|---|---|
| 1   My partner *is/isn't* going to watch TV this evening. | |
| 2   My partner *is/isn't* going to visit family next weekend. | |
| 3   My partner *is/isn't* going to cook dinner tonight. | |
| 4   My partner *is/isn't* going to work tomorrow. | |
| 5   My partner *is/isn't* going to travel to another town or city next month. | |
| 6   My partner *is/isn't* going to see a film next weekend. | |
| 7   My partner *is/isn't* going to go to bed late this evening. | |
| 8   My partner *is/isn't* going to buy some new clothes or shoes next weekend. | |

## 12C Revision board game

All the language in the Students' Book

© Pearson Education Limited 2002

# Question Cards

---

1   What is the plural of these words?

child      man
woman    person

---

2   Correct the sentences. There is one mistake in each sentence.

a)   I going to watch TV tonight.
b)   Where did she went yesterday?
c)   Do she speak English?

---

3   Match the verbs with the nouns.

move      your partner
get        children
have      house
meet      married

---

4   How do you say these numbers?

1,000,000    12,000
450          33

---

5   Put *'m*, *are* or *'s* in the gaps.

Tim: "...... you a teacher?"
Sue: "No, I ...... not, but my brother ...... a Spanish teacher."

---

6   What are these 'food and drink' words?

B _ E _ D
W _ T _ R
F _ U _ T
V _ G _ T _ B _ E _

---

7   Match the verbs with the nouns.

have      the cinema
play       shopping
go to     football
go         dinner

---

8   Put the correct verb in the gaps.

a)   ......... the guitar
b)   ......... homework
c)   ......... in a flat
d)   ......... television

---

9   Which sentence is correct? Correct the two wrong sentences.

a)   I can to swim well.
b)   Can you play tennis?
c)   I don't can speak German.

---

10   Choose the correct answer.

a)   There *is/are* five people in my family.
b)   There *isn't/aren't* any parks in my town.
c)   *Is/Are* there a cinema near your house?

---

11   Choose the correct answer.

a)   Where *did/was* he born?
b)   Why *did/were* you late?
c)   Where *did/were* you go yesterday?

---

12   Name ten jobs in thirty seconds.

---

13   What is the Past Simple of these verbs?

become    start
meet       be

---

14   What is the opposite of these adjectives?

rich        slow
dangerous   beautiful

---

15   Which question word?

a)   .........'s your mother's name?
b)   ......... did you go on holiday?
c)   ......... is your favourite singer?

---

# Question Cards

---

**16** Do these phrases talk about *the past* or *the future*?

- six weeks ago
- tomorrow
- yesterday
- last week
- next week

---

**17** These are the answers. What are the questions?

a) I'm an engineer.
b) I'm 22.
c) I'm from Brazil.

---

**18** Read and complete the sentences.

Tom is Sally's brother, and their parents are Ana and Steve.
a  Steve is Tom's ......... .
b  Ana is Steve's ......... .
c  Sally is Ana's ......... .

---

**19** Choose the correct answer.

a) There are *some/any* people in the café.
b) There aren't *some/any* children here.
c) Is there *a/some* post office near here?

---

**20** Which preposition?

a) ......... the morning
b) ......... the weekend
c) ......... Monday
d) ......... June

---

**21** What's the Past Simple of these verbs?

leave        make
sell         play

---

**22** Say the months of the year, starting with *January*. You have twenty seconds!

---

**23** Choose the correct answer.

a) *Do/Does* you like tennis?
b) Where *do/does* your brothers live?
c) Where *do/does* your husband work?

---

**24** Make these sentences negative.

a) I like dance music.
b) She plays tennis every day.
c) They went on holiday last year.

---

**25** Put this conversation in order.
a) Yes, can I have these postcards, please?
b) *Two pounds fifty.*
c) *Hello, can I help you?*
d) No, thanks. How much is that?
e) *Sure. Anything else?*

---

**26** Put *was* or *were* in the gaps.

a) Where ......... you yesterday?
b) My friends ......... here six months ago.
c) He ......... in England last year.

---

**27** Say ten places in a town or city (e.g. *a park*) in thirty seconds!

---

**28** Put these phrases in order, starting with *I love*.

I like ...        I love ...
I hate ...        I don't like ...
It's okay ...     I really like ...

---

**29** Choose the correct answer.

a) I like *he/him* a lot.
b) *She/Her* lives in Thailand.
c) *They/Their* dog's name is Mark.

---

**30** What's the Past Simple of these verbs?

write        get
study        go

---

© Pearson Education Limited 2002 **159**

# Modules 1-2

TIME: 30 MINUTES

## Test A

Name: ........................................................

**A** Write the questions.

**For example:**

*How old are you?* ............ I'm 25.

1 ................................................ ?
Alvarez.

2 ................................................ ?
Julia.

3 ................................................ ?
58 Highland Avenue, London.

4 ................................................ ?
No, I'm not. I'm Spanish.

5 ................................................ ?
0208 421 8310.

6 ................................................ ?
I'm a Spanish teacher.

| 6 |
|---|

**B** Correct the spelling.

**For example:**

footbaler   *footballer* .........

1   teecher        ....................
2   docter         ....................
3   bussinesswoman ....................
4   actoress       ....................
5   waitor         ....................
6   police oficer  ....................
7   politishian    ....................
8   shop asistant  ....................

| 4 |
|---|

**C** Put ' in the correct places.

**For example:**

I̷'m a singer.

1   Whats your full name?
2   It isnt a French car. Its an Italian car.
3   Open your books.
4   Her names Caroline and shes from Switzerland.
5   Youre Russian, yes?

| 6 |
|---|

**D** Write the numbers.

**For example:**

..... *forty-five* .....

1 .........................

2 .........................

3 .........................

4 .........................

5 .........................   6 .........................

| 6 |
|---|

**E** Complete the sentences with one word.

**For example:**

*My.* name is Bond, James Bond.

**A:** Hi, John. (1) ......... are you?

**B:** (2) ......... well, thank you. And (3) ......... ?

**A:** I'm fine. (4) ......... is Monika Henriksen from my company.

**B:** Hello, nice to (5) ......... you.

**A:** Monika's (6) ......... engineer.

**B:** That's interesting. – Oh! Here's my taxi. See you (7) ......... , Monika.

| | 7 |
|---|---|

**F** Tick (✓) the correct word.

**For example:**

open ✓
work     your book

1   write
   listen    your name

2   say
   read    your book

3   work
   listen    in pairs

4   he's from
   she's    France

5   Germany
   capital    city

| | 5 |
|---|---|

**G** Put the countries, cities and nationalities in the correct place.

| O | O o | o    O |
|---|---|---|
| ............... | ............... | *New York* |
| ............... | ............... | ............... |
| O o o | o o O | o O o o |
| ............... | ............... | ............... |
| ............... | ............... | ............... |

New York     Japanese     London
Spain     American     Germany
Turkish     Brazil     Italy

| | 8 |
|---|---|

**H** Write *a* or *an*.

1 ...... actor

2 ...... nice pen

3 ...... Argentinian

4 ...... big number

5 ...... Hungarian city

6 ...... email

7 ...... question

8 ...... Italian car

| | 8 |
|---|---|

| | 50 |
|---|---|

# Modules 1-2

TIME: 30 MINUTES

# Test B

Name: ................................................

**A** Write the questions and answers.

STUDENT I·D
Full name:
DOCTOR TONI PESCI
Nationality:
AMERICAN
Age:
23
Marital status
MARRIED

**For example:**

What / first name?
*What's your first name?* ............ *Toni.*
...................................... ..............................

1 What / surname?
.......................................? ..............................

2 Italian?
.......................................? No, I'm ..............

3 old?
.......................................? ..............................

4 married?
.......................................? Yes.

5 job?
.......................................? I'm ....................

[9]

**B** Put the words in the correct places in the sentences.

| an His her from you a ~~'m~~ She's |

**For example:**

I Jennifer. ......*I'm Jennifer.*......

1 What's job? ..............................

2 It's English car. ..............................

3 name's John. ..............................

4 He's politician. ..............................

5 thirty-five. ..............................

6 He's Scotland. ..............................

7 Are Polish? ..............................

[7]

**C** Write the jobs.

.......... doctor ..........

1 ..........................

2 ..........................

3 ..........................

4 ..........................

5 ..........................

6 ..........................

7 ..........................

8 ..........................

[8]

**D** Write the numbers.

**For example:**

(45) . *forty-five* .........

1 ......................

2 ......................

3 ......................

4 ......................

5 ......................

6 ......................

7 ......................

[7]

**E** Write the negatives.

**For example:**

My city's very big.   *My city isn't very big.* ....

1   My name's Ming-mei

......................................................

2   You're British.

......................................................

3   I'm married.

......................................................

4   She's from Korea.

......................................................

5   Sanyo's a Turkish company.

......................................................

[5]

**F** Mark the stress on the countries and nationalities.

**For example:**

Rússian

American        Turkey      Japan      Polish

Brazilian       Italy       the USA    Great Britain

[8]

**G** Tick (✓) the correct answer.

**For example:**

Where are you from?

a) Argentina. ✓     b) I from Japan.     c) German.

1   Hello, my name's Susanna.
   a)  I'm Jo. Nice meet you.
   b)  I'm Jo. Nice to meet you.
   c)  Are you?

2   – Hello, Stefan.
   – Hi, Miguel,
   a)  This is Franco.
   b)  He is Franco.
   c)  This Franco.

3   She's a politician.
   a)  How spell 'politician'?
   b)  What spelling 'politician'?
   c)  How do you spell 'politician'?

4   Students: Good morning, Mr Greene.
   Teacher:
   a)  Work in pairs.
   b)  Say your books.
   c)  Open it.

5   Bye, Paula.
   a)  Hi.
   b)  See you later.
   c)  Please.

6   Hi, James. How are you?
   a)  I'm fine, thanks.
   b)  I'm nice, thanks.
   c)  Are you well?

[6]

[50]

© Pearson Education 2002          **163**

# Modules 3–4

TIME: 30 MINUTES

# Test A

Name: ...................................................

**A** Write the missing letters in these food and drink words.

**For example:**

r _i_ c _e_

1  b r _ _ _          6  m _ _ k
2  m _ _ t            7  e _ _ s
3  c _ f _ _ _        8  p _ _ _ a
4  f r _ _ _          9  c h _ _ _ _
5  w _ t _ _          10  v _ g _ _ _ _ _ _ s

**10**

**B** Complete the conversation.

**For example:**

They ....._aren't_..... students. They're teachers.

**A:** Good morning, Miss Page, Mr Komoto. How (1) ............ your rooms?

**B:** We (2) ............ very happy with (3) ............ rooms. (4) ............ small and very cold.

**A:** I'm (5) ............ sorry. Let me look. (6) ............ rooms are 102 and 103, yes?

**B:** Yes. (7) ............ room is 102 and Miss Page's room is 103.

**A:** OK. Here are the keys for rooms 104 and 105. They're (8) ............ the right of room 103.

**B:** Thank you very much.

**8**

**C** Write the words for places. What is the extra place?

| | | | | | | | | |
|---|---|---|---|---|---|---|---|---|
| 1 | | P | A | R | K | | | |
| 2 | L | _ | _ | _ | | | | |
| 3 | | B | _ | S | _ | _ | _ | _ |
| 4 | | _ | T | _ | _ | _ | _ | |
| 5 | | | C | _ | _ | _ | | |
| 6 | | _ | Q | _ | _ | R | _ | |
| 7 | S | _ | P | _ | _ | _ | _ | _ | _ |
| 8 | | | _ | _ | N | _ | | |
| 9 | | C | _ | _ | _ | M | _ | |
| 10 | M | _ | _ | _ | T | _ | _ | N |

**10**

**D** Write these sentences in the plural. Make fourteen changes.

**For example:**

It's expensive. ....._They're expensive._.....

1  Is this your pen?

   ..............................................................?

2  There's a child.

   ..............................................................?

3  Is that person from Italy?

   ..............................................................?

4  (*in a taxi*) This address, please.

   ..............................................................?

5  Is there a bus from London to Oxford?

   ..............................................................?

**7**

**E** Mark the stress.

**For example:**

•
awful

1 expensive   2 beautiful   3 fantastic   4 hotel
5 interesting   6 restaurant   7 address

**7**

**F**  Tick (✓) the correct answer.

**For example:**

Where are you from?

a) Argentina. ✓    b) I from Japan.    c) German.

1  Do you like fish? – Yes, but …

    a) … is this restaurant expensive?

    b) … is expensive this restaurant?

    c) … this restaurant expensive.

2  A sandwich and a coke, please.

    a) How many?

    b) How much is that?

    c) How much this cost?

3  Excuse me, …

    a) … where the post office?

    b) … is a post office near?

    c) … where's the post office?

4  Vo ist der … ?

    a) Sorry, no understand.

    b) Sorry, I don't understand.

    c) Sorry, I'm not understand.

5  Bye, Sonya!

    a) See you later.

    b) Good evening.

    c) Hello, Juan!

6  Teacher: I like chocolate.

    Student:

    a) What's spelling 'chocolate'?

    b) How do you spell 'chocolate'?

    c) How spell 'chocolate'?

7  Hi, Melanie.

    a) Here is Ildiko from Hungary.

    b) This is Ildiko from Hungary.

    c) She is Ildiko from Hungary.

8  Hello, Ildiko.

    a) Nice meet you.

    b) How are you?

    c) Nice to meet you.

|  | 8 |
|---|---|
|  | **50** |

# Modules 3-4

TIME: 30 MINUTES

Name: ...................................................................

**Ⓐ  Write the missing letters in the words.**

**For example:**

The hotel is very b _i_ _g_

> Hello everyone!
> I'm on holiday in Ljubliana, the
> capital city of Slovenia, and it's
> (1) f_ _ _ _ _ _ _c here! The
> city is (2) s_ _ _ _ and very
> (3) o_ _ and the buildings are
> (4) in_ _ _ _ _ _ _ _ _ _. There
> are a lot of restaurants and the
> food is  (5) ex_ _ _ _ _ _ _
> but very (6) g_ _ _. Our hotel is
> very (7) n_ _ _ and the weather is
> (8) h_ _.
> See you soon.
> Angie

**8**

**Ⓑ  Write these sentences in the plural. Make fourteen changes.**

**For example:**

It's English.   ....*They're English*......

1  Is this your sandwich?

   ...........................................................?

2  Is that car Italian?

   ...........................................................?

3  Who's that person?

   ...........................................................?

4  Your baby is beautiful.

   ...........................................................?

5  Is there a taxi?

   ...........................................................?

**7**

**Ⓒ  Look at the pictures. Write the places.**

**For example:**

*bank*
..........................

1 ..........................

2 ..........................

3 ..........................

4 ..........................

5 ..........................

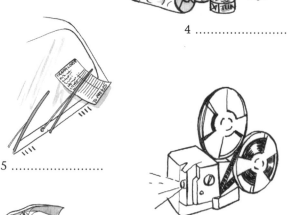

6 ..........................

7 ..........................

8 ..........................

**8**

© Pearson Education 2002   PHOTOCOPIABLE

**D** Complete the conversation.

**For example:**

They *aren't* students. They're teachers.

**Keiko:** Is this your hotel?

**Leila:** Yes.

**Keiko:** Where (1) ................. it?

**Leila:** It's (2) ................. Turkey.

**Keiko:** How many rooms are (3) .................?

**Leila:** Fifty. And (4) ................. is our town. Its name's Side. (5) ................. a big park in the centre of town and our hotel is (6) ................. the left of the park.

**Keiko:** And who are these?

**Leila:** My family. (7) ................. are my children.

**Keiko:** How (8) ................. are they?

**Leila:** (9) ................. four and seven.

☐ **9**

**E** Correct the spelling of these food and drink words.

**For example:**

rise .......*rice*.......

1 bred ..................

2 piza ..................

3 cofee ..................

4 vegtabels ..................

5 froot ..................

6 milch ..................

☐ **6**

**F** Put the words in the correct places.

| 0 | 0   o | 0   o   o |
|---|------|-----------|
| *chips* | *taxis* | *companies* |
| .................. | .................. | .................. |
| .................. | .................. | .................. |

~~companies~~   ~~taxis~~   ~~chips~~
mountains   holidays   names
beaches   waitresses   squares

☐ **6**

**G** Tick (✓) the correct answer.

**For example:**

Where are you from?

a) Argentina. ✓     b) I from Japan.     c) German.

1   Where are those students from?
    a) Their Argentinian.
    b) Argentinian.
    c) They're Argentinian.

2   Where's the bank?
    a) It's over.
    b) It's near restaurant.
    c) It's over there.

3   – A burger, please.
    – Here you are.
    a) How many?
    b) How much is that?
    c) How much this cost?

4   An aubergine, please.
    a) Sorry, I don't understand.
    b) Sorry, I'm not understand.
    c) Sorry, no understand.

5   Good morning, Jim.
    a) Hello, Bill. Here is Doctor Sarah Miller.
    b) Hello, Bill. This is Doctor Sarah Miller.
    c) Hello, Bill. She is Doctor Sarah Miller.

6   Bye, Claudia.
    a) Good evening.
    b) Hello Juan!
    c) See you later.

☐ **6**

☐ **50**

**167**

# Modules 5-6

TIME: 30 MINUTES

## Test A

Name: ...........................................................

---

**(A)** Peter and Diana are married. They have two sons, Paul and Steve, and one daughter, Amy. Write sentences.

**For example:**

Amy is ...*Peter's daughter*... (Peter)

1  Paul is ................................................ (Steve)

2  Diana is ................................................ (Amy)

3  Diana is ................................................ (Peter)

4  Peter and Diana are .........................................

    ................................................(Amy and Steve)

5  Amy is ................................................ (Paul)

6  Peter is ................................................ (Diana)

7  Peter is ................................................ (Paul)

| | **7** |

---

**(B)** Correct the mistakes in each sentence.

**For example:**

A bottle ~~of~~ coke, please.    *A bottle of coke, please.*

1  David no understand Spanish.

.........................................................

2  These books isn't interesting.

.........................................................

3  – Where are these pizzas from?
   – Their from Pizza in the Park.

.........................................................

4  Your son like his work?

.........................................................

5  Do you like burgers?
   Yes, I like.

.........................................................

6  It's George car.

.........................................................

| | **6** |

---

**(C)** Look at the pictures and write the words in the correct places. What is the extra word?

| | **9** |

---

**D** Complete the gaps with a pronoun or adjective (e.g. *I*, *me*, *my*, *he*, *him*, *his*, etc.).

**For example:**

My son really likes Indian food but I don't like ..*it*... .

1 Do you like children?

Yes, I love ................. .

2 *(in a hotel)* Good afternoon.

Good afternoon, ................. names are Tony and Kay Bush.

3 Is Penélope Cruz a good actress?

Yes, I like ................. a lot.

4 These are my sons. ................. names are Mohamed and Ahmed.

5 Do you eat meat?

Yes, but I don't like ................. very much.

6 Is this ................. pen?

Yes, it is. Thank you very much.

| 6 |

**E** Write a verb in the Present Simple, positive or negative, in each gap.

**For example:**

I ..*have*. a computer but it ..*isn't*. very good.

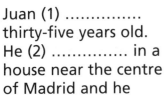

## This Month's Weightwatcher

Juan (1) .............. thirty-five years old. He (2) .............. in a house near the centre of Madrid and he (3) .............. for *Allo* magazine. He's married but he (4) .............. any children. He (5) .............. seven burgers and a lot of chocolate every day. He (6) .............. a lot of football on the television, but he (7) .............. football. 'I'm 120 kilos. I want to be 90 kilos,' he says.

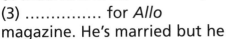

| 7 |

**F** Put a preposition from the box into the correct place in the sentences.

| on   from   in   with   of   ~~at~~ |

                    *at*
1   Maria's/school.
2   Michael Owen, the footballer, is England.
3   Is Lake Titicaca Brazil?
4   Are you holiday?
5   The bus stop's on the left the station.
6   Do you live your son's family?

| 5 |

**G** Correct the spelling of these words.

**For example:**

theetre ....*theatre*.........

1   shoping   .............   4 caretoons   .............
2   danceing   .............   5 clasical music   .............
3   traveling   .............

| 5 |

**H** Tick (✓) the correct answer.

**For example:**

Where are you from?

a) Argentina. ✓      b) I from Japan.      c) German.

1 Can I help you?

a) Yes, you have stamps?

b) Yes, have you any stamps?

c) Do you have any stamps?

2 Can I have three cheeseburgers, please?

a) Sorry, we haven't cheeseburgers.

b) Sorry, we don't have no cheeseburgers.

c) Sorry, we don't have any cheeseburgers.

3 Can I help you?

a) Where the station?

b) Is a station near?

c) Where's the station?

4 What's Susanna's job?

a) She's an engineer.

b) She's engineer.

c) She's a engineer.

5 Do you like dance music?

a) Yes, I like.

b) Yes, we do.

c) Yes, we like.

| 5 |

| 50 |

© Pearson Education 2002      **169**

# Modules 5–6

TIME: 30 MINUTES

## Test B

Name: ...............................................................

**Ⓐ** John and Hilary are married. They have 4 children, 2 boys, Sam and Ben, and 2 girls, Penny and Abby. Write sentences.

Hilary is (1) ......*Sam's mother*..................... ( Sam).

and (2) .................................................... (John).

Ben is (3) .................................... (Penny and Abby).

and (4) ..................................................... (Hilary).

John is (5) .................................................... (Sam).

and (6) ..................................................... (Hilary).

Penny and Abby are (7) ..........................................

.................................................(John and Hilary).

John and Hilary are (8) ..........................................

.................................................(Sam and Ben).

☐ **7**

**Ⓑ** Write a verb in the Present Simple, positive or negative, in each gap.

**For example:**

I ...*have*... a computer but it ...*isn't*... very good.

## Teacher of the Month

Margarita Da Silva
(1) ..................
Portuguese and she
(2) .................. with
her family in Lisbon.
She (3) ...............
three languages, Portuguese, Spanish and English and she (4) .................. for a language school in the centre of the city. She (5) ................. English to children from four to six years old. She really (6) .................. her job: 'It's fantastic!', but she (7) ................. the hours. 'I work from eight o'clock to eight o'clock: twelve hours every day!'

☐ **7**

**Ⓒ** Look at the pictures. Write the words.

**For example:**

1 ......................

...... *CD* ......

3 ......................

2 ......................

4 ......................

5 ......................

6 ......................

7 ......................

8 ......................

☐ **8**

**Ⓓ** Correct the mistakes in each sentence.

**For example:**

A bottle⁄coke, please. ....*A bottle of coke, please.*....

1 Mr Kohl speak English?

.................................................................

2 Colin no like cats.

.................................................................

3 Do you like classical music? – Yes, I like.

.................................................................

4 How old are you're grandchildren?

.................................................................

5 These eggs isn't good.

.................................................................

☐ **5**

**E**  Complete the gaps with a pronoun or adjective (e.g. *I*, *me*, *my*, *he*, *him*, *his*, etc).

**For example:**

My son really likes Indian food but I don't like ...*it*. .

Dear Grandmother,

How are you? I'm very well. I'm in class 2 now. I have three new teachers. Mr Carey is great. (1) ................'s from the USA. I like (2) ................. a lot because (3) ................. lessons are interesting. Miss James and Mrs Brown are from England and I don't like (4) ................. very much. (5) ................. lessons are awful! Miss James is 26 or 27 and she's (6) ................. French language teacher and Mrs Brown is very old and teaches cooking. I hate (7) ................. and she doesn't like (8) ................. !

Lots of love,

Binnie.

| | 8 |
|---|---|

**F**  Look at the pictures and complete the sentences.

1 Sarah likes ............ .

2 Miko likes ............

.............................. .

3 Tom likes ............

.............................. .

5 Patsy likes ............

.............................. .

4 José likes ............ .

| | 5 |
|---|---|

**G**  Put a preposition from the box into the correct place in the sentences.

| on   from   on   with   of   ~~at~~   in |
|---|

**For example:**

Elizabeth's ᵃᵗ school.

1   The White House is the USA.

2   We live our grandparents.

3   Maria lives in the centre the city.

4   The bank's the left of the cinema.

5   We're here in India holiday.

6   Tomas comes Poland.

| | 6 |
|---|---|

**H**  Tick (✓) the correct answer.

**For example:**

Where are you from?

a) Argentina. ✓     b) I from Japan.     c) German.

1   Can I have six bananas, please?
   a) Sorry, we don't have no bananas.
   b) Sorry, we don't have any bananas.
   c) Sorry, we haven't bananas.

2   What's Tom's job?
   a) He's an actor.
   b) He's actor.
   c) He's a actor.

3   Do you like shopping?
   a) Yes, we like.
   b) Yes, I like.
   c) Yes, we do.

4   Can I help you?
   a) Do you have any postcards?
   b) Yes, have you postcards?
   c) Yes, you have postcards?

| | 4 |
|---|---|

| | 50 |
|---|---|

# Modules 7–8

TIME: 30 MINUTES

Name: ...............................................................

**A** Write one word in each gap.

**For example:**
*When*. do you start work? – At nine o'clock.

## Mothers and Children

Q: (1) .....*What*.'s your full name?
A: *Maria Elisabetta Prodi.*
Q: And (2) ............ (3) ........... you live?
A: *In the centre of Rome.*
Q: Do you have a (4) ............ ?
A: *Yes, usually I'm a dancer, but not now!*
Q: (5) ............ (6) ............ people are (7) ............ in your family?
A: *Four. My husband, my son and my two daughters.*
Q: What are (8) ............ names?
A: *Toni, Marco, Sonia and Ana.*
Q: And (9) ............'s this?
A: *This is Ana.*
Q: (10) ............ (11) ............ is she?
A: *She's just eighteen months old!*
Q: She's beautiful!

[10]

**B** Match a word from A with a word from B.

**For example:**

| A | | B |
|---|---|---|
| 1 watch | .....*f*.... | a work |
| 2 get | .......... | b the Internet |
| 3 have | .......... | c chess |
| 4 use | .......... | d home |
| 5 go to | .......... | e a magazine |
| 6 play | .......... | f television |
| 7 speak | .......... | g breakfast |
| 8 read | .......... | h guitar |
| 9 play the | .......... | i French |

[8]

**C** Put a word/words from the box into the correct place in each sentence.

| every on doesn't never in can't ~~do~~ |
|---|

1  How ^*do* you spell 'magazine'?
2  My husband reads newspapers. He hates them.
3  I like dancing but I dance very well.
4  Mr Fenton usually works from seven to twelve o'clock the morning.
5  I go shopping weekend.
6  Rachel really like jazz music.
7  I go to the cinema Fridays.

[6]

**D** Write the missing letters in these verbs.

1  r *u* n
2  w _ l _
3  t _ _ k
4  s t _ _ _
5  w r _ _ _
6  c _ _ k
7  h _ _ r

[3]

**E**  Write the words:

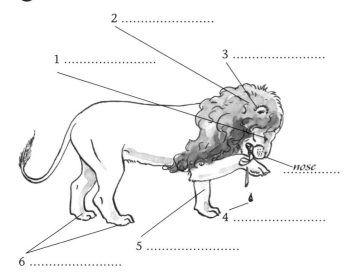

2 ........................

1 ........................

3 ........................

nose ........................

4 ........................

5 ........................

6 ........................

| 6 |

**F**  Correct the mistakes.

**For example:**

Does Natasha live with her the parents?
*Does Natasha live with her parents?*

1  My sister not usually watch cartoons.

   ..................................................

2  Do you can drive well?

   ..................................................

3  Do you work in the night?

   ..................................................

4  I wear shoes in the home always.

   ..................................................

5  Is that Sonia brother?

   ..................................................

| 5 |

**G**  Write the words.

**For example:**

73  *seventy-three*

1  105  ..................................

2  25%  ..................................

3  10,000 ..................................

4  7 cm  ..................................

5  ⏰  ..................................

| 5 |

**H**  Tick (✓) the correct answer.

**For example:**

Where are you from?

a) Argentina. ✓    b) I from Japan.    c) German.

1  Do you have the time?
   a) I'm sorry.
   b) I'm sorry, I don't.
   c) Yes, it's half to seven.

2  Can I help you?
   a) Yes. When the bus goes?
   b) Yes. When does go the bus?
   c) Yes. When does the bus go?

3  When is breakfast?
   a) On eight.
   b) At eight.
   c) At eight to nine.

4  Can I help you?
   a) How much are these pens?
   b) How much those pens?
   c) How much cost those pens?

5  Yes?
   a) Who is the bank?
   b) Where is the bank?
   c) Is near a bank?

6  Hello, Jon.
   a) Hi. Here is my sister, Paula.
   b) She is my sister, Paula.
   c) This is my sister, Paula.
   Hello, Paula. Nice to meet you.

7  Can you please turn round?
   a) Sorry, no understand.
   b) Sorry, I don't understand.
   c) Sorry, I'm not understand.

| 7 |

| 50 |

# Modules 7-8

TIME: 30 MINUTES

# Test B

Name: ........................................................

**A** Write a question word(s) in each gap.

**For example:**

*When*. do you start work? – At nine o'clock.

## Paul Owen: What does he like?

**Q:** (1) ............'s your favourite day of the week, Paul?

**A:** *Sunday.*

**Q:** (2) ............ ?

**A:** *Because I always play football with my son.*

**Q:** (3) ............ children do you have?

**A:** *Two.*

**Q:** (4) ............ are their names?

**A:** *Chris and Martin.*

**Q:** And (5) ............ are they?

**A:** *Nine and five years old.*

**Q:** (6) ............ do you live?

**A:** *Near Dublin, in Ireland.*

**Q:** And (7) ............'s your favourite footballer?

**A:** *David Beckham. He's fantastic!*

**Q:** (8) ............ is your next football game?

**A:** *Saturday. We play Manchester United.*

**Q:** Good luck!

**A:** *Thank you.*

| 8 |

**B** Put a cross (✗) next to the incorrect word.

**For example:**

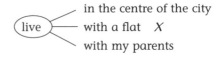

live — in the centre of the city / with a flat ✗ / with my parents

1 go to — home / work / the bank

2 drive — a car / well / a bicycle

3 watch — picture / TV / football

4 use — the Internet / a camera / lunch

5 have — twenty-one years old / a job / breakfast

6 get — the station / home / up

7 play — chess / guitar / football

8 read — music / a magazine / the Internet

9 speak — German / Italy / three languages

| 9 |

**C** Correct the mistakes.

**For example:**

Does Natasha live with her the parents?
*Does Natasha live with her parents?*

1 Is this you're pen? ........................................

2 Does Tanya can walk? ........................................

3 Mrs Carter not usually read newspapers. ................

4 I work in night. ........................................

5 My daughter hates cat. ........................................

| 5 |

**174**

© Pearson Education 2002  **PHOTOCOPIABLE**

**D** Put a word/words from the box into the correct place in each sentence.

every   on   doesn't   never   in   can't   ~~do~~

1   How  you spell 'magazine'?
2   Greg like shopping at all.
3   I go dancing weekend.
4   I like swimming but I swim very well.
5   Does Patrick go to work Saturdays?
6   Mr Jones uses a mobile phone. He hates them.
7   Julia sleeps from ten o'clock to twelve o'clock the morning.

**6**

**E** Write the parts of the body.

**For example:**

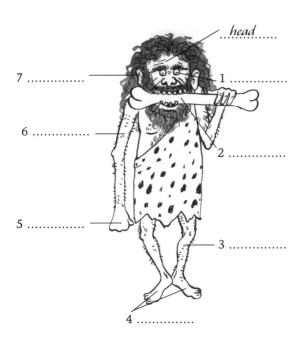

......head......

7 ...............   1 ...............
6 ...............
2 ...............
5 ...............   3 ...............
4 ...............

**7**

**F** Write the words.

**For example:**

73   ......seventy-three......

1   ......................................
2   50% ..............................
3   22,000 ..........................
4   108 ................................
5   ......................................
6   9 km .............................

**6**

**G** Write the verbs.

1 ...............   2 ...............   3 ...............

4 ...............   5 ...............   6 ...............

**3**

**H** Tick (✓) the correct answer.

**For example:**
Where are you from?
a) Argentina. ✓   b) I from Japan.   c) German.

1   When is our lesson?
    a) At nine.
    b) On nine.
    c) At half to nine.
2   Can I help you?
    a) Yes. When the football starts?
    b) Yes. When does start the football?
    c) Yes. When does the football start?
3   Do you have any stamps?
    a) Yes, they are.
    b) I'm sorry, we don't.
    c) I'm sorry.
4   Can I help you?
    a) How much are these eggs?
    b) How much cost those eggs?
    c) How much those eggs?
5   Yes?
    a) Is near a post office?
    b) Who is the post office?
    c) Where is the post office?
6   Do you have a penknife?
    a) Sorry, I'm not understand.
    b) Sorry, I don't understand.
    c) Sorry, no understand.

**6**

**50**

**175**

# Modules 9–10

TIME: 30 MINUTES

## Test A

Name: ................................................

### Ⓐ Write a verb in the past.

My grandfather (1) ................. in 1925. He
(2) ...................... school when he was six years old
and when he was twelve he (3) ................. school and
(4) ................. to live in Manchester with his sister's
family. He (5) ................. for a bus company and
when he was eighteen he (6) ................. a bus driver.
He (7) ................. his wife in 1944 and they got
married in 1946. They (8) ................. four children:
my father and three daughters.

| **8** |

### Ⓑ Write the opposite adjectives.

**For example:**

a good lesson    ...*a bad lesson*....

1  an old building        ...................................
2  a poor country         ...................................
3  a beautiful city       ...................................
4  a slow train           ...................................
5  a quiet road           ...................................
6  an expensive holiday   ...................................
7  a tall boy             ...................................
8  a dangerous sport      ...................................

| **8** |

### Ⓒ Put the sentences in the correct order.

**For example:**

time / bus / does / go / the / What / ?
  *What time does the bus go?*

1  Roald Dahl / Where / born / was / ?
   ...................................................

2  name / your / 's / full / What / husband / was / ?
   ...................................................

3  were / family / children / How many / there /
   your / in / ?
   ...................................................

4  always / Saturday / They / football / on /
   played / evenings / .
   ...................................................

5  from / were / their / Where / parents / ?
   ...................................................

| **5** |

### Ⓓ Write the full date in words.

**For example:**

14/1/1976  *January the fourteenth, nineteen seventy-six*

1  16/5/1992   ...................................................
2  21/7/1965   ...................................................
3  10/10/2001  ...................................................
4  4/2/1853    ...................................................
5  12/3/2006   ...................................................

| **5** |

### Ⓔ Put the words in the correct columns.

| 0 | 0  o | 0  o  o |
|---|------|---------|
| *liked* | ................ | ................ |
| ................ | ................ | ................ |
| ................ | ................ | ................ |

~~liked~~  beautiful  watched  dangerous
started  lived  listened

| **6** |

**F** Correct the sentences.

**For example:**

My names Susan.

......*My name's Susan.*......

1 My flat's very confortable.

....................................................

2 We studied Japanese at school.

....................................................

3 Were Stefan at school on Thursday?

....................................................

4 It's a job important.

....................................................

5 English is a very dificult language.

....................................................

6 My parents was very happy.

....................................................

| 6 |

**G** Write the missing letters.

**For example:**

　　g o　　　　　　w _e_ _n_ t

| | PRESENT | PAST |
|---|---|---|
| 1 | m _ k _ | m _ _ _ |
| 2 | w _ _ _ | w _ _ k _ _ |
| 3 | b _ g _ n | b _ g _ _ |
| 4 | o p _ _ | o p _ _ _ _ |
| 5 | d i _ | d _ _ _ |
| 6 | h _ t _ | h _ _ _ _ |
| 7 | f _ n _ _ h | f _ _ _ _ _ _ |

| 7 |

**H** Tick (✓) the correct answer.

**For example:**

Where are you from?

a) Argentina. ✓　　b) I from Japan.　　c) German.

1 Where were you born?
　a) In 1965.
　b) In Louisiana.
　c) On Saturday.

2 How much was your computer?
　a) This was $500.
　b) It sold $500.
　c) It was $500.

3 How old was your mother when she got married?
　a) About twenty-two.
　b) She had twenty-one years old.
　c) I'm not know.

4 When were you at home?
　a) At the morning.
　b) On five o'clock.
　c) In the afternoon.

5 Can I help you?
　a) Yes, do you have any postcards?
　b) Yes, have you postcards?
　c) Yes, you have postcards?

| 5 |

| 50 |

© Pearson Education 2002　　　　　　**177**

# Modules 9–10

TIME: 30 MINUTES

# Test B

Name: ................................................................

**A** Write a verb in the past.

My sister is Amy Hunt, the famous writer. She
(1) .................. in 1982 in Boston, USA, when I was
four years old. Our family (2) .................. in the centre
of the city and Amy (3) .................. school when she
was five in Boston. In 1990 we (4) .................. house
and (5) .................. to live in Chicago. Amy
(6) .................. school when she was eighteen and she
(7) .................. her first book, *Chicago Blues*, when she
was nineteen. It (8) .................. 100,000 copies in one
month! My sister was rich! She (9) .................. John,
her husband, one year later and they got married in
December 2001.

| **9** |

**B** Write the opposite adjectives.

**For example:**

a good lesson ......*a bad lesson*......

1   a safe road          ..................................
2   a rich family        ..................................
3   a new hotel          ..................................
4   a beautiful house    ..................................
5   an expensive school  ..................................
6   a clean room         ..................................
7   a fast train         ..................................
8   a busy city          ..................................

| **8** |

**C** Put the sentences in the correct order.

**For example:**

time / bus / does / go / the / What / ?
......*What time does the bus go?*......

1   were / people / class / How many / there / your /
    in / ?
    ..................................................................

2   the / never / We / TV / in / watched / evenings / .
    ..................................................................

3   Leonardo da Vinci / When / born / was / ?
    ..................................................................

4   English / difficult / your / Were / lessons / ?
    ..................................................................

5   was / wife / job / What / 's / first / your / ?
    ..................................................................

| **5** |

**D** Write the full date in words.

**For example:**

14/1/1976   *January the fourteenth, nineteen seventy-six*

1   17/4/1982   ..................................................
2   22/11/1969  ..................................................
3   2/2/2000    ..................................................
4   6/6/1876    ..................................................
5   10/5/2007   ..................................................

| **5** |

**E** Put the words in the correct columns.

| 0 | 0   o | 0   o   o |
|---|-------|-----------|
| *watched* | .................. | .................. |
| .............. | .................. | .................. |
| .............. | .................. | .................. |

~~watched~~   difficult   loved   beautiful
opened   played   hated

| **6** |

**F**   Correct the sentences.

**For example:**

My names Susan.

............*My name's Susan.*...............

1   There wasn't any people in the square.

   ...................................................................

2   It's a house very comfortable.

   ...................................................................

3   Your CD player is very nosy.

   ...................................................................

4   I were very naughty when I was young.

   ...................................................................

5   The train leaved the station at half past nine.

   ...................................................................

   | 5 |

**G**   Write the missing letters.

**For example:**

   g o                    w _e_ _n_ t

|   | **PRESENT** | **PAST** |
|---|---|---|
| 1 | b _ c _ _ _ | b _ _ _ _ _ |
| 2 | t _ _ k | t _ _ k _ _ |
| 3 | st _ _ t | s t _ _ _ _ _ |
| 4 | m _ k _ | m _ _ _ |
| 5 | l _ k _ | l _ _ _ _ |
| 6 | s _ n g | s _ _ _ |
| 7 | l i _ _ | l _ v _ _ |

   | 7 |

**H**   Tick (✓) the correct answer.

**For example:**

Where are you from?

a) Argentina. ✓     b) I from Japan.     c) German.

1   How much was your camera?
   a) This was £100.
   b) It costed £100.
   c) It was £100.

2   When were you at home?
   a) At the afternoon.
   b) On half past seven.
   c) In the evening.

3   When were you born?
   a) In 1988.
   b) In South Africa.
   c) On Wednesday.

4   Were you at home on Friday?
   a) Yes, I wasn't.
   b) Yes, we were.
   c) Yes, I was at.

5   How old was your father when he died?
   a) Sixty-two.
   b) He had sixty-five years old.
   c) I'm not know.

   | 5 |

   | 50 |

© Pearson Education 2002                    **179**

# Test A

Name: ..........................................................

**A** Complete the conversation.

**Ana:** Hello, James. (1) ...*Did*.... you (2) ............ a good holiday?

**James:** Yes, it (3) ............ very good. Do you (4) ............ to see my photographs?

**Ana:** Oh, yes. Did you go (5) ............ ?

**James:** No, I (6) ............ with my friend, Pete.

**Ana:** And (7) ............ did you (8) ............ ?

**James:** In a small hotel (9) ............ the beach.

**Ana:** What did you (10) ............ every day?

**James:** We relaxed on the beach and we (11) ............ shopping or walking and (12) ............ the evenings we sometimes (13) ............ to music in the cafés.

[  12  ]

**B** Put one word from the box into each sentence.

are  by  to  an  last  ago  any  on  in  ~~the~~  every

**For example:**
My son Jack lives in ~~centre~~ of the city.  *(the inserted above)*

1  We went to Moscow car.
2  Did you see Beverly Kinley week?
3  I'm sorry. I didn't buy eggs.
4  When I was young I always read bed.
5  Chris's birthday is December 15th.
6  What you going to do tomorrow evening?
7  Do you want see the new *Star Wars* film?
8  We go shopping weekend.
9  I met my wife ten years.
10  Yoko is engineer.

[  10  ]

**C** Put a cross (✗) next to the incorrect word.

**For example:**

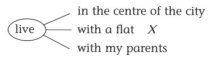
live — in the centre of the city / with a flat  *X* / with my parents

1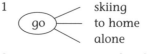
go — skiing / to home / alone

2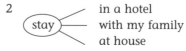
stay — in a hotel / with my family / at house

3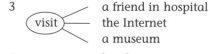
visit — a friend in hospital / the Internet / a museum

4
have — lunch / nice time / three brothers

5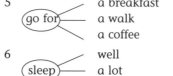
go for — a breakfast / a walk / a coffee

6  sleep — well / a lot / good

7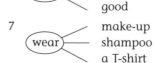
wear — make-up / shampoo / a T-shirt

[  7  ]

**D** Join the sentences with *and* or *but*.

**For example:**
I like classical music ...*and*... I like jazz music.

1  We went to the station ............ there weren't any trains.
2  Are you going to go to Rome ............ Milan?
3  Mark can speak Chinese ............ he can't speak Russian.
4  We went to Ibiza on holiday ............ had a good time.
5  I want to go to university ............ study engineering.
6  We're going to meet Ray Smith ............ his wife.

[  6  ]

**E** Write the words.

1  *shampoo*  2  ...............  3  ...............

4  ...............  5  ...............  6  ...............

7  ...............  8  ...............  9  ...............

| | 8 |
|---|---|

**F** Tick (✓) the correct answer.

**For example:**

Where are you from?

a) Argentina. ✓     b) I from Japan.     c) German.

1  Can I help you?
   a) Yes. Can I have a single to Paris?
   b) Yes. I like a single to Paris.
   c) Yes. I want single to Paris.

2  What size is this T-shirt?
   a) £6.50.
   b) It's expensive.
   c) Large.

3  I'm going to do a test tomorrow.
   a) Have a nice time.
   b) Good luck.
   c) See you later.

4  When's the last train to Belfast?
   a) On Friday.
   b) At 11.30.
   c) It's very late.

5  Are you going to go to the shops?
   a) No, I am.
   b) Yes, why?
   c) Yes, yesterday.

6  Two burgers, please.
   a) Here are you.
   b) Over there.
   c) Here you are.

7  Do you want to watch television?
   a) Yes, I want.
   b) Yes, I like.
   c) Yes, I do.

| | 7 |
|---|---|

| | 50 |
|---|---|

  © Pearson Education 2002

# Modules 11–12

TIME: 30 MINUTE

# Test B

Name: .......................................................

## A Complete the conversation.

**Tom:** Hello, mother?

**Vicky:** Hello, Tom. How are you and (1) ..*where*.. are you?

**Tom:** (2) ............ the Hilton Hotel, Tokyo and I'm fine. We got here twenty minutes (3) ............ . Our room is on the sixteenth floor and it's very small! And yesterday we (4) ............ in Kyoto. It (5) ............ beautiful.

**Vicky:** Where did you (6) ............ ?

**Tom:** In an old hotel in the centre of the city.

**Vicky:** And what did you (7) ............ there?

**Tom:** I spent a lot of money!

**Vicky:** (8) ............ are you going to go to Australia?

**Tom:** We' (9) ............ going tomorrow night (10) ............ ten o'clock.

**Vicky:** (11) ............ a good journey (12) ............ telephone me from Sydney! Give my love to Theresa.

**Tom:** OK. Bye!

**Vicky:** Goodbye.

| 11 |

## B Put a cross (✗) next to the incorrect word.

**For example:**

live — in the centre of the city
— with a flat   X
— with my parents

1 have — a mobile phone
— nice week
— breakfast

2 stay — with my friend
— at home
— at house

3 wear — a handbag
— a jacket
— a jumper

4 go for — lunch
— a walk
— swimming

5 do — his homework
— sport
— the Internet

6 go to — the beach
— home
— a restaurant

7 visit — your grandmother
— the capital city
— the cinema

| 7 |

## C Join the sentences with *and* or *but*.

**For example:**
I like classical music ..*and*.. I like jazz music.

1 John went to an Italian restaurant ............ he wasn't hungry.

2 We're going to meet Ray Smith ............ his wife.

3 We went to Paris ............ we didn't see the Eiffel Tower.

4 I got up early ............ started work at 7.30.

5 They went to the cinema ............ had a good time.

| 5 |

**D**  Put one word from the box into each sentence.

| any every ~~the~~ last a to are on ago by the |
|---|

**For example:**

My son Jack lives in ̶centre of the city.  *the*

1   They don't want spend a lot of money.
2   Do you play football week?
3   We travelled to Cape Town plane.
4   We're going to go on holiday Saturday.
5   Do you play guitar?
6   Sorry. There weren't vegetables.
7   Did you play tennis week?
8   I finished university three years.
9   I work for ICI and Stuart is doctor.
10  What you going to do tonight?

| **10** |
|---|

**E**  Write the words.

.....*jumper*.....

1  .......................

2  .......................

3  .......................

4  .......................

5  .......................

6  .......................

7  .......................

8  .......................

9  .......................

| **9** |
|---|

**F**  Tick (✓) the correct answer.

**For example:**
Where are you from?
a) Argentina. ✓        b) I from Japan.        c) German.

1   It's my birthday tomorrow.
   a) Good luck!
   b) See you later.
   c) Have a good day!
2   Can I have three coffees, please.
   a) Here you are.
   b) Here are they.
   c) Here are you.
3   Can I help you?
   a) How size is this jacket?
   b) What size is this jacket?
   c) Do you have large jacket?
4   Do you want to watch *The Matrix*?
   a) Yes, I like.
   b) No, I don't.
   c) Yes, I want.
5   Are you going to the post office?
   a) Maybe, why?
   b) Yes, two hours ago.
   c) No, we are.
6   Can I help you?
   a) Yes, I want return to Geneva.
   b) Yes, I like a return to Geneva.
   c) Yes, can I have a return to Geneva?
7   Did you see Paula?
   a) Yes, I saw.
   b) Yes, I did see.
   c) No, I didn't.
8   When's the last train to Belfast?
   a) On Friday.
   b) At 11.30.
   c) It's very late.

| **8** |
|---|

| **50** |
|---|

# Test Answer Key

## Modules 1–2 Test A

**A**
1 What's your surname?
2 What's your first name?
3 What's your address?
4 Are you British? (or any other nationality)
5 What's your telephone number?
6 What's your job?

**B**
1 teacher  2 doctor  3 businesswoman  4 actress
5 waiter  6 police officer  7 politician
8 shop assistant

**C**
1 What's your full name?
2 It isn't a French car. It's an Italian car.
3 Open your books.
4 Her name's Caroline and she's from Switzerland.
5 You're Russian, yes?

**D**
1 twenty-two  2 eighteen  3 one hundred
4 sixty-four  5 thirteen  6 eleven

**E**
1 How  2 Very  3 you  4 This  5 meet  6 an
7 later

**F**
1 write  2 read  3 work  4 he's from  5 capital

**G**

| O<br>Spain | O  o<br>London<br>Turkish | o  O<br>Brazil |
|---|---|---|
| O  o  o<br>Italy<br>Germany | o  o  O<br>Japanese | o  O  o  o<br>American |

**H**
1 an  2 a  3 an  4 a  5 a  6 an  7 a  8 an

## Modules 1–2 Test B

**A**
1 What's your surname? (1)   Pesci (2)
2 Are you Italian? (3)
   American./not Italian, I'm American. (4)
3 How old are you? (5)   I'm 23./23. (6)
4 Are you married? (7)
5 What's your job? (8)   I'm a student./A student. (9)

**B**
1 What's **her/his** job?
2 It's **an** English car.
3 **His** name's John.
4 He's **a** politician.
5 **She's/He's** thirty-five.
6 He's **from** Scotland.
7 Are **you** Polish?

**C**
1 teacher  2 footballer  3 police officer  4 actress
5 businessman  6 waiter  7 singer
8 shop assistant

**D**
1 twenty-one  2 thirty  3 eight  4 one/a hundred
5 fourteen  6 twelve  7 ninety-five

**E**
1 My name isn't Ming-mei.
2 You aren't British.
3 I'm not married.
4 She isn't from Korea.
5 Sanyo isn't a Turkish company.

**F**

A•merican   Turk•ey   Jap•an   Po•lish
Brazilian   Italy   the U•SA   Great Britain

**G**
1 b  2 a  3 c  4 a  5 b  6 a

## Modules 3–4 Test A

**A**
1 bread  2 meat  3 coffee  4 fruit  5 water
6 milk  7 eggs  8 pasta  9 cheese  10 vegetables

**B**
1 are  2 aren't  3 our / the / these  4 They're
5 very / really  6 Your / The  7 My  8 on

**C**

| | | | | | | | | |
|---|---|---|---|---|---|---|---|---|
| 1 | | P | A | R | K | | | |
| 2 | L | A | K | E | | | | |
| 3 | | B | U | S | S | T | O | P |
| 4 | S | T | A | T | I | O | N | |
| 5 | | C | A | F | E | | | |
| 6 | | S | Q | U | A | R | E | |
| 7 | S U | P | E | R | M | A | R | K E T |
| 8 | | B | A | N | K | | | |
| 9 | | C | I | N | E | M | A | |
| 10 | M O | U | N | T | A | I | N | |

The extra word is RESTAURANT.

**D**
1 Are (1) these (2) your pens (3)?
2 There are (4) some (5) children. (6)
3 Are (7) those (8) people (9) from Italy?
4 These (10) addresses (11) please.
5 Are (12) there any (13) buses (14) from London to Oxford?

**E**
1 expensive   2 beautiful   3 fantastic   4 hotel
5 interesting   6 restaurant   7 address
**F**
1 a   2 b   3 c   4 b   5 a   6 b   7 b   8 c

## Modules 3–4 Test B

**A**
1 fantastic   2 small   3 old   4 interesting
5 expensive   6 good   7 nice   8 hot
**B**
1 Are (1) these (2) your sandwiches (3) ?
2 Are (4) those (5) cars (6) Italian?
3 Who are (7) those (8) people (9) ?
4 Your babies (10) are (11) beautiful.
5 Are (12) there any (13) taxis (14) ?
**C**
1 post office   2 hotel   3 café   4 supermarket
5 car park   6 cinema   7 beach   8 station
**D**
1 is   2 in   3 there   4 this / here / that   5 There's
6 on   7 These / Those   8 old   9 They're
**E**
1 bread   2 pizza   3 coffee   4 vegetables   5 fruit
6 milk
**F**

| 0 | 0   o | 0   o   o |
|---|-------|-----------|
| names<br>squares | beaches<br>mountains | holidays<br>waitresses |

**G**
1 c   2 c   3 b   4 a   5 b   6 c

## Modules 5–6 Test A

**A**
1 Steve's brother   2 Amy's mother   3 Peter's wife
4 Amy and Steve's parents   5 Paul's sister
6 Diana's husband   7 Paul's father
**B**
1 David doesn't understand Spanish.
2 These books aren't interesting. / This book isn't
   interesting.
3 They're from Pizza in the Park.
4 Does your son like his work?
5 Yes, I do.   6 It's George's car.
**C**

| 1 | | | | C | A | M | E | R | A |
|---|---|---|---|---|---|---|---|---|---|
| 2 | | | P | U | R | S | E | | |
| 3 | M | O | B | I | L | E | P | H | O | N | E |
| 4 | | | | C | D | | | | |
| 5 | M | A | G | A | Z | I | N | E | |
| 6 | W | A | L | L | E | T | | | |
| 7 | | | W | A | T | C | H | | |
| 8 | | | | G | L | A | S | S | E | S |
| 9 | L | I | G | H | T | E | R | | |
| 10 | | | | R | A | D | I | O | |

The extra word is CREDIT CARD.
**D**
1 them   2 Our   3 her   4 Their   5 it   6 your
**E**
1 is   2 lives   3 works   4 doesn't have   5 eats / has
6 watches   7 doesn't play
**F**
2 Michael Owen, the footballer, is **from** England.
3 Is Lake Titicaca **in** Brazil?
4 Are you **on** holiday?
5 The bus stop's on the left **of** the station.
6 Do you live **with** your son's family?
**G**
1 shopping   2 dancing   3 travelling   4 cartoons
5 classical music
**H**
1 c   2 c   3 c   4 a   5 b

## Modules 5–6 Test B

**A**
2 John's wife   3 Penny and Abby's brother
4 Hilary's son   5 Sam's father
6 Hilary's husband   7 John and Hilary's children
8 Sam and Ben's parents
**B**
1 is   2 lives   3 speaks   4 works   5 teaches
6 likes / loves   7 doesn't like
**C**
1 camera   2 mobile phone   3 magazine   4 watch
5 lighter   6 purse   7 wallet   8 tissues
**D**
1 Does Mr Kohl speak English?
2 Colin doesn't like cats.
3 Yes, I do.
4 How old are your grandchildren?
5 These eggs aren't good.
**E**
1 He   2 him   3 his   4 them   5 Their   6 my / our
7 her   8 me
**F**
1 cooking
2 TV *or* watching TV
3 newspapers / reading a newspaper / newspapers
4 dancing
5 computers / the Internet *or* using a computer /
   computers / the Internet
**G**
1 The White House is **in** the USA.
2 We live **with** our grandparents.
3 Maria lives in the centre **of** the city.
4 The bank's **on** the left of the cinema.
5 We're here in India **on** holiday.
6 Tomas comes **from** Poland.
**H**
1 b   2 a   3 c   4 a

## Modules 7–8 Test A

**A**
2 where   3 do   4 job   5 How   6 many   7 there
8 their   9 who   10 How   11 old
**B**
2 d   3 g   4 b   5 a   6 c   7 i   8 e   9 h

**C**
2 My husband **never** reads newspapers. He hates them.
3 I like dancing but I **can't** dance very well.
4 Mr Fenton usually works from seven to twelve o'clock **in** the morning.
5 I go shopping **every** weekend.
6 Rachel **doesn't** really like jazz music.
7 I go to the cinema **on** Fridays.

**D**
2 walk   3 talk   4 stand   5 write   6 cook   7 hear

**E**
1 eye   2 head   3 ear   4 blood   5 leg   6 feet

**F**
1 My sister doesn't usually watch cartoons.
2 Do you drive well?
3 Do you work an night?
4 I always wear shoes at home.
5 Is that Sonia's brother?

**G**
1 a/one hundred and five   2 twenty-five per cent
3 ten thousand   4 seven centimetres
5 ten to seven

**H**
1 b   2 c   3 b   4 a   5 b   6 c   7 b

## Modules 7–8 Test B

**A**
1 What   2 Why   3 How many   4 What
5 how old   6 Where   7 who   8 When

**B**
1 home   2 a bicycle   3 picture   4 lunch
5 twenty-one years old   6 the station   7 guitar
8 the Internet   9 Italy

**C**
1 Is this your pen?
2 Can Tanya walk?
3 Mrs Carter doesn't usually read newspapers.
4 I work at night.
5 My daughter hates cats.

**D**
2 Greg **doesn't** like shopping at all.
3 I go dancing **every** weekend.
4 I like swimming but I **can't** swim very well.
5 Does Patrick go to work **on** Saturdays?
6 Mr Jones **never** uses a mobile phone. He hates them.
7 Julia sleeps from ten o'clock to twelve o'clock **in** the morning.

**E**
1 eye   2 bone   3 leg   4 feet   5 hand   6 arm
7 ear

**F**
1 half past nine
2 fifty per cent
3 twenty-two thousand
4 a/one hundred and eight
   (a/one hundred eight in US English)
5 twenty five to four
6 nine kilometres

**G**
1 sitting   2 standing   3 walking   4 running
5 writing   6 cooking

**H**
1 a   2 c   3 b   4 a   5 c   6 b

## Modules 9–10 Test A

**A**
1 was born   2 started / began   3 left / finished
4 went   5 worked   6 became   7 met   8 had

**B**
1 a new building   2 a rich country   3 an ugly city
4 a fast train   5 a busy road   6 a cheap holiday
7 a short boy   8 a safe sport

**C**
1 Where was Roald Dahl born?
2 What was your husband's full name?
3 How many children were there in your family?
4 They always played football on Saturday evenings.
5 Where were their parents from?

**D**
1 May the sixteenth, nineteen ninety-two
2 July the twenty-first, nineteen sixty-five
3 October the tenth, two thousand and one
4 February the fourth, eighteen fifty-three
5 March the twelfth, two thousand and six

**E**

| 0 | 0  o | 0  o  o |
|---|------|---------|
| watched lived | started listened | beautiful dangerous |

**F**
1 My flat's very comfortable.
2 We studied Japanese at school.
3 Was Stefan at school on Thursday?
4 It's an important job.
5 English is a very difficult language.
6 My parents were very happy.

**G**
1 make    made
2 walk    walked
3 begin   began
4 open    opened
5 die     died
6 hate    hated
7 finish  finished

**H**
1 b   2 c   3 a   4 c   5 a

## Modules 9–10 Test B

**A**
1 was born   2 lived   3 started / began   4 moved
5 went   6 finished / left   7 wrote   8 sold   9 met

**B**
1 a dangerous road   2 a poor family   3 an old hotel
4 an ugly house   5 a cheap school   6 a dirty room
7 a slow train   8 a quiet city

**C**
1 How many people were there in your class?
2 We never watched TV in the evenings.
3 When was Leonardo da Vinci born?
4 Were your English lessons difficult?
5 What was your first wife's job? / What was your wife's first job?

**D**
1 April the seventeenth, nineteen eighty-two
2 November the twenty-second, nineteen sixty-nine
3 February the second, two thousand
4 June the sixth, eighteen seventy-six
5 May the tenth, two thousand and seven

**E**

| 0 | 0   o | 0   o   o |
|---|-------|-----------|
| loved | opened | difficult |
| played | hated | beautiful |

**F**
1 There weren't any people in the square.
2 It's a very comfortable house.
3 Your CD player is very noisy.
4 I was very naughty when I was young.
5 The train left the station at half past nine.

**G**
1 become      became
2 talk         talked
3 start        started
4 make         made
5 like         liked
6 sing         sang
7 live         lived

**H**
1 c   2 c   3 a   4 b   5 a

## Modules 11–12 Test A

**A**
2 have   3 was   4 want   5 alone   6 went
7 where   8 stay   9 near / on   10 do   11 went
12 in   13 listened

**B**
1 We went to Moscow **by** car.
2 Did you see Beverly Kinley **last** week?
3 I'm sorry. I didn't buy **any** eggs.
4 When I was young I always read **in** bed.
5 Chris's birthday is **on** December 15th.
6 What **are** you going to do tomorrow evening?
7 Do you want **to** see the new *Star Wars* film?
8 We go shopping **every** weekend.
9 I met my wife ten years **ago**.
10 Yoko is **an** engineer.

**C**
1 to home   2 at house   3 the Internet   4 nice time
5 a breakfast   6 good   7 shampoo

**D**
1 but   2 and   3 but   4 and   5 and   6 and

**E**
2 jumper   3 jacket   4 handbag   5 lamp   6 table
7 chair   8 carpet   9 shoes

**F**
1 a   2 c   3 b   4 b   5 b   6 c   7 c

## Modules 11–12 Test B

**A**
2 In   3 ago   4 were   5 was   6 stay   7 do
8 When   9 re   10 at   11 Have   12 and

**B**
1 nice week   2 at house   3 a handbag
4 swimming   5 the Internet   6 home   7 the cinema

**C**
1 but   2 and   3 but   4 and   5 and

**D**
1 They don't want **to** spend a lot of money.
2 Do you play football **every** week?
3 We travelled to Cape Town **by** plane.
4 We're going to go on holiday **on** Saturday.
5 Do you play **the** guitar?
6 Sorry. There weren't **any** vegetables.
7 Did you play tennis **last** week?
8 I finished university three years **ago**.
9 I work for ICI and Stuart is **a** doctor.
10 What **are** you going to do tonight?

**E**
1 lamp   2 make-up   3 T-shirt   4 clothes   5 shoes
6 shampoo   7 table   8 chair   9 flowers

**F**
1 c   2 a   3 b   4 b   5 a   6 c   7 c   8 b

# Resource bank key

## Classroom language

| | | | |
|---|---|---|---|
| 1 | f | 4 | b |
| 2 | c | 5 | a |
| 3 | e | 6 | d |

## Module 1

### Vocabulary Booster – Jobs

**Exercise 1**

a nurse
b salesperson
c travel agent
d secretary
e musician
f taxi driver
g lawyer
h journalist

**Exercise 3**

```
            S E C R E T A R Y
            A
  T R A V E L   A G E N T
            E
        M U S I C I A N
            P
    L       E           N
  T A X I D R I V E R   U
    W       S           R
    Y     J O U R N A L I S T
    E       N           E
    R
```

## Module 2

### Vocabulary Booster – Nationalities

**Exercise 1**

| | | | |
|---|---|---|---|
| 1 | The USA | 9 | Poland |
| 2 | (Great) Britain | 10 | Turkey |
| 3 | Japan | 11 | Germany |
| 4 | France | 12 | Australia |
| 5 | Russia | 13 | Egypt |
| 6 | Italy | 14 | Thailand |
| 7 | Spain | 15 | China |
| 8 | Brazil | 16 | England |

**Exercise 2**

| -n, -an, -ian | -ish | -ese | other |
|---|---|---|---|
| American Russian Italian Brazilian Australian Egyptian | British Spanish Polish Turkish English | Japanese Chinese | French German Thai |

## Module 3

### 3A What are their names?

**Exercise 2**

a What are their names?
b Where are they from?
c What are their jobs?
d How old are they?
e Are they married?
f What's their address?
g What's their phone number?

### Vocabulary Booster – Food and drink

**Exercise 1**

1 chicken
2 beer
3 chocolate
4 tomatoes
5 orange juice
6 sausages
7 tea
8 bananas
9 wine
10 apples
11 potatoes

**Exercise 2**

| meat | vegetables | fruit | drinks | other words |
|---|---|---|---|---|
| sausages chicken | tomatoes potatoes | bananas apples | orange juice wine beer tea | chocolate |

# Module 4
## Vocabulary Booster – Places in a town

**Exercise 1**
1 a football stadium
2 a bookshop
3 a museum
4 a clothes shop
5 a market
6 a theatre
7 a pharmacy
8 a bus station
9 an airport
10 a library

## 4C Spot the difference

1 In picture A there are some mountains. In picture B there aren't any mountains.
2 In picture A there's one taxi. In picture B there are two taxis.
3 In picture A there are three trees. In picture B there are four trees.
4 In picture A there are two children near the bus stop. In picture B there are three children.
5 In picture A there's a bank on the right of the supermarket. In picture B it's a post office.
6 In picture A there's a man near the hotel. In picture B there isn't.
7 In picture A there are two boys near the supermarket. In picture B there are two girls.
8 In picture A there's a dog, in picture be there isn't.
9 In picture A there are six people in the café, in picture B there are five.
10 In picture A there are three bottles of water on the table in the café, in picture B there's only one bottle.

# Module 5
## Vocabulary Booster – Rooms in a house

**Exercise 1**
a bedroom
b living room
c kitchen
d bathroom
e hall
f balcony
g toilet

**Exercise 2**
1 a cooker
2 a sofa
3 a bath
4 a table
5 a shower
6 a fridge
7 a bed
8 a chair
9 a picture

# Module 6
## Vocabulary Booster – Sports

**Exercise 1**
a golf
b volleyball
c basketball
d motor racing
e jogging
f swimming
g boxing
h tennis
i cycling
j skiing

## 6C Does he or doesn't he?

a speak
b watch
c like
d use
e read
f like
g play
h read
i watch
j eat
k like

# Module 7
## 7A A footballer's day

**Worksheet A**
1 What time does he get up?
2 What does he have for breakfast?
3 What does he do in the morning?
4 What time does he have lunch?
5 What time does the match start?
6 What does he do after the match?
7 What does he do when he gets home?

**Worksheet B**
a What time does he have breakfast?
b What does he do in the morning?
c What time does he go to the stadium?
d What does he have for lunch?
e What time does the match start?
f What does he do in the evening?
g What time does he go to bed?

## Vocabulary Booster – Verbs and nouns

**Exercise 2**

| go to | go | play | have |
|---|---|---|---|
| a concert the theatre the gym the beach | shopping swimming dancing running | basketball cards golf volleyball | a meal a bath a shower a cup of coffee |

**Exercise 4**
a  go
b  play
c  have
d  go to; go
e  have
f  have
g  go; go to
h  go; play
i  go to
j  play

# Module 8
## Vocabulary Booster – Parts of the body

**Exercise 1**
a  head
b  nose
c  mouth
d  teeth
e  face
f  arm
g  fingers
h  hair
i  ear
j  eye
k  back
l  stomach
m  hand
n  leg
o  foot

**Exercise 4**

## 8B  Question word quiz

1  Where; c
2  How many; b
3  What; c
4  Who; b
5  Where; a
6  Why; b
7  Where; c (it's in Kenya)
8  How many; b
9  When; a (or c if used after 2004!)
10 What; b

# Module 9
## Vocabulary Booster – Describing people

**Exercise 1**
a  Chris
b  Alan
c  Chris or Alan
d  Mark
e  Chris
f  Alan
g  Mark or Chris
h  Mark
i  Alan or Chris
j  Mark
k  Alan

**Exercise 2**
a  has
b  has; 's
c  has
d  's; has
e  has; 's
f  's; 's

# Module 10
## 10A  Past Simple quiz

1  was; a
2  got; c
3  started; b
4  lived; b
5  became; was; b
6  sold; c
7  had; c
8  wrote; painted; made; a
9  was; played; a
10 went; b

## Vocabulary Booster – Irregular verbs

**Exercise 2**
a  know
b  understand
c  drink
d  eat
e  do
f  see
g  come
h  read
i  give
j  buy

**Exercise 3**
a  understood
b  drank
c  gave
d  bought
e  ate
f  did
g  saw
h  read
i  came
j  knew

## Module 11

### 11D Past Simple snakes and ladders

1. left, made, walked
2. What did you do last weekend?
3. Where did you go last month?
4. Were; was
5. Did; didn't
6. various answers
7. was; didn't
8. I didn't go for a walk on Monday.
9. studied; sold; hated
10. Did; did
11. Frank studied French at school.
12. Where did you go on holiday last year?
13. the sentence is correct
14. watched; met; had
15. He didn't start work at nine o'clock in the morning.
16. We lived in a big house, and we were rich.
17. was; were
18. various answers
19. didn't; was
20. finished; became; wrote
21. How many people were there in your school?
22. did; didn't
23. Tom and Susan didn't study English at school.
24. I didn't do my homework last night.
25. wanted; went; got
26. did; was
27. various answers
28. were; was
29. the sentence is correct
30. What time did you get up this morning?

### Vocabulary Booster – The weather

#### Exercise 1

| | |
|---|---|
| It's dry. | Tokyo |
| It's hot. | Abu Dhabi |
| It's cloudy. | Cape Town |
| It's cold. | Moscow |
| It's sunny. | Madrid |
| It's wet. | London |
| It's warm. | Buenos Aires |
| It's windy. | Chicago |

## Module 12

### Vocabulary Booster – Clothes

#### Exercise 1

1. trainers
2. a shirt
3. a dress
4. a suit
5. a hat
6. a coat
7. boots
8. trousers
9. a skirt
10. a tie

### 12C Revision board game

1. children; men; women; people
2. a) I'm going to watch TV tonight.
   b) Where did she go yesterday?
   c) Does she speak English?
3. move house; get married; have children; meet your partner
4. one million; twelve thousand; four hundred and fifty; thirty-three
5. Are; 'm; 's
6. bread; water; fruit; vegetables
7. have dinner; play football; go to the cinema; go shopping
8. a) play    b) do    c) live    d) watch
9. a) I can to swim well.    b) is correct
   c) I can't speak German.
10. a) are    b) aren't    c) Is
11. a) was    b) were    c) did
12. various answers
13. became; started; met; was/were
14. poor; fast; safe; ugly
15. a) What    b) Where    c) Who
16. six weeks ago, yesterday and last week all talk about the past; tomorrow and next week talk about the future.
17. a) What's your job?    b) How old are you?
    c) Where are you from?
18. a) father    b) wife    c) daughter
19. a) some    b) any    c) a
20. a) in    b) at    c) on    d) in
21. left; made; sold; played
22. January, February, March, April, May, June, July, August, September, October, November, December
23. a) Do    b) do    c) does
24. a) I don't like dance music.
    b) She doesn't play tennis every day.
    c) They didn't go on holiday last year.
25. c, a, e, d, b
26. a) were    b) were    c) was
27. various answers
28. I love ..., I really like ..., I like ..., It's okay. I don't like ..., I hate ...
29. a) him    b) She    c) Their
30. wrote, got, studied, went

**Pearson Education Limited**
Edinburgh Gate, Harlow
Essex CM20 2JE, England
and Associated Companies throughout the world

*www.longman.com/cuttingedge*

First published 2002
Eighth impression 2010

Set in 9/12pt ITC Stone Informal
And 9/12pt Congress Sans

Printed in China     SWTC/08

ISBN 978-1-4058-4365-2 (Teacher's Resource Book and Test Master CD-Rom pack)
ISBN 978-0-582-50180-5 (Teacher's Resource Book)
Prepared for the Publishers by Stenton Associates
Photocopiable pages by Jennifer Coles

**Acknowledgements**
Special thanks to Frances Eales for writing the progress tests in
this book.

Illustrated by: Kathy Baxendale, Jackie Harland, Bob Harvey
(Pennant), Graham Humphreys (The Art Market), Ed McLachlan
and Chris Pavely.

**Author acknowledgements**
Chris Redston: I would like to thank my co-authors Sarah
Cunningham and Peter Moor for their help and advice, Tricia
Moss for her careful editing of the Resource bank, Frances Eales
for writing the Tests, Adrian Stenton and his team for his
detailed editing of the Teacher's notes, Naomi Tasker for her .
patience and cheerfulness under pressure, and all these people
for not phoning me before lunchtime. I would also like to thank
the following people for their help and inspiration during the
writing of this book: Mark and Laura Skipper, Dylan Evans, Polly
Kirby, Joss Whedon, Dan Castellaneta, Ali Bond, John and Avis
Hilder, Rupert Giles, Will Ord, Albert Hofmann, Margie Baum,
Frank Moon, Nancy Cartwright, Alan Sadler, Alexander Harris,
Matt Stone, Trey Parker, James Marsters, Jacopo Barigazzi, my
sisters Anne and Carol, and particularly my father Bill Redston
for all his love and support.